Two Lives During the English Civil War

Two Lives During the English Civil War

Cavalier's Note Book
William Blundell

Autobiography of Joseph Lister
Joseph Lister

LEONAUR

Two Lives During the English Civil War
Cavalier's Note Book by William Blundell
Autobiography of Joseph Lister by Joseph Lister

First published under the titles
Cavalier's Note Book
and
Autobiography of Joseph Lister

Leonaur is an imprint of Oakpast Ltd

Copyright in this form © 2010 Oakpast Ltd

ISBN: 978-0-85706-090-7 (hardcover)
ISBN: 978-0-85706-089-1 (softcover)

http://www.leonaur.com

Publisher's Notes

In the interests of authenticity, the spellings, grammar and place names
used have been retained from the original editions.

The opinions of the authors represent a view of events in which he
was a participant related from his own perspective,
as such the text is relevant as an historical document.

The views expressed in this book are not necessarily
those of the publisher.

Contents

Cavalier's Note Book

William Blundell

Contents

To
NICHOLAS BLUNDELL
OF CROSBY, LANCASHRE, ESQ., J.P., D.L,
COLONEL OF DUKE OF LANCASTER'S OWN RIFLE MILITIA
THIS VOLUME
WHICH ENSHRINES SOME OF THE WISDOM
OF A WORTHY ANCESTOR
IS
RESPECTFULLY INSCRIBED

CHAPTER 1

The Blundells of Crosby

This village lies near the sea-coast, six miles from the great maritime town of Liverpool At the present moment the suburbs of this vast town, soon to be dignified with the title of city, have stretched out almost to the park walls, and its long line of docks commences with the newly-constituted borough of Bootle. The family is of Norman descent, and French representatives of the race are still to be found in good position, using the original form 'Blondell,' as the name appears in the roll of Battle Abbey. Both surnames, Blondell and Blundell, are indeed to be met with in this famous catalogue, but the former is supposed to be the more ancient

The author of the following notes makes mention of a deed, tempe. Henry II., in which his ancestor is styled Nicholas Blondell, but this deed cannot at present be found. The earliest charter now in possession of the family is one of that reign, in which John, Earl of Morton, gives Great Crosby and its appurtenances to Robert de Ennuylesdale (Ainsdale), his forester, for homage and service, and a reserved rent of 100 *solidi*. This deed is very clearly indited, and the strong ligature of silk and silver tissue to which the seal was originally attached is well preserved. The seal itself has disappeared, and its loss may perhaps be due to the custom of enclosing valuable seals in linen bags. Most of the seals so covered have crumbled away, whilst others of an equally early date, to which this attention has not been paid, are in good preservation.

It is perhaps worthy of remark that the green wax has proved more durable than the white, and a friend who was for many years in the Record Office declares that his experience in this matter coincides with that of the writer. The grant above referred to was confirmed by King John in the year of his accession to the throne (1199). Blundell

Sands, now the site of numerous villas, and a portion of the property thus acquired, is still held by the family; but the manor and bulk of the township passed in very early times to the neighbouring family of Molyneux of Sefton. On the other hand, the manor and township of Little Crosby, the present seat of the Blundells, is said to have been derived from the Molyneuxs.

It is somewhat curious that the first possessions of the Blundells in this country are intimately connected with the early fortunes of Liverpool.. In 1208, King John gave Ravinesmols,[1] Annolnesdale, &c., to Henry Fitz-Warine of Lancaster (whose father, Warine, had been the King's falconer), in exchange for Liverpool and Uplitherland.[2] He then ordered his vassals at Toxteth to settle in the new town, and by a grant, dated the same year, constituted it a free *burgh*. This was the origin of what is now the most important seaport town in England. Ainsdale, though under a new feudal lord, remained in the hands of the Blundells, whose representative, Nicholas Blundell, was called upon in 1292 to show why he claimed wreck of the sea on this manor, without the King's licence. This was at Lancaster, before Hugh de Cressingham and his associates, itinerant judges.

> And Nicholas appeared and said that he and all his ancestors from time immemorial had held the said manor, and in like manner had the wreck of the sea all the time, and considered it something annexed and appertaining to the manor; and had used that liberty up to this time without any interruption of time, and he was prepared to verify this in Court.
>
> And William Inge answered for the King, that in England no one can have or receive wreck but the King and those to whom he concedes the privilege, and as Nicholas the aforesaid can produce no concession of such right from the King or his ancestors, he claims judgment for the King. Moreover, it was urged that in point of fact the ancestors of Nicholas had not exercised this liberty *ab antiquo*, [Enquiry is asked]
>
> The jury declare upon oath that the aforesaid Nicholas had

---

1. Raven-meols, formerly a separate lordship, is. now included in Formby. A large farm still bears the name, which, is clearly of Danish origin, as are Formby, Crosby, &c.

2. Up-litherland was likewise for a long period a separate lordship, until absorbed into the township of Aughton. Here, in a secluded spot, amidst low-lying meadows, stands Walsh Hall, occupying the site of the ancient residence of a branch of the powerful family of Waleys, a name frequently met with in early local charters.

acquired the manor from his father. And they say that Henry, father of the King, gave to the father of Nicholas a certain vessel from a certain wreck which happened in the manor, and no other of the ancestors of Nicholas had ever taken wreck, nor has Nicholas himself, since no wreck has happened. Hence it follows that the King recovers his seisin of the aforesaid wreck when it may happen in the aforesaid manner. [Judgement for the King.] [3]

In 1328 Ainsdale was transferred, apparently by marriage settlement, to Gilbert de Halsale, and in 1631 it was purchased from Sir Cuthbert Halsall, along with Birkdale, Meanedale, and Formby, by Robert Blundell of Ince Blundell, Esq., at that period a lawyer of Gray's Inn. It has descended to Thomas Weld Blundell, Esq., and the fortunate position of this property (between Liverpool and Southport) has led to the conversion of a large tract of rabbit warrens into a valuable estate.

Robert de Ainsdale had a son Adam, whose son Robert assumed the name of Blundell, to which family no doubt the grantee of King John belonged. Norman races of distinction were careful to preserve their patronymics, whilst members of less distinguished families suffered themselves to be designated from the properties which they acquired. Thus, the descendants of William Gemet became De Lydiates and De Halsalls from these attained possessions. In the same way the De Scarisbricks, De Aghtons, De Maghulls and others are found in this neighbourhood early in the thirteenth century seated at their respective manors, while the Molyneuxs and Blundells alone in these parts retained their ancestral surnames.

There were several knights amongst the first Blundells, who were probably all soldiers and knighted for their prowess in battle. Sir Robert Blundell accompanied Edward I. in his Welsh expedition, 1277, and the following year, in view of eventualities, he made over his estates to his son Nicholas, reserving to himself 'wreck of the sea' and certain rents. A curious clause, in which Nicholas in case of failure in the fulfilment of the conditions is to pay five *marks* to the King for his new work constructing at 'Roye Lane,' confirms the circumstance of his presence in Wales, where Edward was then fortifying Rhuddlan Castle. The Welsh proved valiant defenders of their native hills, and it seems probable that Sir Robert Blundell was one of the fourteen

---

3. *Placita de quo Warranto*, p. 369.

knights banneret who perished during the absence of the King, in an engagement which was very disastrous to the English arms. The Lion rampant, the present crest of the family, appears on the seal of this interesting deed of Sir Robert Blundell's, whose name encircles the device.

We pass on to notice an early specimen of an English deed, bearing date 1405, which shows the remarkable tenacity of provincial phrases. This document is a declaration of uses by 'Robyn ye Molyneux' of Melling, in which the same terms are often repeated, so that it affords little scope for variety of phraseology. Still, a few of the expressions used may be worthy of notice. Thus, in the passage, 'Yf he dee bowte hayr of hys bode geyton i weddyd bed yen to,' &c., we find several terms still employed. 'Dee' for die, 'bowte' for without, 'geyton' for begotten, 'i' for in, 'yen' then, are frequently heard in this neighbourhood. At the same time it cannot fail to strike the observer, that the number of those who speak the broad vernacular of their forefathers is yearly decreasing. The Fylde country has long been considered the stronghold of Lancashire provincialisms, but even there a notable change is manifest This change is due not so much to the spread of education, as to the increased facilities of intercommunication leading to a greater refinement of speech, and in some respects of manners.

In 1414 we find Nicholas Blundell of Crosby, one of the knights of the shire for the county of Lancashire, in conjunction with Ralph de Radcliffe, son and heir of Sir Ralph de Radcliffe, Knight, of Smithells and Blackburn. Alice, his daughter, married William Blundell of Ince Blundell, Esq., the representative of the neighbouring branch of this ancient race. It is somewhat curious that this is the only ascertained alliance between the two families. This is the more remarkable as the properties lie contiguous to each other, and both have had resident proprietors for nearly seven centuries, united by the bonds of religion and friendly intercourse. There is no trace of any feud existing between the two houses, at any period of their history, and scarcely even of a passing estrangement on the question of boundaries, that fruitful source of dissension betwixt neighbours.

A century later we meet with a document enumerating the wrongs which Nicholas Blundell, his wife and children, suffered at the hands of Dame Anne Mulnes (Molyneux), and Sir Edward Mulnes, Parson of the Church of Sefton, 'by thare grat myzgth and power.' The Molyneuxs, whose seat was at Sefton, only a short distance from Crosby, had always been a warlike race, and had risen to eminence by their prowess in the field. Sir William Molyneux distinguished himself at Agincourt, and Dame Anne, daughter of Sir John Dutton, was the widow of his son, Sir Thomas, who died 1491. Their eldest son, Sir William, in conjunction with Sir William Stanley, led the Lancashire bowmen at Flodden Field, and contributed greatly to the success of that memorable engagement

At the date of the events recorded in the document he was absent in the service of his sovereign, leaving his mother lady paramount at Sefton. The allegations of the Blundells show an abuse of power and a defiance of law on the part of this great family, which we should hardly have expected to find in the reign of Henry VIII., although the *Paston Letters* have made us familiar with similar instances of the violence and lawlessness of powerful nobles at a somewhat earlier date. The difference between the parties appears to have sprung from a disputed claim to certain lands in Sefton, which the Blundells had possessed from time immemorial, and for which they were entitled to receive from the Molyneuxs twenty *marks per annum*, which sum the latter refused any longer to pay.

This land they seized upon, and when the Blundells endeavoured to regain possession, they proceeded against them with a high hand, refusing to abide the award of four 'indifferent' men, to whom both parties had agreed to refer the question. Mr. Blundell declares that they took from him his right of waifs and strays, and wreck of the sea, and would not suffer his family to follow hunting, fishing, and hawking, 'qwech was to yam grat plesure and tresure.' They carried off his tenants at their will, and 'retayned yam to do yam s'v's in yar time of pleasure.' Sir Edward Molyneux, the Parson of Sefton, seems to have gone the length of practically excommunicating Mr. Blundell, who complains that he took from him the right of the Church, and would not suffer him to 'kneel or tarry' in his chapel on the north side of Sefton Church.

They broke into his house, spoiling his goods, and carried off a fat ox; when he would have defended his premises, they took him and his son to Lancaster, where they cast them into prison, and kept them fourteen weeks to his utter undoing. They further took possession of a ward of George Blundell, and parted Nicholas and his wife, after they had been united three-score years and had had twelve children together, and 'nev'r nod'r cold find fote nod'r w't od'r' a picture of domestic felicity which would have entitled the couple to the flitch of Dunmow. In fine, they drove him out of his house, and kept it by force, putting in his brother, and they 'occupy his proper goods moveable and unmoveable.'

This document is in the nature of a petition to the Crown, for redress, and the matter was finally adjudicated upon by Cardinal Wolsey, who in 1526 issued a decree in favour of the Blundells.

At the period of the Reformation the family adhered to the ancient faith, and had much to suffer from the oppressive laws which signalised the latter portion of the reign of Elizabeth. In 1590, Richard Blundell of Crosby was indicted at the Lancaster Assizes, before Judges Church and Walmsley, for having harboured Robert Woodroff, a seminary priest, and being convicted, was committed to prison at Lancaster Castle, along with his son William.

A letter to his wife, dated September 28, 1590, has been preserved, in which he speaks of the sickness prevalent within the walls of the prison. He mentions the death of Mr. Worthington of Blainscoe, and the grievous illness of Mr. Latham of Mosborough, both fellow-sufferers in the cause of religion. He himself died there on March 19, 1591-2, the restrictions of confinement and the unwholesomeness of the prison no doubt contributing to hasten his end. William, his son and heir, followed the same course, and, until James I. came to the throne, two-thirds of his lands were in the hands of the Crown for recusancy. He was then able to obtain a royal pardon, and resumed possession of his lands, but after the Gunpowder Plot, the odium of which fell upon the whole Catholic body, they were again seized by rapacious courtiers, who had begged them from the King. The following statement, written by himself, gives a precise and circumstantial account of the troubles in which he had been involved for conscience' sake:—

In the yeare of our Lord God 1590, the 11th June, the Right Honorable Henrie, Earl of Darbie, sent certaine of his men to searche the house of Richard Blundell of little Crosbie, in the Countie of Lancaster, Esq., for matters belonging to Catholicke Religion; &c, where they apprehended and took away with them to his honor's house (the new Parke) one Mr. Woodroffe, a seminary priest, and the said Richard Blundell, and mee, William Blundell, son of the said Richard: and the day next following we were severally examined by the Earle: and on the thirteenth day of the said month wee were all sent to be imprisoned in Chester Castle. About the 5th or 6th of August next following, wee were all by the Earle's men featched from

Chester and brought to Knowesley, one of his honor's houses, where wee were (as alsoe my mother, and one John Carre, my Other's man) severally examined by Chatterton the Bishopp of Chester, who was joyned in Comission with the Earle to examine us uppon interrogatories by the Lords of the Councell.

And the day following, the priest, my father, and I were sent prisoner to Lancaster (where we found prisoners there before us, Mr. Henrie Latham of Mosborowe, and Mr. Richard Worthington of Blainschouge, committed for their conscience), where also my fether and I remained for the most part until the 19th day of March of the year 1592, on which day my saide ffather changed this life for a better. Within about a ffortnight after, I had a license, obtained from the Right Honorable the Earle of Derbie, to come to Crosbie for one onely month. And then returned to Lancaster againe, whence, about Michselmas ensuing or somewhat before, I was againe dismissed by his honor's warrant

And uppon the 20th or 21st November next after, I was againe apprehended (in the time of Bell's persecution) by John Nutter, Parson of Sephton, and divers others assisting him, and my wyfe also was taken, and both of us first weare carried to the Parsonage of Sephton, and theire staide all night, whence on the morning wee were brought to my Lord his house, the New Parke, before the Earle, the Bishopp Chatterton, and Mr. Wade, one of the Clearkes of the Councell; where my wife was dismissed, and I with others sent to London with 2 Pursevants or Messengers. And on the 8th Decr, (being the Feast of the Conception of Our bl. Ladie), I, with an'r Henrie Latham of Mosborowe, was by the afforesaid Mr. William Wade brought before Docter Whyt(gift), Archbishop of Canterburie, att his house, Croydon in Surrey, where we were adjudged to prison, Mr. Latham to the Fleete, and I to the Gatehouse of Westminster, where I remained prisoner till the 12th July 1595.

Then was set at libertie uppon bonds to appeare and come in within 20 dayes after warning given, since which time I was never imprisoned And soe coming home with my wyfe, who had come upp to London with her brother Edward Norres, and he returning after a few dayes, she stayed in prison with mee till my said deliveries which was some 6 or 8 weeks. And after, we lived at Grosbie untill the 27th May 1598, at what tyme my house was searched by Sir Richard Mollinex, Knt and John Nutter, Parson of Sephton, when, I escaping, my wyfe was taken for her conscience and carried first to Sephton, and examined, and returned home for that night uppon bonds or promise of my ffather Norres (as I thinke) to appeare at Chester before the Bishopp such a day. Accordingly, the last of the same month, she, together with other Catholicks, as namely Hector Stock, Elin Baron, the wyfe of Laurance Baron of the Edge, Jane Melling, widow, Elin Blundell, the wyfe of Thomas Blundell of the Carrside in Ince Blundell, were committed to prison in the Castle of Chester.

And within a little more than a month after (as I take it), some man (but I never knew who it was) caused the old indictment for entertaineing a Seminary Priest, which had been in the yeare 1590 afforesaide, to be prosecuted against me. Whereuppon proclamation was made according to theire custome at the Countie Courts at Lancaster, that I should come in and appeare, which I not doeing, was condemned of felonie by the Coroner.

After this condemnation I tarried secretly at countrie houses some 3 quarters of a yeare. And in the meanwhile my wife, getting out of prison in Chester Castle uppon bonds for her appearance againe &c., she and I, for feare of being apprehended, went first to Wrixham in Wales, where our brother Bannister dwelt And thence after a good while (my wyfe being great with childe) returned into Lancashire to the Spekes, and I ridde to Weme, where my brother Bannister had another dwelling house. And thence to London to get a pardon, where, sending home my horses, I with my man Peter Stocke staide there about ffive weeks. And, without getting a pardon, I came into Staffordshire, changing my name, whither my wyfe came to mee, and theire we staide about two yeares att six several places until the Queen's death; when cominge home, I soone after obtained from K. James a free and large pardon, which cost me in all but either 40 or 50 shillings.

He also gives a list of all those who begged his lands from the Crown, and the result, but this document is too long for insertion here.

In connection with the long imprisonment of Mrs. Blundell at Chester, mentioned in the foregoing narrative, a curious letter is extant at Crosby, dated August 23, 1598, which bears the signature of Sir Richard Molyneux, Knt, and Rev. John Nutter, Parson of Sefton, the 'Golden Ass' of Queen Elizabeth. This is an application to the Bishop of Chester on behalf of Mrs. Blundell, whose release they ask for on the ground of ill health. One very suggestive passage may be noticed:—

> And for that common experience doth too well teach us that ye evill examples of such Archpapists and disobedient persons doe greatlie hinder the race of ye Gospell (especiallie in these maritime parts) and daylie threaten dangerous events, if ye same be not wislie foreseene and speedilie prevented: wee could wish our selves likewise altogether freede from the company of Mr. Blundell if by any lawful way or meanes he (being a confyned Papist) might be removed from among us.

It is not clear whether the death of Mr. Blundell or only his banishment is here hinted at.

This staunch recusant has left behind him in manuscript several treatises on controversial matters, and many poems of a religious character. One of the latter consisting of seventeen *stanzas* was written, as he states, at the time of the above persecution. He appears to have wooed the muses with little success, but we give the following *stanza* of this poem, not for the sake of its versification, but to show what sort of trials those had to endure, who in this country, three centuries ago, refused to accept the new ordinances in matters of religion, which were then being forced upon the nation:—

Husbands and their wives parted are asunder.
Parents severed are from their children dear.
Sucking babes do cry
Which at home do lie;
Mothers do bewayle
Being fast in gaol;
All the country talketh
Every way one walketh,
What in Sefton we endure
For no strange opinion
But that old religion
Austin planted here most sure.

In 1611, Mr. Blundell, finding his fellow Catholics refused burial at their Parish Church (Sefton), ordered a plot within his own grounds to be set apart for this purpose. The place selected was called Harkirke—the hoary or ancient church—and the tradition that a church had once existed there probably influenced his choice. In preparing the ground many scores of Saxon coins were discovered, chiefly of the reign of Alfred the Great; and Mr. Blundell caused a copper-plate to be engraved in which thirty-two of these coins are represented.

This plate has been preserved at Crosby, as well as a description of the coins written by himself; but not altogether correct: the coins themselves have disappeared. Later on, this act of humanity, coming to the knowledge of Government, was the occasion of a severe sentence being pronounced against him. For when the Sheriff and his followers, in attempting a levy upon his goods for recusancy, had met with some resistance on the part of his tenants, he was summoned before that all-potent tribunal, the Star Chamber. This happened in the year 1629, and the result is thus given in Rushworth's *Historical Collections* vol. 2 p. 21:—

> And ye defendant Blundell being a Popish Recusant convict, and living in little Crosby in Lancashire, enclosed a piece of ground and fenced it, part with a stone wall and part with a hedge and ditch, and kept and used the same for the space of 10 years for the burial of Popish Recusants and Seminary Priests, and for these offences 2 of the rioters were fined 500*l.* a piece and 3 others 100*l.* a piece, and Blundell for procurement of the riots and erecting the Churchyard, 2,000*l.* All committed to ye Fleet, and the walls and mounds of the Churchyard to be pulled down by the Sheriff, and ye ground laid waste, by decree to be read at ye assizes.

From further documents it appears that the fine was afterwards reduced to 500*l.* The sum of 80*l.* was awarded to the Sheriff, Sir Ralph Ashton, whose acknowledgment to Mr. Blundell for the payment of this amount on July 20, 1629, is now before the writer.

This stout sufferer for conscience sake died at Crosby, at the age of 78, on July 2, 1638, and was succeeded in his estates by his grandson William, the author of the following notes.

CHAPTER 2

William Blundell the Cavalier

William Blundell the Cavalier was born at Crosby Hall on July 15, 1620, and lost his father Nicholas in 1631, when he was but eleven years of age. His mother, Jane, daughter of Roger Bradshaigh, Esq. of Haigh, near Wigan, survived till August 26, 1640. It seems probable that he received his early instruction from his father or grandfather, and was afterwards sent to one of the secret places of education well known to those who adhered to the ancient faith. That there were several such in various parts of the kingdom, is evident from the frequent reference made to them in the reports of the Government spies and informers.

In 1635 a draft warrant was issued by the Privy Council for the search of Stanley Grange, the residence of the Hon. Anne Vaux, where the Jesuit Fathers had established a school. In this case, timely notice of the intended visit having been received, the school was found to be broken up and the boys dispersed. A more successful raid on Mr. Levison's house, near Wolverhampton, resulted in the capture of several youths, who were in the end restored to their parents. It does not appear that Mr. Blundell was trained at St Omer's College, for though he speaks favourably of the system of education pursued at that famous Jesuit Seminary, yet he expressly says that he derived this opinion from the fruits of learning and virtue which he perceived in others. Moreover, the circumstance of his never having acquired the French language until late in life sufficiently proves that he never resided in a foreign seminary.

In fact, the period allowed him for education was too short for him to have spent his time abroad, for he was summoned to take an active part in life at an unusually early age. But whoever taught him did the work well, securing for his pupil a solid foundation of learning and a love of letters which he never lost In consequence of the death of his eldest son and heir, the grandfather was anxious to make a fresh settlement of his estates during his own lifetime. This was of particular importance in the case of recusants, as two-thirds of their landed property lay at the mercy of the crown, and hence it was very desirable that the holder should only possess a life interest in the estate.

This rendered necessary the early marriage of William Blundell, who, when but fifteen, espoused Ann, daughter of Sir Thomas Haggerston, of Haggerston, co. Northumberland, Bart In one of his letters to Lady Haggerston, written in 1651, there is an interesting reference to his youthful and martial appearance when he came as a suitor to the fair Northumbrian home, from which he drew his partner in the joys and sorrows of a long career:—

> I remember there was a young fellow not far from Haggerston, that told a friend of ours that would gladly have drawn him to the wars, that it was a great pity 'so gude a like man as he should be knocked o'th head.' You will remember what a pretty, straight young thing, all dashing in scarlet, I came to Haggerston, &c.

The dashing scarlet attire must have added to the attraction of his youthful figure, and such an apparition would have found favour at other places besides Haggerston. If he could not entice a sturdy yeoman to the field, another voice answered more readily to his call. His wife happily proved all that he had hoped for, and in 1665, writing to the same lady, he alludes to her thus pleasantly:—

> And now, when I speak of your ark, I must here acknowledge that the dove which was sent from thence, some thirty years ago, hath saved from sinking our little cock-boat at Crosby in many a storm.

In the early part of his wedded career, Mr. Blundell led a life of gaiety, and readily gave himself to the pursuit of pleasure with little thought of the morrow. He afterwards bitterly lamented his great and continual charge at this time in horses, dogs, hawks, play, apparel, and a thousand other excesses. A few lively poetical pieces written at this period evince the delight he took in plays, dances, and other country amusements. He visited Dublin in 1638, and was entertained at the court of the unfortunate Earl of Strafford, then at the height of his short-lived glory.

He describes the almost regal state assumed by the Lord Deputy, the first nobleman of Ireland, the Marquis (afterwards Duke) of Ormond being amongst his retainers. In these pursuits, without the aid of more destructive sources of expenditure, he was gradually involving himself in debt, when he was called to a sense of his duty and to more serious occupations by the summons of war.

The King was rallying his adherents round his standard, and had gratefully responded to the applications of certain loyal Lancashire Catholics to be permitted to take up arms in his defence. With all the ardour of youth Mr. Blundell threw himself into the struggle, accepting a captain's commission from Sir Thomas Tildesley, Knt, authorising him to raise a company of 100 dragoons for the royal cause. This commission, dated Leigh, December 22, 1642, bearing the neat signature of the famous Lancashire General, is still preserved at Crosby, and is couched in the following terms:—

> By virtue of his Majestie's commission under his signe manuall to mee directed, I doe hereby constitute and appointe you William Blundell Esquire to bee Captaine of one companie of Dragoones in my Regiment And I doe hereby give you full power and authoritie for his Majestie and his name to raise, impresse and retaine the said companie, raised or to bee raised by sound of Drumme or anie other waie (and in anie of his Majestie's Dominions) for the defence of his Majestie's royall person, the 2 houses of Parliament, the Protestant religion, the lawe of the land, the libertie and propertie of the subject and Priveledge of Parliament, and when soe raised to bringe together and employ in his Majestie's service as you shall from tyme to tyme receive directions for. And I doe hereby require all the inferiour officers and souldiers of ye companie you to obey as their Capitane, you likewise obeying your superiour officers according to the discipline of warre.[1]

The quota was still incomplete, when Mr. Blundell was called upon to join Lord Strange in the neighbourhood of Preston. The latter no-

---

1. A reduced facsimile of this Commission is given as a frontispiece; it is taken with permission from a full-size impression which accompanies two papers by the editor, entitled *A Century of Recusancy,* read before the Historic Society of Lancashire and Cheshire, and printed with the proceedings for 1879. In these papers a few of the documents and letters here given are made use of, with several additional ones having reference to that particular subject. It may likewise be here mentioned, that four articles from the same pen were inserted in the Month (October 1878, to January 1879), under the title of *A Loyal Catholic Cavalier.* In these will be found some specimens of the following notes, and of the numerous letters of Mr. Blundell.

bleman, by the death of his father, had become Earl of Derby before the march to Lancaster was undertaken. A work by Madam Guizot de Witt, entitled *The Lady of Latham*, which contains several particulars derived from family documents, gives the following account of this expedition:—

> Lord Derby left Latham House on 17th March (1642-3) after nightfall, and after a forced march of about 30 miles, the little army appeared the next morning before the walls of Lancaster. The garrison were summoned to surrender, and indignantly refused; the soldiers hesitated to make a second attack, when the Earl of Derby, seizing a short pike, sprang forward, crying, 'Follow me.' Some gent.lemen volunteers immediately joined him, and urged the soldiers on. The assault was made, the city taken, and the fortifications raised.'

Mr. Blundell was one of those who responded with alacrity to the call of their leader. The gallantry of this little band exposed it to the severe fire of the garrison, and he received a serious wound, having his thigh shattered with a musket-shot Seacome—of whom Dr. Ormerod, the historian of Cheshire, remarks that, though untrustworthy in other matters, he may be relied on in what relates to the civil war—in describing this engagement, says, 'Mr. Blundell, that gallant, loyal, and worthy gentleman,, was wounded on entering the city.' He was carried to Dinkley, the residence of Colonel Talbot, then engaged on the King's side, where every attention was paid him.

In after years, writing to Mrs. Talbot, he recalls his obligations to her, reminding her of the long week which he spent in her hospitable mansion, where he was nursed with so much tenderness in his sore infirmity. This wound had the effect of rendering him a cripple for life, and in his own neighbourhood, his tenants, indulging the Lancashire propensity for nicknames, commonly called him, 'Halt-Will.' He himself tells us that he had to wear a very high-heeled shoe, and calculated that he had lost three inches in height by reason of his accident From this period till the close of the civil war, his life was one of privation and anxiety.

He resided during these disastrous years chiefly in the houses of friends and acquaintance, his constant good humour making him a general favourite. As he was in continual danger of being taken prisoner, he was compelled to leave his own house at Crosby to the care of his wife, or of his sister Frances, a woman of rare courage and prudence. So exposed were they, while the war lasted, to domiciliary visits, in which the soldiers carried off anything they could lay their hands upon, that they were obliged to bury their bread from meal to meal.

One advantage which Mr. Blundell undoubtedly drew from his misfortunes, was the conviction that they were sent him as a wholesome correction, to withdraw him from the vain pursuit of pleasure, and to fix his mind on more lasting possessions. This is evident from numberless letters and remarks, some of which will be found in the following pages. *Periissem nisi periissem*, was the motto to which he clung in after life, for he declares that he would have been lost, as regards his fortunes both here and hereafter, if it had not been for this merciful visitation.

Being totally disabled from all active employment, he could do little to aid his party, and must have watched the waning cause of the Royalists with dismay. A letter of his to a friend in the Isle of Man sends intelligence which he desires may be communicated to the Earl of Derby. He was thrice imprisoned at this period, and again a fourth time, in 1657, at Liverpool, which he describes as a loathsome prison. From a letter dated March 17, 1657-8, it appears that his confinement had then lasted ten weeks. This was probably in some part of the Castle, which had been dismantled during the civil war. Here he had for a companion his uncle, Christopher Bradshaigh, and the Hon. Richard Butler, heir to the title and impaired fortunes of Viscount Mountgarret.

When this young man was released, after a long imprisonment, his uncle. Colonel Mervin Touchet, requested Mr. Blundell to receive him for a time at his house at Crosby. There he remained for two years, his father and friends being unwilling, perhaps unable, to assist him with the means necessary for his return to Ireland. It is not surprising that, under these circumstances, he formed an attachment to Emilia, Mr. Blundell's eldest daughter. This resulted in a marriage in 1661, but the young couple had many privations to endure, until their accession to the title in 1679. The Duke of Ormond, the head of the house of Butler, proved a warm friend, and for many years they resided at Kilkenny, near the mansion of their noble benefactor. From this couple, the present Henry Edmund, thirteenth Viscount Mountgarret, descends.

By the law of 1646, no Papist delinquent could compound for his estate; consequently, all Mr. Blundell's estate was seized and remained in the hands of the Commissioners for nine or ten years. His trials at this period, in the loss of goods and the ravages committed upon his lands, were very severe. The following is a record preserved in his handwriting:—

The war between Charles I. and his Parliament began *a.d.* 1642. That year, March 18, my thigh was broken with a shot in the King's service. *a.d.* 1643, all my goods and most of my lands were sequestered for being a Papist and delinquent, as the prevailing party call the King's partakers. In the year 1645, my wife farmed my *demesne* at Crosby, and all her quick goods being lost, she bought one horse and two oxen to make up a team. *a.d.* 1646, November 13, I valued all my goods, and comparing them with my debts, I found myself worse than nothing by the whole sum of 81*l.* 18s., my lands being all lost *a.d.* 1653: Till this year, from 1646 inclusively, I remained under sequestration, having one-fifth part allowed to my wife, and farming only from the sequestrators my *demesne* of Crosby and the mill. About Midsummer 1653, my whole estate was purchased and compounded for with my own money, for my use, so that in the month of February 1653-4, I was indebted 1,100*l.* 7s., after which time I was so overcharged with care, debts, business, and imprisonments, that I think I took no account of the value of my goods till the year 1658.

In the repurchase of his estate, Mr. Blundell employed the intervention of two Protestant friends—his cousin, Sir Roger Bradshaigh, Bart, of Haigh, and Mr. Gilbert Crouch. The sum paid appears to have been 1,340*l.*, representing, no doubt, his life interest in the property. In addition to this Mr. Blundell found himself saddled with the arrears of rents reserved to the Crown, arising out of frequent grants for recusancy, some of which had never been discharged. These went as far back as the reign of Elizabeth, and though Mr. Blundell represented the injustice of charging him with rents which should have been paid by those who had the benefit of the forfeitures, the Government was inexorable, and he was compelled to pay on this score 1,167*l.* 15s. 6½d. Moreover, the cost of making out this prodigious bill was added to the account, making an addition of 34*l.* 10s. 2d. to the foregoing sum. This remarkable document, a roll of twenty feet in length, has been carefully preserved at Crosby. May it long serve to remind his descendants of the faith and loyalty of their ancestor.

In 1658, Mr. Blundell procured a pass from Colonel Gilbert Ireland to go abroad, which he made use of to conduct two of his daughters to Rouen, where they were desirous of embracing a religious life. An incidental reference to the journey, which he makes in a letter written subsequently to these daughters, reveals some of the inconveniences to which travellers were subjected at that period.

> When you went from my poor house to Rouen, part of your journey was on horseback, some little part on foot, the most by coach, and the rest in a tottering bark or cockboat upon the unstable element of water, not without crosswinds and perhaps a tempest Besides these you may remember some other varieties in that journey, as our stop at Liverpool water, the brawls, the lets, and other accidents in the coach and in the inns; and at the last, when we came to London, the unexpected death of the greatest person (Oliver Cromwell), as we esteemed him, upon the whole earth, was the occasion, by shutting up of the sea-ports, of a notable stop in your journey.

Our Cavalier was still abroad in 1660, when England was preparing to welcome again her legitimate monarch. Attracted by the gathering of royalists at Breda, he hastened thither and had an interview with Charles the night before his embarkation. He renewed on this occasion to his King the offer of his fortunes and life, and no doubt heard him utter those promises of toleration which were so soon forgotten. He accompanied him in the same ship to Dover, where he was a witness of the joy and acclamations which greeted his arrival. An interesting anecdote, recorded in the following pages, in which we find King Charles measuring his height against the lintel of the cabin door, shows that the King was of more than ordinary stature. None of his followers could attain the measure of royalty; but perhaps the tallest practised a wise abstention, qualifying themselves thus early for the *rôle* of courtiers.

Whatever benefits some of the party may have derived from the Restoration, those of an obnoxious faith had little to expect. At first there was a gleam of sunshine and a certain degree of relaxation from the severities of the penal laws; but soon the Anti-Popery cry was renewed, and persecution became the order of the day. The King's easy nature induced him to accede to fresh measures of repression, and the report of the conversion of the Duke of York was not calculated to alter the temper of the nation. At length the audacious plot concocted by Titus Oates found the country ready to listen to any extravagance, and worked it into the frenzy of a religious panic. The voice of justice and reason was no longer heard, and many innocent Catholics, both priests and laymen, became the victims of popular fury.

Among the sufferers was Richard Langhorne, Esq., a lawyer of eminence and a consistent Catholic, with whom Mr. Blundell had long before contracted what he styles, in the language of the day, 'an entire friendship.' Many letters had passed between them, and in 1666 Mr. Langhorne sent his friend an interesting account of the Great Fire of London, of which he was an eye-witness. A remarkable letter, bearing date May 14, 1673, written by Mr. Blundell, we cannot forbear quoting in part. It reveals the consternation with which Catholics beheld the signs of the times, and their apprehension of what was to follow. It will be seen that Mr. Blundell echoes a sentiment of his correspondent, which, taken in connection with his subsequent fate, seems couched in the language of prophecy. It is clear also that Mr. Blundell would have been equally ready to suffer death in the same cause.

> You think we are all asleep, and that we shall be eating and drinking, marrying and giving in marriage, when the storm and the flood come. Shall I tell you my fancy? Perhaps you will say it is a wild one. I think that none but madmen can execute those cruel things that are threatened against His Majesty's Catholic subjects. And if men be really mad, there is no defence against them by paper walls. In my younger days our next Justice of the Peace (Colonel Moore, of Bank Hall) sent one of my tenants, a soldier of the trained bands, to the gaol for refusing the oath of allegiance. He was prisoner a year or two, and being at last released in time of the war, he took up arms for the King, and lived and died (with his poor estate sequestered) a loyal Catholic subject; whilst that very same Justice of the Peace was one of the King's Judges and died (for aught I know) an unrepenting rebel I knew no leading rebel about those times who was not, as I confidently think, a notable taker or tenderer of the oath of allegiance, nor any one Catholic refuser who proved disloyal to his King. God grant us a better test of allegiance, a more lucky oath.
>
> I have a villainous book of Prynne's printed in 1643, where he endeavours to prove by the records of sundry kingdoms, that the people had authority to depose and resist their kings, to call them to strict account, and, when they saw just cause for

it, to proceed capitally against them. According to these same grounds, King Charles I. was beheaded. When the bloody deed was done, Milton and sundry others by writing, and thousands of others by the sword, defended it as just Yet Milton and those are pardoned and live in security. Prynne, as is very well known, was an eminent Parliament man, a mortal foe to the Papists, and was cherished with a very fair salary and with singular places of trust since the King came in. I think we do not seek for preferment.

For my own part, I am sure I only plead *pro domo mea*, for the same house and lands which I lost for my duty to the King, to a pack of those arch villains, and purchased it from them again after 9 or 10 years' sequestration, with money which I borrowed. My limbs, my goods, my liberty, I lost on the same account Many others of ours lost life and all. And ours and our greatest enemies' principles are still the same. If we must therefore beg or hang, I pray God bless the King, and the will of God be done. My dearest sir, I wish as much as you that *we were together one day before we suffer,* and I shall not despair of this happiness, neither will I be cross or wilful in refusing advice, &c.

In a letter to the same gentleman,, dated February 22, 1677, Mr. Blundell speaks of the fresh exactions in his neighbourhood, to which the revival of the persecution had given rise.

. . . Many seizures have here (in these parts) been made of ye estates of convicted Recusants. If ye Inquisitions had not been indifferently favorable, they had been utterly ruined. Ye Papists, I presume, do take it a little unkindly, after an 18 years' sequestration suffered under ye usurpers, to be sequestered again by ye King, and to be jeered no doubt for theire loyalty by ye old oppressors. Here is one of my poore neighbours hardly put too't by many expenceful shifts to keepe off for a tyme a judgement and ye execution necessarily following, upon a verdict given against him about 18 months agoe by force of ye statute for 20*l.* a month for his absence from church service. For my own part, you know I am wholly for liberty of conscience;\ yet would I have them humbly to submit their fortunes to the secular power. . . .

In a letter to Lady Bradshaigh dated December 26, 1678, he writes:

Notwithstanding the great disloyalty of very many persons (as it seems) who had lived in good repute, I cannot accuse myself of any such crime. And although by confinement, disarming and other waies I may appear to be one of ye wicked, yet, for as much as concerns either my allegiance to ye King, or my hearty true respects to my worthy friends, I defy ye whole world and ye Devil himself to prove it

Another letter relating to this eventful period, and dated April 4, 1679, is addressed to Mr. John North, of Dublin. It is valuable, as expressing the personal sentiments of Mr. Blundell on a matter regarding which the religion of Catholics has often exposed them to the suspicion of disloyalty. But neither the past sufferings of our Cavalier on behalf of the Crown, nor his present protestations, could avail him as long as he adhered to the proscribed creed of his forefathers.

I have been inwardly no little afflicted to see and hear those many astonishing particulars which have filled ye world with wonder, and to be constrained either to believe that many of those very same persons, who being of my own profession had once been active assertors of ye Royal cause, and painful sufferers for it, have since contrived ye worst of treasons against it; or else to believe or think . . . that there hath been an unchristian confederacy against ye reputation, lives and fortunes of many innocent men. I was troubled a little som months agoe to see my trusty old sword taken from me (which had been my companion wen I lost my limbs, my lands, my liberty for acting against the rebels in the King's behalf) by an officer appointed for ye purpose, who in that former old war had been a captaine against ye King.

Yet I hear no personal charge against me, nor do I fear any at all, saving purely upon ye account of ye religion which I have ever profest In that particular I conceive that my estate and my liberty, as well as many others, may incur no little damage, if ye Parlements will be done; and if that be ye King's will too, I shall most heartily and humbly submit I have formerly suffered the loss of a fair personal estate and sequestration of all my lands for lo long years and upwards. After which I bought ye same lands off ye rebels in ye year 53 with ye money which I borrowed off my friends.

I was 4 tymes taken prisoner and paid my ransom twice All this was for my loyalty to ye King. I deny, as in ye presence of God, yet I have ever entertained any designe whatsoever contrary to ye duty of a subject eyther against that K. or this. And as for invasions, it hath ever been my professed principle, that all even Catholic subjects of a lawful Protestant king (such as King Charles ye 2nd) are obliged faithfully to adhere to that King in all invasions whatsoever, though made by Catholic princes or even by the Pope himself.

Mr. Langhorne suffered resolutely on July 14, 1679, asserting in his last speech that he had an offer of a free pardon if he would have renounced his religion. The judge who condemned him (Justice Scroggs) afterwards declared that he was convinced of his innocence, for which he was taken to task by Oates and Bedloe. This must have been a very anxious time for Mr. Blundell, as, in addition to his friend's prosecution, his own son Nicholas had been marked out as one of the victims for destruction. He had entered the Society of Jesus in 1662, and was arrested at Lambeth by the pursuivants of Oates, who declared that he had revealed to him the plan for the burning of London.

He must have been speedily released from custody, and was present at the trial of the accused, of which he gives many particulars in a letter to a nun at Cambray, which has found its way into the State Archives at Brussels. Extracts from the letter may be seen in the ample account of this conspiracy, contained in the fifth volume of Foley's *Records of the English Province*, S. J. This work, of which the last volume has only recently appeared, is not sufficiently known. It embodies more original information respecting the Catholic body during the operation of the penal laws than any work hitherto published.

Another of Mr. Blundell's correspondents was the well-known political writer Roger l'Estrange, Esq. (afterwards knighted), who published an *Intelligencer,* which his friend was able to join a neighbour in procuring twice a week. From some passages in his letters, it is probable that he furnished occasional items of news for this journal. Mr. Blundell seems to have had some difficulty in getting his correspondent to put the right address upon his letters. Thus on June 1, 1664, he says in a postscript:

> If you do ever remember me again, I pray forget not Liverpool, for your two last letters being directed to Preston (20 miles off) came late to my hand. Liverpool is 5 from hence and even from thence the passage to us dependeth very often upon the

market day.

Writing the following month from 'Westchester,' he says:

Yours of the 2nd, directed to Crosby in Cheshire, I have caught today in my journey to Chester. You shot 6 bows over Crosby when you aimed at Preston, and now at Cheshire you are three or four short. Surely I shall take myself for some great body, for every shaft will hit me though shot at random.

Chapter 3

William Blundell the Cavalier—Continued

Notwithstanding his lameness, Mr. Blundell's activity, both of mind and body, was very great He visited, as may be seen from the following notes, many places of interest at home and abroad, concerning which he has several curious notices. His hurt does not seem to have prevented him from riding, or from following the diversion of hunting, of which he was particularly fond. His cousin, Sir Roger Bradshaigh of Haigh, kept a pack of hounds, as also did his kinsman and neighbour, Laurence Ireland, of Lydiate, Esq. He carefully records the bugle notes of Sir Roger's huntsman, also his 'recheat' or recall of the hunting party. He gives also the 'recheat' (a much longer one) of his friend Mr. Ireland.

This gentleman,, the last of the Lydiate branch of the Irelands of Hutte and Hale, when a widower at the age of thirty-one, having settled his estates on his elder daughter Margaret (afterwards married to Sir Charles Anderton, Second Baronet of Lostock), left the world and became a Jesuit and a priest Mr. Blundell, in his letters to his friend and to Sir Thomas Preston, of the Manor, Furness, Bart, who some time afterwards, under similar circumstances, entered the same Society, seems to envy their lot, and tells them that they have chosen the better part He reminds Laurence Ireland of the last house but one at which they had met to join a hunting party.

On this occasion his friend remarked to him that whenever he heard the triple note of the bugle sounding to the chase, it seemed to cry out to him 'Dead, Dead, Dead.' Whilst abroad, Mr. Blundell furnished him, at his request, with what he calls 'bills of mortality.' Three or four of these very interesting communications have been copied into his letter-book, and they contain, besides much local news, many matters of general interest In a letter dated 1668 occurs this passage:

> The noble Countess of Southampton hath been here four or five weeks amongst us, bowling on Sephton Green; the country came flowing in, and she kept a public table at the Hall of Maile (Maghull). I could have soured her cheer by giving her bills of mortality since the last scene she acted in this neighbourhood. But I was so sour myself, that I saw not so much as a brace of rubbers on the Green during the whole play. *Quantum mutatus.*

It must be presumed that the once fashionable pastime alluded to was the attraction which drew Barbara Villiers, Duchess of Cleveland and Countess of Southampton, one of the numerous mistresses of Charles II., from the fascinations of a Court to so remote a spot as Maghull. From a letter written about this time by the Cavalier's son William to his brother-in-law, Lawrence, son of Rowland Eyre of Hassop, co. Derbyshire, Esq., it would appear that a bowling club had been established at Sefton under distinguished auspices:

> If you could have time to make a step into Lancashire, I would show you once a week a meeting of a dozen or fourteen gent. lemen, or more, who, after a dinner had at Sefton, spend the afternoon at bowls. My Lord Molineux and his son (who is lately come out of Italy), Sir Edward Stanley, my cousin Scarisbrick, and others have engaged to meet at Sefton every week. Sir Edward Stanley has set afoot bows and arrows, and follows the sport very eagerly. My Lord Molineux his son intends to do the like. So that you will find other diversion besides downright drinking.

From the last expression it may be inferred that the praiseworthy encouragement given to these innocent recreations by the heads of the chief families in this part, was with the view of counteracting that evil. That it was a great evil at that period, is evident from Mr. Blundell's correspondence.

In his bills of mortality the number of deaths amongst the gentry, which he attributes to what he calls 'the vice of our country,' is very large. He mentions the appalling circumstance of a 'notable observing youth' having reckoned no fewer than fifty burials of rich and poor within the space of one year in Prescot parish alone, all caused by immoderate drinking. This shows the prevalence of this vice to an alarming extent, fostered as it was by the example of the higher orders. Mr. Blundell gives more than one example of a young man challenged and shot dead by his host, who chose to think himself insulted when his guest refused his cups. Whatever may be the case at present with regard to the lower orders, it is certain that there is a manifest improvement amongst those of the higher class, since the days of deep drinking have gone out.

In the following notes frequent reference will be found to the subject of duelling, another prevalent vice of the times. Mr. Blundell's mind seems to have been much exercised by this question; but he was clearly of opinion that it was unlawful either to give or to accept a challenge. He says that a man whose courage has been proved can refuse a challenge without imputation of cowardice, and he brings an example to show how a man should act whose valour has not been put to the test How Mr. Blundell himself would have acted in such a case, is evident from the following remarkable answer which he had prepared in anticipation of a challenge. Here we find the noblest sentiments of a Christian and the exalted courage of a cavalier happily blended:

I have lost much blood in defence of the laws, and will not hazard any to break them. I confess I dare not be damned upon any account, and am unwilling to be hanged upon this. I have not learnt the ways to evade the hand of justice when I am guilty of blood. In short, I will neither meet you nor any man, how strong or weak he may be, with so bad a design, and I propose, by God's assistance, that the most public or great affront that malice shall devise against me, shall not move me from this resolution. If I have done wrong to you or any man else, I will hazard my blood and fortune (in a just and honourable way) so far to make amends; and in this I shall always be willing to submit to indifferent judges. In the mean time, if this answer displeases you, I shall never decline the walks to which my business leads me out of any fear of your sword, &c.

Mr. Blundell says that the party from whom he had good reason to expect a challenge was a person of great repute, and from another passage we gather that it was Colonel Moore, his neighbour of Bank Hall. This gentleman, was the only Protestant magistrate in the neighbourhood, and had given much annoyance to him and his tenants on the score of religion. Mr. Blundell had written some verses concerning him which were not of a complimentary character, and possibly had expressed his sentiments in language which would be called in these days 'unparliamentary.'

As Colonel Moore died in Dublin about 1650, having accompanied Cromwell to Ireland at the head of a force, this answer must have been written before that period. He was one of the members of Parliament whose names we find appended to the warrant for the execution of Charles I. Notwithstanding the injuries received from the family, Mr. Blundell, on occasion of an epidemic (said to have been smallpox), when Mrs. Moore had her husband (Edward, afterwards Sir Edward Moore, Baronet, son of the Colonel) sick and three children dead in the house, went no less than four times to visit and console her. At this time none of her friends would come near the place, and it is a curious sign of the credulity of the age, that Mrs. Moore could not be persuaded that her children had succumbed to any natural distemper, but ascribed their death to witchcraft

So great was the excitement produced throughout the country by the accusations of Titus Oates, that besides the exclusion of the Catholic Peers from the House of Lords, which was effected in 1678, the banishment of all the leading Catholics of the kingdom was seriously contemplated. This was perhaps found to be too severe and impolitic a measure to be carried out Lists of the intended victims were prepared in 1680 by the aid of the returns of the names of recusants made at that time. Sir Roger Bradshaigh sent Mr. Blundell a catalogue of Popish recusants of the greatest quality in Lancashire, whom it was proposed to banish.

This he had procured from the Earl of Ancram, and we find Caryll Viscount Molyneux at the head of the list, which comprises sixty-four names, including those of Mr. Blundell and his son William. He had previously applied to Government for a pass to go abroad, and was informed that he could not have one, unless he entered into recognisances not to return into England without a licence. Mr. Blundell indignantly refused a permission coupled with so hard a condition, and thus expresses himself in a letter to Lord Ancram:—

22 Aug. 1679. . . . . . I have engaged in 500*l.* already not to travel to Rome, and now to banish myself by a deliberate act of my own from my native and best beloved country, I have not the heart to do. I should certainly forfeit my bond if nothing else would effect my return. I would rather be confined again (as once in the prime of my youth for the noblest cause in the

world) to my plundered bare walls and a pair of crutches, than to lead the life of an outlaw. I desire, as the case now stands, rather to keep my possession till the law of the land or of nature do turn me out

Later on he procured a licence free from the obnoxious condition, and passed over into France, where he spent a good part of the following year. He resided chiefly at La Fleche, for the sake of his grandson the Honourable Edmund Butler, who was then pursuing his studies at the Jesuit Academy.

During the short reign of James II. our Cavalier was frequently in London, where he had many friends at Court, who encouraged him with the hope of at length obtaining some compensation for his many trials. At their suggestion he prepared a petition to the King, and was led to expect that he might receive some post, though, as he himself says, he hardly knew what sort of an office would suit a man of his years and infirmities. This petition, which is inserted at the conclusion of this sketch, does not appear to have been actually presented, and the end of his hopes and those of his friends came very speedily.

When the news of the Prince of Orange's intended landing reached England, the martial instincts of the old cavalier were aroused, and he addressed a letter to the Honourable Robert Strickland, Vice-Chamberlain to the Queen, suggesting a plan for the discomfiture of the enemy's troop of horse, which was said to be incomparably strong. This plan was the planting of a number of sharp-pointed rods (tipped with iron, if possible) to be so placed as to impale the horses of the troopers when they rushed to the attack. He goes into details, describing, with the precision of a quartermaster, the size of the rods, the quantity required, and the wagons desirable for their transportation.

Whatever military men may think of this scheme, to a non-combatant it wears rather an impracticable appearance, as its success seems wholly to depend upon the enemy adopting the exact position necessary for their impalement. As they might possibly have declined to be parties to their own destruction, in this case the rods were as likely to be a hindrance to the King's troops as damaging to the enemy. Our cavalier must have been considerably disgusted to find the kingdom delivered up without a struggle; but, considering the then temper of the nation, it was perhaps the wisest course the King could have adopted.

In 1689 Mr. Blundell underwent, at Manchester, his fifth imprisonment, being confined with others of his religion, by virtue of a warrant from Lord Gerard of Brandon, Lord Lieutenant of the county. This step was no doubt taken as a measure of precaution to prevent the disaffected from joining King James in Ireland. This confinement lasted seven weeks, and was rendered less irksome by the company he met with. Of Mr. Towneley of Towneley, one of the prisoners, he says that his cheerful society would make life pleasant anywhere.

From the period of his release till the close of his life, Mr. Blundell remained at his own house, or rather within the tether of what he calls his five miles' chain. This was the limit of travel then prescribed for recusants, who had to enter into recognisances not to exceed it without a licence. In January 1691, he thus writes to a Protestant friend in London:—

> Since my discharge at the assizes, I have not stirred from home; yet my son and servant have made good use in my behalf (so far as their five miles' chain will reach) of those two horses for which you were kindly pleased to procure me a licence. We have now no disturbance at all, and if I be not greatly mistaken, all my friends here and hereabout are so sensible of this present ease, that they will not easily lose it through any demerit It is but nine or ten months since my own in-foal mares were taken out of my grounds, and sold to my neighbours. Our colts were then taken at two or three years of age, and about that time it was, that my servant, returning unarmed from the next market, was assailed upon the road with pistol and bayonet, whereby some blood was drawn, because he would not yield his horse (which, in truth, was a very mean one) to an officer of our country's militia, who refused to show an order for seizing the same. We have none of these doings now. We may sit very securely under our own vines, and we have reason to pray for the King. I am sure without his favour (a favour, I confess, unexpected) we had all been a prey to the law, or, rather, perhaps, to the rabble.

The record of the death of one of Mr. Blundell's tenants, in 1692, brings to light a remarkable proof of the patriotism and loyalty of our cavalier. This man, Robert Tomson, had been a seaman in the reign of Charles I., and had performed some conspicuous act of gallantry, for which Mr. Blundell gave him a free lease of his tenement in Little Crosby. The grant is thus recorded in the tenants' book:—

> 24th June 1669. Gave unto Robert Tomson, the seaman, a lease *gratis*, for the great service he had done to his late Majesty in

time of the war, which was truly great and remarkable in many respects.

We regret that we have not succeeded in finding any particulars of this deed. The ingratitude and injustice with which Mr. Blundell had been treated enhance the generosity of this act. Himself a great sufferer for his loyalty, he would not allow an inferior man, who had done a service to the King, to go without his reward, although his own reduced fortunes could ill afford the sacrifice.

Another trial awaited Mr. Blundell, before his long and eventful career came to a close. He was one of the Lancashire Catholics of position accused of participation in the sham plot of 1694. The late Bishop Goss, in *Manchester State Trials*, which he edited for the Chetham Society from papers at Crosby, gives the following account of his transaction:—

On Monday, July 30, 1694, at half-past five in the morning, three of the King's messengers, with two of the informers, invaded the hall at Crosby, with the intention of carrying off old Mr. Blundell. As, however, he was then in his seventy-fifth year, and had been lame for many years, in consequence of the injuries he had received while fighting in the royal cause, they did not take him with them: but they carried off a case of pistols, two swords, and a fowling-piece, with seven horses and two hackney-saddles. Mr. William Blundell, jun., having shown them to his father's room, left the house; but, finding on his return that they carried off his horses, he went to Liverpool, to Mr. Norris of Speke, who gave him into the custody of the Mayor, by whom he was handed over to Captain Baker, who sent him to Chester Castle and thence to London, where, having been examined, he was committed and taken to Newgate. None of the authorities concerned in this illegal arrest seem to have doubted the justice of committing the son for the supposed crime of the father.

The trial resulted in the acquittal of the prisoners, who were dismissed by the Judge with the injunction to '*go and sin no more:*' a singularly inappropriate application of Scripture in the case of these much injured gentlemen.

The brave, loyal, and virtuous Cavalier whose life we have been attempting to sketch ended his days peaceably at Crosby Hall, on May 24, 1698, He was interred at Sefton Church, in the Blundell Chapel, where the bones of so many of his ancestors repose. He was succeeded in his estates by his son William Blundell, who only survived him a few years, dying in 1702. This gentleman,'s son Nicholas, who married the Honourable Frances, daughter of Marmaduke, third Lord Langdale, and died in 1737, was the last in the male line of this ancient race. The family succession was kept up through the marriage of Frances, surviving daughter and heiress of Nicholas, with Henry Peppard, Esq., of Drogheda, whose son Nicholas took, in 1772, the name of Blundell, and was ancestor to Colonel Nicholas Blundell, its present worthy representative. To the courtesy of this gentleman, our readers are indebted for whatever pleasure or interest they may derive from the perusal of these pages.

The following is the petition to King James II. referred to above, which was prepared by the Cavalier, but never presented. It is interesting as containing the summary of his claims upon the merciful consideration of his sovereign. It is headed—

The Family of William Blundell

The family of W. B. hath continued in ye place where it is now seated for very many generations, during which time there is no memory left that any son or daughter of ye house hath professed any other than ye Roman Catholick Religion. This hath been ye cause that since ye pretended Reformation, it hath suffered persecution for the same in an extraordinary degree. The story would be here over long: and so much thereof as happened before our memory, may be found by ancient writings, that give us an account of many imprisonments of ye ancestors of ye said W. B., *viz.* at Chester, Lancaster, and London; the begging of ye real estate by sundry court favourites in Queen Elizabeth's dayes, and ye seizure of ye moveable goods with ye utter loss of ye same in later times.

The persecution occasioned by ye late plott, and especially the execution of ye statute for 20*l. per mensem*, hath been an extraordinary damage by reason it hath also involved and very sorely impoverisht ye greatest part of his tenants. For whereas W. B. is ye Lord or owner of one small Lordship or Manor consisting of forty houses or thereabouts, there are not (thro ye grace of God) any other but Catholicks in it, except, peradventure, one or two dayly labourers, which being born in other places are come to live there for work. And as it hath pleased

God to grant such grace to that neighbourhood dureing a long persecution. His goodness has been greatly remarkable to ye kindred of W. B. which is scattered farther abroad; as appears by a list of one hundred Catholic Priests and Religions of both sexes, whereof seven of his own children and all ye rest in the 2nd, 3rd, and 4th degree; many of which are liveing and many dead If none of these had renounced ye world, it is probable that an extraordinary great number of that kindred had engaged in defence of ye Crown in our late unfortunate warrs. And yet there has likewise been very many such, and some of them greatly remarkable, whereas there were none at all that fought on ye Rebells' side.

It is known that W. B. himself was sorely maimed in ye service at ye very beginning of ye warr, in the year 42, and that he was for ye same divested of goods and land; which lands were sequestred and wholly detained from him for ye space of ten years, and then were exposed to sale by virtue of a Rump act Yet true it is, that they were purchased in the name of his friends with moneys which he himself procured, for his own proper use and behoofe.

This case of sequestration and sale under a monstrous pretence of delinquency, involved all ye visible fortunes of very many hundreds of other Catholick familyes, as well as ye family abovesaid of W. B.; altho it may be hard at ye present to find one other English subject liveing, that in other respects and according to his small quantum has suffered so much as he by loss of blood, imprisonment, decimation, and sundry other wayes. There are liveing this present year, 1687-8, no fewer then 13 sons and daughters (besides the teeming wife of his most dutiful eldest son and som children already preferred) that are yet to be provided for out of his small estate: and this estate at ye present is so sorely charged, that altho ye family hath long subsisted in ye worst of times, it is now in danger to fail when ye times are good

. . . . It is very well known that ye small township abovesaid was many years remarked for these things,—

That it had not a beggar;

That it had not an alehouse;

That it had not a Protestant in it

Yet our troubles have so much increased for some later years, that ye case as to ye matter of beggars is sorely changed.

This document reminds us that time brings about its revenges. It is curious to find one who had suffered constant persecution and had experienced the severe displeasure of the Crown because he refused to become a Protestant, pleading the absence of Protestantism in himself, family, and township, as an argument likely to find favour with his sovereign. It is perhaps still more curious to notice that after the lapse of two centuries things remain in this respect almost wholly unchanged. A direct descendant of the Cavalier, occupying his mansion and estate, can say at this day of his village, that there is neither beggar, alehouse, nor Protestant within it This cannot altogether be spoken now of the *township*, although the truth is not far from it.

The village of Little Crosby lies on the northwest of the park, almost within shelter of its walls. Many of the cottages have been rebuilt of late years, and the place has a neat and clean appearance. The school is under chaise of the Sisters of Charity of St Vincent of Paul, with whose habit those who have travelled abroad will be familiar. One of the sisters of the present squire is a member of this religious Order. The church stands at the northern extremity of the village, and is the result of a bequest of the late William Blundell, Esq., who died in 1854. This gentleman, married Katharine, daughter of Sir Thomas Massey Stanley, Bart, of Hooton, Cheshire, the chief of that famous race.

Little Crosby Church is a neat Gothic edifice, complete with spire, &c. The interior decorations were designed and executed by the patient and skilful hand of the present squire in his younger years.

CHAPTER 4

Character and Literary Productions of William Blundell

The following notes show that Mr. Blundell possessed much of that honourable and open character which is said to belong to Lancashiremen of the best type. He speaks his mind in a straightforward, manly way. The impression we have in reading his letters and remarks is highly favourable to his integrity. We seem to be listening to a man who would rather suffer any torments than tell a lie or deny his principles. And that such was his real character, the whole tenor of his life bears witness. His friends reposed the greatest confidence in him, and he was frequently selected as umpire in family differences, where the circumstances called for the exercise of much tact and judgment Ladies who presided over religious houses abroad found in him a faithful financial agent.

His carefulness and exactitude in managing this troublesome business, which he undertook solely out of charity, is manifest from the account-books which he has left behind him. Considering the many troubles in which he was involved, it is difficult to see how he contrived to bring up a large family in tolerable comfort He says in one of his letters, that three generations of his race were then living on the estate, and that he does not believe that there is in Lancashire another housekeeper who has so many mouths to feed. One element in his character was of the most essential service to him at all times, and that was his unfailing good-humour.

Whatever he had to endure, he never desponded; nor did he give way to any murmuring or repining at Divine Providence. How he combated temptations of this nature (which happened to him as to others), may be gathered from some of the following reflections. He was of a hasty temperament, and frequently yielded to sallies of anger. This propensity, however, he much subdued by watchfulness, and we learn from his own observations, how continually he laboured to repress other excesses, not by general resolutions, but by particular and approved methods. His witty and agreeable manner made him a delightful companion, and his society was eagerly sought for by a large circle of acquaintance. He reckoned amongst his dearest friends many who were not of his own faith, and exercised towards all an hospitality that was only bounded by his means.

If his career as a soldier had not been cut short, Mr. Blundell was likely to have proved a good commander. He was of an enterprising, hardy, and valorous nature: qualities which would have gone far to endear him to his troops. Nor was he wanting in that discretion and ability without which a general can neither combat difficulties nor achieve successes. To the close of his life he took much interest in military matters, and made many observations relative to cannon and other implements of war. As has been already remarked, one of his latest letters, addressed to the Vice-Chamberlain of King James II.'s consort, contained details of a plan for the defeat of the Prince of Orange's troop of horse.

His letters are no hasty scrawls, but bear marks of the careful revision of the writer. They must have been charming reading to his correspondents, from the pleasant vein of humour which runs through them. One addressed to a recently married daughter, which he wrote towards the end of his life, is full of fun, showing that he retained to the last the same happy and contented mind. They contain many proofs of the influence which he possessed over young men of his own position in life, and of the excellent use which he made of that influence. Whilst his neighbours, the young squires of Ince Blundell and Scarisbrick, are still at college, he writes to them in his pleasant manner, giving them details of country news, but does not fail to exhort them to lay up such a stock of learning and virtue as will enable them to combat the temptations to which they will soon find themselves exposed.

His nephew, Thomas Selby of Biddlestone, Northumberland, Esq., who had come early into possession of his estate, experienced a large share of this tenderness and solicitude. In a long letter written to him at St. Omer's College, he confesses his own mistakes in early life, the better to warn him against those dangers which beset unguarded youth. He uses many motives to urge his correspondent to aim at a high standard, while he enjoys the advantage of residing at a place so renowned for virtue and learning. One sentence we give as a sample of his earnest and impressive manner:

> I would have you, nephew, to think often (it is a lawful and honourable ambition), that the time will come when you shall sit like an oracle in the Highlands of Northumberland, giving counsel and assistance to all your friends and neighbours. So did Roger Widdrington, your late neighbour and kinsman, who, besides a general reputation for wisdom, raised himself merely by his own wit, tempered finely with learning and seconded by a commendable frugality, from a most inconsiderable to a fair and eminent fortune. This example is familiar (*nam nota loquor*), and yourself cannot choose but remember him.

It may be thought that this was the outcome of the wisdom of his riper age, but he had only attained his thirtieth year when he penned these lines. They represent, therefore, the excellent form which his mind had thus early assumed. So great an interest did he take in the welfare of youth, that for some years he acted as tutor to his grandsons Edmond and Richard Butler, the children of Lord Mountgarret. His assiduity and perseverance in this laborious office were incessant The result he communicates in a letter to their father, in which he commends the proficiency of his pupils, and boasts, not unreasonably, that this success has been attained without the help of a rod. He says that he had found better means of stimulating their industry, and urges their father to send them abroad, to pursue their studies under a better master. He says of the elder—

> I would have him to dance and fence, to speak Latin and French readily, and to see the world. We are here so far from speaking good Latin, that our English is barbarous. You may find us now and then up to our ears in Plutarch, in a hot dispute whether Alexander the Great or Caesar was the braver man. And perhaps, within an hour or two afterwards, the gallant fierce disputant will be up to the knees in the brambles, at the head of a whole regiment of our pitiful tatterdemalions, beating to start a hare. I blame not but pity him for it; he hath seldom better company with which to divert himself And yet, to my great admiration, he contracts as little rusticity as any I have ever met with in so hard a case.

The elder of these youths became, in 1706, the sixth Viscount

Mountgarret, and retained to the close of his life a strong attachment to Crosby, the scene of his happy and careless boyhood When obliged to leave Ireland, through the troubles in which his family was involved by its fidelity to King James, he sought with his father an asylum in England. They settled in the neighbouring town of Ormskirk, then the residence of a number of the local gentry, as the petty capital of a rural district Edmund, Lord Mountgarret, was restored in blood and honours in 1721.

In matters of religion, as may easily be discovered from the following notes, Mr. Blundell was not only staunch in belief, but faithful in the practice of the duties of his creed. And yet he must have had many difficulties to encounter in securing opportunities for its observances. At a time when no Catholic chapel except the Queen's, and those of foreign ambassadors, were tolerated in England, the services of the Church were necessarily performed in secret in some obscure part of the dwelling. To this the tenants and neighbouring Catholics had access, and the priest attended to their spiritual wants with as much precaution as possible. All this was accompanied with great risk to the host, and still greater to the priest, whose life was at the mercy of the meanest informant The chaplain had generally, for greater security, his room at the upper part of the house, and in time of danger was obliged to keep very close and retired. Mr. Blundell, in his letters to Haggerston, often desires to be remembered to the gentleman, at the ' top of the house.' Here too he was, when necessary, served from the family table. In the *Breifie Narration* of Rev. Gilbert Blackball (published in 1844 by the Spalding Club), the writer says

—In great houses, if the priests eat in their private chambers, they must stay till the lady send them from the table, upon trenchers, such pieces as she pleaseth. I have seen this done in England to priests eating in their chambers (1638).

A frequent change of residence was very necessary, and we do not find that any priests had a settled abode till the close of the civil war. Curiously enough, it happens that Crosby Hall is the first place in Lancashire named in conjunction with a resident priest The Rev. John Walton, S. J., became Mr. Blundell's chaplain about 1652, but was obliged to leave through ill-health in 1656. Mr. Blundell, who was then staying with his wife at Haggerston, sent him a farewell letter, which we quote, to show the affectionate relations subsisting between them:

I received your letter of farewell long since, and if ye had dealt lesse cruelly by writing lesse kindly, I could sooner have returned an answer. That part which belongs to my wife, she returns ye in prayers and tears; but those (as ye know best) are generally much wanting in her husband. Yet I confidently believe now that he prayes very heartily amongst other blessings for your health. Just so do I pray for my purgatory in this world, both wishing and fearing ye smart. If ye recover now, Sir, we would not murther ye againe at Crosby for all ye world. If ye linger in ye same maner still, I have petitioned your master to return ye thither. And as long as those fearefull hopes of ours are lyk to continew, so long shall ye poore old cabin be undisposed to any other, &c.

The Rev. John Walton, S. J., who belonged to an old Lancashire family, was sent on the mission in 1652, and it is probable that Crosby was the first place that he served. When absent from home, for the reasons already assigned, we find Mr. Blundell saying in a letter to his sister Frances at Crosby, in 1656, 'Mr. Walton is welcome to stay and do nothing;' from which it would appear that his health was very bad. He did not return to Crosby; but died in London on December 30, 1677, at the age of fifty-five. The next chaplain at Crosby was the Rev. Francis Waldegrave, S. J. He was a great grandson of Sir Edward Waldegrave, Knight, the stout servant of Queen Mary, who was imprisoned for refusing to enforce the mandate of King Edward VI.'s Council, which forbade the celebration of mass at Copped Hall, in Essex, the then residence of the Princess.

Losing his father in early youth, his mother, Lucy, daughter of Dean Mervin, sought an asylum with her brother, a clergyman of the Established Church. Notwithstanding her conversion, he received her and her children with the utmost kindness, and made no objection to her son Francis going to St Omer's College, which was accomplished with the assistance of his aunt Frances, who had married Richard, Lord Weston, Lord High Treasurer of England, and subsequently. Earl of Portland. He was ordained priest in the church of St John Lateran, at Rome, on March 25, 1651, and left college for the English Mission in the autumn of the following year.

After three years he embraced the Society of Jesus, having long had this desire. Mr. Blundell says that he was the dear friend of his brother Richard, who had the same desire, and, impatient of delay, sought the intercession of several cardinals to obtain a dispensation from his College oath. Making many journeys for the object through the streets of Rome, during the summer heats of 1649, he contracted a fever, of which he died the same year. He had the consolation of being clothed, before his death, with the habit of St Ignatius. In another place will be found Mr. Blundell's memoir of his brother, from which it appears that he was a youth of remarkable virtue and ability.

After having served Crosby for many years. Father Waldegrave went to Lydiate Hall, the residence of old Mrs. Ireland, where, he died in 1701. He was buried in the ruined chapel of St Katharine, and a copy of the inscription, still to be seen on his tombstone, will be found in *Foley's Records, S.J.*, vol. 5. He was a man of zeal and talent, and Mr. Blundell contracted a friendship with him which lasted through life. After he had left Crosby, his friend continued to employ him as his spiritual director, and consulted him in weighty matters. He speaks of a horse to which he had given the name of 'Waldegrave.'

The amusing incident which Mr. Blundell relates of his chaplain refusing, on one occasion, to join him and his family in a particular act of devotion, no doubt refers to Mr. Waldegrave. It did not, however, disturb the amicable relations subsisting between them, and the squire's momentary irritation passed off in the act of recording it There is no doubt that, although priests had only their patrons to look to for the supply of all their wants, yet they occupied a perfectly independent position in the household. They were by no means that abject servile class which chaplains of the Established Church are represented by some popular writers to have been. They were, for the most part, men of family, often the equals in point of birth to those at whose table they sat, and not rarely their superiors in culture and learning.

Add to this the advantages derived from a long residence abroad, and it may readily be imagined that a Catholic squire of those days found in his chaplain a polished and agreeable companion. Moreover, their wide acquaintance with the Catholic gentry, would furnish them with topics of conversation very acceptable to those knit together by the powerful bonds of faith and mutual suffering. Much information on family matters was thus obtained, and introductions with a. view to marriage were frequently furnished through their agency.

When Mr. Blundell wanted a wife for his son and heir, he received very exact particulars of two matches proposed to him, and in one case his informant was a priest Although his choice did not fall upon either of these parties, yet he was indebted to a priest for an intro-duction to his future daughter-in-law. In a letter to the Rev. Henry

Heaton, S. J. (probably Lord Montague's chaplain); he takes occasion to thank him for the good wife which he had procured for his son. This lady was Mary, daughter of Rowland Eyre, of Hassop, Derbyshire, Esq., who married William Blundell in 1668. We are tempted to bring to light a loveletter, written shortly before their union, which tends to show the immense distance between that age and the present one. The courtly and chivalrous terms in which this Cavalier's son greets the lady of his heart will fall on modern ears like the strains of an ancient roundelay.

> It is near ten days since I was torn away from your presence, where I desire ever to live, having left my heart behind me. Yet I bear the separation with the less impatience, because you did not reject me when I came from thence. I shall never desire to live without your favour, nor shall your favours ever raise me to a higher degree of confidence than becomes your humble servant This paper shall take the boldness to kiss your fair hand, from whence I am encouraged to hope for such a favourable return as may keep my hopes alive. I will still confide in your goodness to allow me the great honour to appear again in your presence about the middle of the next month. Oh! my most honoured dear lady, how shall I count those unkind hours that keep me from so great a joy! I could wish your heart like mine in all but the pain it feels. I told you once before (as I hope I did not offend), that your goodness hath cause to pardon what your virtue and beauty have done.

The accomplished object of these stately sighs brought her husband a numerous family, but was always delicate in health, and was more than once on the brink of the grave. In her youth she had wished to consecrate herself to God in religion, but yielded to the representation of her friends, who thought her health too infirm for such a vocation. On the death of her husband in 1702, her longing for a religious life returned, and she went to join the Benedictine Nuns at Ghent, where two of her daughters had been professed. One of these was the Superioress, and under her rule she spent happily the last years of her pilgrimage. She died in 1707, and a sitting portrait of her in her religious habit is amongst the family pictures at Crosby Hall.

We have said that the priests in the times we are alluding to were frequently men of good birth, and Mr. Blundell names no fewer than eighty-seven of his relatives, without reckoning any of his own family, who had embraced a religious life. In speaking of the disastrous civil wars and the large number of Catholics who had fallen on the royal side, he says that the number would have been much greater if so many had not entered a better militia. Out of a family of three sons and seven daughters who grew to man's estate, two sons and five daughters of our Cavalier became religious.

Taking together the three generations in the midst of which he stood, no less than seventeen Blundells, male and female, devoted themselves to a religious life. Unless the sons of the gentry had adopted this vocation, the necessary succession of priests, humanly speaking, could not have been kept up. By debarring Catholic gentlemen from any worldly employment suitable to their position in life, the Government, in its blind policy, promoted to the best of its power the cause of that religion which it was its object to stifle. It threw into its arms those who alone had the means and the opportunity of becoming priests.

Moreover, it furnished a class of priests which in the circumstances of the times was more acceptable to the gentry, and therefore more serviceable to religion, than any other could have been. Not the least valuable portion of the work to which we have already alluded (*Foley's Records, S. J.*), is the revelation it makes of the real names of the priests whose lives it recounts. It will there be seen that they worked under assumed names, not only on account of the danger which threatened themselves, but also for fear of that in which their kindred might be involved through their means. For this reason priests and religious were carefully excluded from pedigrees presented at Visitations or entrusted to Heralds' College. Many ancient and honourable houses will be able to fill up these *lacunae* in their genealogical tables by the aid of the pedigrees in which Brother Foley introduces, for the first time, not the least worthy branches of their stock.

We must now devote a short space to some cursory notice of the literary occupations of Mr. Blundell. These pervaded his life, or rather a certain calm and studious life ran alongside his public troubled career, tending much, no doubt, to sweeten the cup of his sorrows. He seems to have begun the practice of taking notes from the various authors he read when about the age of forty. These notes are contained in three books, called *Historia*, *Adversaria*, and *Hodge Podge*. The two first are small *quartos* of perhaps 1200 pages each, and these are for the most part well filled, and closely written in a neat and clear hand. *Hodge Podge* is a large *quarto*, and, in addition to Mr. Blundell's notes, contains literary productions in poetry and prose of his grandfather, besides matters of later date.

Most of the extracts and notes have a Latin heading in the margin, and the same heading recurs in several places, if the number of selections requires it This plan of common-place book has obvious advantages. With a general threefold grouping there is ample scope to embrace every subject Within very elastic folds. Although he nowhere mentions it, it seems highly probable that Mr. Blundell adopted this plan from *Drexelius* a learned Jesuit writer of the early part of the seventeenth century. It is certain that he was well acquainted with his treatise called *Aurofodina*, in which this system is recommended and elucidated by examples. He quotes at the beginning of *Historia* the Latin *dictum* found in this work, and followed it in practice, '*Modo tui armenti pecus sit, de stabulo non litigemus:*' 'Only let it be one of your herd, and you need not care where it is housed.'

This plan of common-place book has found favour with many literary men. William Windham, the statesman, had his *Historia* and *Adversaria*, as we learn from his diary (a very disappointing book), and it is highly probable that Dr. Johnson, to whom he deferred in such matters, recommended to him the adoption of this system. The result in Mr. Blundell's case is an accumulation of extracts and quotations, which, while they bespeak his industry, must have helped materially to enlarge his knowledge and correct his judgment.

Common-place books are of all publications the most dreary and uninviting, and hence it happens that even the names of Southey and Buckle cannot invest their compilations of this kind with any flavour of interest We need not stop, therefore, to speak of these selections, which derive whatever value they possess from the books from which they were taken. These are now for the most part obsolete, yet it is a pleasure to find that Mr. Blundell appreciated the writings of Bacon, the great luminary of his age. He quotes Ben Jonson, Sidney, and numberless travellers in whose strange accounts of newly discovered regions he much delighted.

Such descriptions have no longer any interest, but the raciness and originality of *Howell's Letters of Foreign Travel*, a work frequently quoted by Mr. Blundell, have preserved it from oblivion. In one of his amusing *Roundabout Papers*, Thackeray says, '*Montaigne* and *Howell's Letters* are my bedside books. If I wake at night, I have one or other of them to prattle me to sleep again.' In religious books he had some special favourites; such as the *Holy Court*, by Caussin, a work that has still many readers, who gather instruction from its ample pages, and regale themselves with its numerous examples. He was well versed in the Holy Scriptures, and applies them frequently in illustration of various headings. Although Mr. Blundell was in his younger days the author of verses by no means despicable, yet he seems early to have abandoned the pursuit

It is quite in conformity with his character to suppose that he relinquished poetry from a religious motive, for fear of it engrossing too much of his mind and time. With the same view, probably, he gave up all desire of seeing plays or comedies, or even of reading such productions. At all events, he very rarely quotes any of them, and considering the general character of such writings in the seventeenth century, no one can say that he did not practise a wise abstinence. Yet it probably deprived him of the opportunity of reading Shakespeare's inimitable works, with which he appears to have been wholly unacquainted. He only mentions his name once, and that in connection with the worst of his plays.

Shakespeare's fame was of slow growth, and he cannot be said to have been really known to his countrymen till the opening years of last century. Even the Rev. John Ward,, who became Vicar of Stratford-on-Avon in 1662, has very little to say in his diary of the man to whom that town is indebted for whatever celebrity it possesses. One passage seems to corroborate the opinion that Shakespeare had little classical learning, but he was evidently then unacquainted with his plays, for he adds this memorandum, 'Remember to peruse Shakespeare's plays, and be much versed in them, that I may not be ignorant in that matter.'

Still it is remarkable that a gentleman, in the position of Mr. Blundell, a literary man, not unacquainted with the contents of London bookshelves, and accustomed to polished if not learned society, should know nothing whatever of our great household poet With his contemporary Milton, as a poet, he was no better acquainted. Of his prose works he speaks frequently, and, as may be imagined, with due abhorrence; but he does not seem to have had any idea that he was the most charming versifier in the kingdom.

The foregoing remarks do not apply to the following notes added by Mr. Blundell himself, which form the matter now given to the public. These are the product of his own thought and observation, and are generally very judicious. He expresses himself in clear and concise terms, free from affectation or pedantry. His good sense revolted against the fashion, common to writers of his day, of decking out their sentences in gaudy trappings. He says of one book (*Loveday's Letters*), that if it was put into plain English, it would look like a plucked peacock. The anecdotes which he recounts are well told, and the quaintness of their dress reminds us of his contemporary Pepys. Several of them regard historical personages, and their authenticity is ensured by Mr. Blundell's careful habit of giving dates and names. His position in life afforded him opportunities of seeing and hearing much that has more than a local interest Thus he speaks of the conversations of Charlotte, Countess of Derby, the famous defender of Latham House. Unfortunately, he does not tell us many of her remarks, which may have arisen from the difficulty which he says he had in catching her observations 'by defect of my Lady's English.'

It will be seen that in many matters of political economy Mr. Blundell was much in advance of his age. He advocates the publication of law reports and of the proceedings in criminal cases, and has an eye to the advantage, if not necessity, of advertising. Notices of sales, &c., he recommends should be put up at the church door or village smithy. He thinks it advisable that when a gentleman, wants to sell his horse, a ribbon should be affixed to the bridle. In days when everybody rode on horseback, it is strange that so good a suggestion was never adopted. He speaks of the advantage of circulating the particulars of the accidents that may happen in a neighbourhood, and instances the case of a man who, while digging for rabbits at the Grange, was smothered by the sand falling upon him.

Shortly after, a similar disaster occurred at Maghull, which is only three miles distant 'Surely,' he says, 'this would never have happened if the last man had been aware of the other's mishap.' He had the satisfaction of finding one at least of his recommendations carried out before his death. His position in life and well-known integrity had caused him to be the depositary of various sums of money, belonging to the ladies who presided over religious houses abroad. This money he was in the habit of lending to gent.lemen of his acquaintance in sums of 50*l*. at the invariable interest of six *per cent*. He sometimes found a difficulty in locating these trusts, and thought the establishment of agencies for the lending and borrowing of money would be of much benefit

Such houses were afterwards established in a few provincial towns, and he made use of them in his later years. The parties who undertook the management of this business appear to have been at first agent.s or attorneys. The system of banking was commenced in London before the end of the seventeenth century, and Mr. Blundell frequently quotes the works of Sir Josiah Child on trade and currency questions. The cavalier's suggestion of a matrimonial mart, conducted by 'sober and discreet persons,' is a good one, and such institutions are successful in France.

In this country they have not been attempted, perhaps through fear of the ridicule which might be thrown upon them. It is well known that the more vulgar method of advertising has given rise frequently to practical jokes not of the most gentle character. In the matter of weights and measures Mr. Blundell had the sagacity to see that great injustice and anomalies might be remedied by a law of uniformity. It is very remarkable that abuses which this country gentleman, saw and spoke of 200 years ago have been permitted to go on to the present day. This very year has witnessed for the first time the attempt to supply the obvious remedy for a great evil which he so long ago suggested.

In addition to the notes of Mr. Blundell which are here given, he left behind him a number of his own letters copied into folio sheets, and since bound up in a volume. He has also inserted in another book those letters of his correspondents which he deemed worthy of preservation. His letters are uniformly well written, and there are few of them that will not bear perusal. In these days of railway haste, correspondence has become an extinct art, and one not likely to be revived. If the present publication meet with the favour of the public, it is intended to publish these letters as the second series of the *Crosby Records*, under the title of *A Cavalier's Letter Book*. We have already in the present introduction given a few extracts from some of these letters for the purpose of illustrating the life of our hero.

A formal work of Mr. Blundell's, entitled *A Short Treatise on the Penal Laws*, exists in MS. at Crosby, but a printed copy cannot be found, though he states that a few copies were printed in London. It is a small *quarto* containing about eighty-five pages, and giving an account of the laws affecting religion and of the hardships arising from them. The author argues that the Catholics are entitled to relief by reason of their great loyalty. He proves this from the fact that, whereas the Catholic gentry of the kingdom were computed before the wars at one-fifteenth of the whole, no less than one-third or one-fourth of the officers of the King's army were Catholics. The majority of those in command who fell at Worcester, he believes to have been Catholics.

A good deal of space is taken up in replying to the extravagances of Prynne and others.

In 1876-7 the Manx Society published *A History of the Isle of Man, by Wm. Blundell, Esq., of Crosby, co. Lancaster, 1648-56,* in two volumes, edited by Wm. Harrison, Esq., and forming Nos. 25 and 27 of the series. The original MS. from which the transcript possessed by the Society was made, appears to be in the Knowsley library. The materials used in the compilation of this work were collected by Mr. Blundell in 1648, when he visited the island under the following circumstances, as recorded in his preface:—

> Wearifed with being so often wakened at midnight to fly from the King's and Parliamentary troops, both equally feared because equally plundering, and finding no shelter under the Snowden Hills, I resolved to banish myself to the Isle of Man.

The Editor mentions in his introduction that Seacome (John Seacome was house-steward to William, ninth Earl of Derby) alludes to this work in his *Account of the Isle of Man,* appended to his *History of the House of Stanley,* and styles the author 'the great and learned Mr. Blundell of Crosby.' He characterises it as the clearest and most correct account of the History and Antiquities of the Island. There does not appear to be a copy of the above MS. at Crosby, and it is somewhat singular that neither in the following notes, nor in the whole series of his letters (occupying three hundred folio pages), does Mr. Blundell make any mention of this history, which he must have completed early in life during the days of his sequestration.

The spelling in Mr. Blundell's MS. notes is generally good, but we have for the most part accommodated it to modern rules. In other respects nothing has been altered, and with the exception of the omission sometimes of a redundant parenthesis, the construction of the sentences remains precisely as he left it.

The editor wishes to express his acknowledgments to J. E. Bailey, Esq., F.S.A., of Stretford, Manchester, for the notes with which he has favoured him, and which are marked with his initials.

T. E. Gibson.

6 Crosby Road,
Birkdale, Southport.

Cavalier's Note-Book

Note such things as are more like to be serviceable many years after the noting than about the present time. For young men do collect such things as to their riper years do appear but toys; therefore be sure to make your notes a little more weighty (*i.e.* of matters somewhat higher) than your present genius and inclination can yet fully relish. Time will bring you to the liking and the use of those which otherwise would be tedious and fruitless.

Collect only the best things, even a few of the very best, to avoid contempt of your own collections no less than confusion.

Do not forbear to note because you know not unto what letter or class to reduce the thing most properly; be sure to insert it '*Modo tut armenti pecus sit, de stabulo nan litigemus*' (Only let it be one of your herd, and you need not care where it is housed).

I did not begin to take these notes until July 15, 1659, being that day 39 years old, yet some few in the *Historia* were notes which I first took in loose papers about the year 1644 and 1645. *Quantum tempus perdidimus!*

Few there are who will give or take advice as they ought I have oft been grievously discouraged in the freedom of my admonishments given to grave persons, men of great virtue and learning, and even sometimes when I had not given the admonishment till themselves had desired me to do it If such men as these did take my plain dealing so ill, what may be thought of such as myself? Perhaps I have offended so oft in taking admonitions unthankfully, that now, by reason of my pride, I meet with few or none.

This will remind the reader of a well-known passage in Dr. Johnson's *Life* in connection with his friend Langton.

On June 3, 1676, I ascended the new tower or monument at Pudding Lane, London, by 310 steps (which I twice counted), to the noble iron balcony which is round the tower; from whence I had an excellent view of the town and country. Above this balcony, the tower, not then quite finished, is raised (as I once counted them), 136 steps. This I take to be the intended full height of the tower. I take the steps on the lower parts to be 6½ inches, but 6 inches from about the middle. They are large and fine, wonderfully held up by ironwork, after the mode of the stairs at Greenwich. The base of the tower is near 26½ feet square. But the tower is round and *egregie structa*, all of stone.

June 3, 1676. I saw about 120 brass guns on the Tower Hill, London. One weighed, as by the figures, 8.1.27. The length appeared to be near 13 feet; the wideness, by my span, 7½ inches. It was said to carry a ball of 63 pounds.

The way to establish trade is to establish fair dealing. Of merchandise some sorts consist of 100 to the hundred, others of 120 and 112. Note the words of *The Complete Tradesman*, printed 1680 for John Dunton, *viz.*, '70 pipe-hoops, 90 hogshead, 120 barrel or kilderkin, no pink or firkin-hoops make a hundred;' glass bottles 21 to the dozen, &c. One agreed to deliver 100 measures of salt for so many hundreds of oats. He took the numbers to be equal, but it was adjudged otherwise at Liverpool, as I have heard, to his great damage. A stone of beef is 8 lbs., of horseman's weight 14, of wool 16, 20, and in some parts of Northumberland 23½.

It was the opinion of Judge Hale (see p. 3 in his *Life*), that to give to such poor as did receive alms of the parish, was to save so much money to the rich, who were bound by law to keep them. He therefore gave to the poor housekeepers who were not kept on the charge of the parish. He laid aside the tenth penny of all he got for the poor. *Ibid* p. 89.

The present January 5, 1686-7, I saw a lusty, strong beggar woman in the street at Wildhouse Gate, who carried upon her back, in a begging way, an old woman, which she said was her mother, and that she was 102 years old. She said that she lived in St Ann's Parish of Soho. I told her the parish was hard-hearted to permit such way of begging, and she did say thereupon that the parish was the most hard-hearted in the world. She got money and farthings apace while I stood by her, and my man Walter Thelwall (who writes this after my dictate) did afterwards meet her in the same street, and saw her receive in a very short time alms from six or seven persons, most of which gave her halfpence, and the rest each one farthing.

Sir Roger Bradshaigh limed the hall croft with lime from Clitheroe, which cost about 8*l.* per acre, each horse-load being 1s. 10d. It hath yielded very good corn since that time, which is now about twelve years, and is like to continue. One year barley, one year fallows, one year wheat for the most part 1660.

Out of Mr. Foxe's note, who got limestones for me in Wales, 1659—

	s.	d.
For getting 12 load of stone at 2d. per load	2	0
„ carriage of do.	17	0
„ slack to burn it 4s., and for carriage 4s.	8	0
„ burning all at 4s. per load	4	0

Sir Roger Bradshaigh, of Haigh, near Wigan, born 1627, created Bart 1679, was the son and heir of James Bradshaigh, Esq., a remarkably learned and pious man, who died in his father's lifetime. His mother was Anne, daughter of Sir William Norris, of Speke, but he had the misfortune to lose his parents, who were both Catholics, in very early life. His guardian, John Fleetwood, of Penwortham, Esq., entrusted his education to the Earl of Derby, by whom he was brought up a Protestant He was throughout life devotedly attached to his cousin Mr. Blundell, and performed for him all the kind offices (and they were very many) which a friendly Protestant could do for one lying constantly under the pressure of the penal laws. Sir Roger died March 31, 1684, and the baronetcy expired in 1731, on the death of Sir Roger Bradshaigh, fourth Bart The property fell through female heiresses to the family of the present Earl of Crawford and Balcarres, one of whose residences is Haigh Hall, the fine mansion of the Bradshaighs, in the neighbourhood of Wigan. This nobleman also possesses the extensive and valuable coalfields with which the estate abounds.

A mason will commonly demand for the getting, working, and setting of such window-work as that in my new building, about 6d. the foot How great their gain will be, we may judge by this. Daniel Sefton (as his prentice told me), doth work upon one day 12 feet of stanchions for those windows, and that in November. It is true that it is the easiest sort of work in my windows, but the said prentice at the same time of the year did work, as he told me, 5 feet of jambs upon one day.

And his master doubtless is able to work more than he can. *a.d.* 1660. But note, the said Daniel, when I hired him by days' wages, did usually work no more (and commonly not so much) than 6 feet of stanchions of the very same stone and the same mould.

I have heard that the wallers about Rivin Pike will make a defensible rough wall for 9d. or 10d. the rood. Inquire of this, for Daniel demandeth more than twice as much.

Hair, if it is grey, may be made black, or of a good dark colour, by rubbing with the light dust of cork which is burnt to ashes. The hair will continue that colour three or four days at the least. You may work the same effect in this manner upon red hair. It likewise drieth the hair exceedingly, and is done in an instant You must slice the cork very thin, and it will take fire and flame and burn quickly into the powder abovesaid. I saw it tried by Mr. Stanton, November 8, 1660.

The tops of green hemp ready to knot or seed, being made into a juice and mixed with cream and olive oil, is singular good to anoint the parts from where your hair is apt to fall, to prevent falling. *Idem narravit*, who hath tried the same, and doth think it causeth hair to come thicker.

Burn southernwood to ashes and mix therewith either thick salad oil, or, which is better, the oil of black snails: anoint the bald part evening and morning, often. This or nothing will make hair to grow upon a bald place. Mr. Stanton had this from Dr. Martin, who magnified the secret very much. The southernwood must be well dried by the fire or the sun. Let it then take fire and burn in an earthen pot of itself almost a day together, still stirring up (if it need), to burn the better. The snails must have salt sprinkled among them, and being then hung up in a net, they will work themselves into a fat, which will drop into a dish which you may set under it.

I was present in the ship (about five miles from Dover), two or three hours before King Charles II. landed in England on Fryday, May 25, 1660, when the King (by reason of an accident), took his own measure, standing under a beam in the cabin, upon which place he made a mark with a knife. Sundry tall persons went under it, but there were none that could reach it After all I went under it myself, and turning in the ends of my thumb and my little finger, I set the knuckle of my thumb, stretched out as much as could be, upon my head, and turning the knuckle of my little finger (borne up as stiflf as might be), I found it did touch directly the mark which the King had made. So that I find myself to be about 5 inches lower than that mark, and I think I am 3 inches lower, as I stand in my high-heeled shoe, than I was before I was lame.

In November 1861, I saw an Irish stripling called (as I take it) Edmund Malone, said to be then under 17 years of age. I found him to be higher than John Dodes by about 1½ inch. I think he was 7ft 2½in. in his shoes, which were not high. He was languid and listless, and not comely, although he was straight I was told he died a few days or weeks after.

On May 23, 1660, the King embarked at the Hague on board a vessel which had hitherto been called the *Naseby*, but to which he now gave the name of the *Royal Charles*, and landed at noon on 25th, at Dover, where Monk awaited him surrounded by an immense crowd.—(*Lady of Latham*, by Madme. Guizot de Witt, p. 244.)

On August 20, 1675, Mr. Blundell of Ince told me that the King (within four months of that time) had said that Lancashire was infamous for perjury and packing of juries. These words, or words to this effect, my cousin Blundell said to me as we came from Croxteth.

This was Henry son of Robert Blundell, of Ince Blundell, Esq., who had succeeded to the estate on the death of his father in 1656. He spoke feelingly on the subject of juries, having himself lost in 1665 a large tract of land, and been mulcted in costs and mesne profits, as the issue of a law-suit with the Gerards, Earls of Macclesfield, on a dispute concerning the boundaries of adjoining properties purchased by the two families. Some account of this tedious and expensive contest will be found in *Lydiate Hall and its Associations*. Mr. Blundell seems to have thought that the power and might of his opponent influenced the adverse verdict of the jury. He married Bridget daughter of the famous Cavalier Sir Thomas Tildesley, Knt, and died on March 30, 1687-8, at the age of 55.

While I am in health, I may do well to make and write down a prayer, protestation, or soliloquy, just such a one as I would desire to say in the extremity of my last sickness. By this I may renounce all thoughts, words, and deeds contrary to a good Christian, which shall happen or to which I shall be tempted at the time. I may beg of God to assist my soul while my body lies in torment, and, by the extreme anguish thereof, hath stupefied or perverted my reason. I may beg likewise grace for my friends that stand by to assist me, that they may not be scandalised either at the rage or stupidity which then may happen unto me by the force of the sickness. And I may offer myself up to suffer more and longer torments, if it be God's pleasure I should do so; and that grace may be allowed me to bear them, I may carry this paper always about me, to the end it may be read to me in my sickness.

The recent admirable biography of Thomas Grant, first Bishop of Southwark, by the lady who writes under the name of Grace Ramsay, contains a passage expressing a similar sentiment In recounting what took place shortly before the death of this saintly prelate, the writer says, 'And then, seeming quite to forget that any one was present, he broke out into a most beautiful prayer, full of sorrow, love, resignation, and every virtue befitting his state. This lasted for a while, wrote the Bishop of Beverley (Dr. Cornthwaite), and then he turned suddenly to me and said, "There, when I can speak no longer, I mean that"' Dr. Grant died at Rome whilst attending the Vatican Council, on June 1, 1870.

We do dispraise ourselves for such and such a thing, that others may thereby have occasion to commend us. And this is called a pride 'by hook or by crook.'

The common people are more easily won by cheap and unprofitable courtesies than by churlish benefits.

Sir William Stanley told me on 14 April, 1668, that he had once at Hooton my Lord M—, the three T's, and I think some few more for 3 or 4 nights, and that there were consumed in his house during their stay 16 dozen bottles of wine, 2 hogsheads of beer, and 2 barrels of ale.

Observe this manner of speaking, *viz.*, 'The thing was done by the King's command,' and thus, 'The thing, no doubt, was done by the King's command.' The first assertion is positive, the second is doubtful, by reason of the words 'no doubt,' which yet ought rather to confirm the position. This happened by the long insincere use of that word. And I fear the same may be said of others. The nobility at the Coronation, 1661, in making homage to the King, said, they would live and die with him, &c., against all manner of 'folks.' In the 8th Edition of *Claudius Maugre's French Grammar* (1678) there is also his short *English Grammar*, which is very pretty and remarkable to be done by an extern. Yet he doth commit some errors in the matter of pronunciation, which I think proceeds from the great conversation he had at London with ladies and nice things.

We translate the words *Utinam* and *Ave* into 'Would to God' and 'God save you,' whereas indeed there is no mention of God. My Protestant Bible Englishes *Ave*, 'God speed.'

We pronounce the letter *i* variously and different from other nations. Consider it in China, ditch, &c. How can it be proper to say *Chyna*, and yet improper and rustical to say *dych'*?

The histories which relate the rebellious wars of the Puritans against Charles I. are (amongst many others) the 1st and 2nd part of Dr. Bate's history in Latin concerning our late wars. This Bate had been Cromwell's physician. Thomas May was the Parliament's Latin historian, and wrote their history partially. Baker's Chronicle, or rather the continuation of Baker by Ph, hath very much of that history, but the man that pleases me best for exactness and brevity is T. Hobbes, who has writ a considerable treatise[1] of 2s, or 3s. price. The name I remember not

Bishop Juxon of Canterbury was a most patient and gentle man. When he was Bishop of London and Lord Treasurer, a distressed gentlewoman, desired him to pay her a good sum of money which was granted her out of the Exchequer. He told her indeed that he could not do it for want of money in the treasury, but that she should be paid when the first money came in. Whereupon observing that she began to weep, he excused himself very humbly by the necessary reason abovesaid, for this dilatory answer. Unto whom the good woman replied, 'Oh, my lord, these are tears of joy. When I made the same suit to my Lord Weston (your Lordship's predecessor), I received a most harsh denial, and now, by your Lordship's most gentle answer, I am put into assured hope. Oh, the great difference (said she) that there is in men!' Mr. Thos. Hawarden told me this July 1st, 1663.

Howell, in his *Familiar Letters* (Book 2 letter 25) confirms this narrative. He says; 'I have known two Lord High Treasurers of England of quite contrary humours, one successively after the other; the one, though he did the suitor's business, yet he went murmuring; and the other, though he did it not, was used to dismiss the party with some satisfaction'
Richard Lord Weston, who contrasts here unfavourably with

---

1. *Behemoth* was the title of Hobbes' treatise on the Civil War.

Archbishop Juxon, was born 1577; sent as Ambassador to Bohemia, 1619'; Chancellor of Exchequer, 1621-4; Ambassador to Brussels, 1622; cr Baron Weston of Keyland, Essex, 1628; Lord Treasurer of England, 1628; cr. Earl of Portland, 1633; ob. Mch. 12, 1635. He married Frances Waldegrave, and had issue, but the titles expired with his own family about 1688, at the death of his son Thomas, who was fourth Earl of Portland

A man who showed a dromedary in most parts of England told me (1662) that he found more profit thereby in Lancashire than in any other county. John Butler the mountebank, born in Berkshire, told me (July 17, 1663) that he found nowhere in England more money stirring among the common people than in Lancashire He commended for the like plenty, Cheshire, Suffolk, and Norfolk. He saith that this is a healthful country, that the moist parts eastward, especially the Isle of Ely, are the most unhealthful. That in the moist parts and in the shires that abound with fruits, are the worst teeth: the worst eyes about the fens: that corns on the feet in Leicestershire, Northamptonshire, and other dry countries are contracted by much ploughing.

Dr. Plot, in his *Natural History of Staffordshire* (published 1686), mentions the burial many years before in a field at Tixall, of a dromedary which had died through the neglect of its keeper. This may not improbably have been the very animal which Mr. Blundell saw. The Doctor speculates upon the curious surmises that the discovery of the bones in after ages may give rise to.

In June 1676 I came from London by coach with Sergeant Edward Rigby, a Parliament man, who told me that some years ago it was moved in the House (and I think it was he who first moved it) that there should be abatement made of the excessive fees in courts, and thereupon a committee was appointed to consider of it, of which he was the chairman. It proceeded far in the matter, and he brought their report concerning the same to the House. After waiting ten days at the bar to deliver the same, the House being busy about a Bill for raising two millions to maintain the war against the Dutch, he could not be admitted, whereupon he told the Speaker, that the matter which he had there to present would advantage the generality of the people of England more than the value of that whole sum, and I think he said that the advantage would be made in as short a time as while the said money was raising. However, he was never admitted to present the report, and he told me he did believe that the men of law in the House, foreseeing their own damage thereby, did hinder the whole matter.

Mr. John Entwistle, the lawyer, held in my hearing, in August 1676, that Mr. Pemberton having received 30*l.* to draw a release (or general release), called it 'Porter's wages.'

Edward Rigby, serjeant-at-law, born 1627, was third son of Colonel Alexander Rigby, and was M.P. for Preston 1661-1678-9, and again re-elected for the subsequent session—

J. E. B.

I did once inquire of a haberdasher of hats, who had a wholesale trade with most parts of England, whether he had observed that any counties of England did produce heads remarkably great or remarkably little; and he told me that the heads of Lincolnshire men were generally smaller than any others that he met with.

The most universal detraction proceeds from State policy. In the reign of Queen Elizabeth, our English books were full of all manner of disgraceful things concerning the Spaniard, because he was then our enemy. Since then, we have stood in fear of the French; at least, we have envied their greatness, and slandered them accordingly. In our late wars with Holland, one Downing, who had been (as I take it) the King's agent. or ambassador there, printed a book (which I have in my library) against the Dutch, charging them bitterly with many foul things, and saying to this effect, that they have cost more coin and Christian blood to Europe than it hath spent and lost by all the wars it has had with the great Turk.

In that speech of the Earl of Shaftesbury, spoken in the Parliament about March 1678-9, which was thought to have occasioned the murder of the Bishop of St Andrews, and the rebellion in Scotland, he was most severe against the Government of that kingdom. He speaks as if the arbitrary power thereof did quite exceed the tyranny used in those which we do esteem the eastward and southern kingdoms of the world. Note the scornful habit of detraction which the English for sundry ages have used against the Welsh and the Scots.

This vice is not peculiar to England, yet we have seen here its dismal effects, especially since the revelations made by Dr. Oates in 1678. Mons. Rob, in his history (written in French) shows how the persecution of the Christians in Japan was grounded upon a malicious lie forged by the Dutch for their own advantage, to discountenance the trade of the Catholic European merchants. The consequence of this persecution, I fear, hath been the destruction of all visible Christianity in Japan. By God's just judgement, the chief author of that contrivance had a punishment even in this world most exemplary strange.

I have heard of one Mr. Fielding, a forward duellist, who notwithstanding did most shamefully misbehave himself (I mean most like a coward) in one of our great battles in the late Dutch war, at sea. And this day, January 29, 1667, my cousin, Margaret Molyneux (who, having waited sundry years upon Madam Eliot, at London, had occasion to know the truth of many such things), told me, for certain, that the said Fielding, coming out of a tavern in London, with his own brother, some months ago, called to a coachman for a coach. The fellow not being willing to take him in, he was so incensed that, drawing his sword, and being hindered by his said brother from hurting the coachman, he presently killed his brother without more ado, and was fairly hanged for his pains.

My good friend, Mr. Da. Sa. (whom I call son) told me this following story, this present May 12, 1668. Mr. Grosvenor, son of Sir Richard Grosvenor, who was killed some time since, said to Mrs. Houghton (now widow of Mr. Gilbert Houghton) that day before he was killed, that if any man was to ride near his footman (who, I think, was to run a race that day), he would kill him, or be killed by him. Mr. D. S. told me that Mrs. Houghton told him this. But the conclusion was this— Mr. Grosvenor that day switched Mr. Roberts, and drew upon him; but Mr. Roberts killed him with his sword, and before he died, he said it was his own fault

It was ridiculous in the beggar (100 years old and odd) who, to move charity, said he was a poor motherless and fatherless creature.

Mr. Howell in 9 letter, sec 5, says, 'I never heard of anything that prospered which, being once designed for the honour of God, was alienated from that use.'

A cross was pulled down at Tewkesbury by the prevailing power of a Puritan minister, long before the general ruin of crosses through England. An inferior townsman of the same sect made use of one the stones of this cross for walling about his well, and some of them (wherein had been pictures of Our Lady and St John) were converted into swine troughs. The event was this: His wife and sundry of his children became blind, and he drowned himself in the same well *Narravit mihi Dnus. Thos. Stanton, qui degens tunc temporis in illo oppido, cum erat admodum juvenis, non semel viderat hominem, qui postea (ut dictum est) sacrilegio suo fatum accelerasset.*[2]

It was proved at Hugh Peter's arraignment that he had said in his sermon that Charing Cross had made more Papists, and done more harm in that way, than any pulpit in London had done good. He was hanged at this place.

I saw Thomas Parr's picture at full length among Cardinal Mazarine's rarities in his Palace at Paris, 1660. In the same year, as I travelled betwixt Antwerp and Breda, I found posted upon the wall of a poor inn the picture of Anthony Haasethus, who was Primus Pastor Gulensis in the Diocese of Liege, where he lived the parson of the parish 100 years together. He died, aged 125, *a.d.* 1586. Being asked by the Bishop of Liege what means he had taken to prolong his life, he answered that he had always abstained from three things, 'women, wine, and anger.' This I have transcribed out of the Latin subscription at the bottom of the same picture, which picture I bought, and have it now in my house.

The King said to the Parliament that the misdemeanours of the Earl of Strafford were so great and many, that he was not fit to serve the place of a Constable. Yet there is no question but these expressions did not proceed from any just will in the King, but only to have saved his life. The loss of this (by his Majesty's consent) did wonderfully afflict and scruple the King; as appeareth by the sad expression he used to the Earl of Camwath, from whom I received it.

I saw the Earl of Strafford in Dublin (June 1639), when he was then Lord Deputy, in far greater state (in some respects) than the King of England. The Earl of Ormond (now Marquis) was pointed out to me riding in the Deputy's own troop. I saw one princely stable of the Deputy's, wherein I judged the worst of 60 horses for the great saddle to be worth 30*l*. He was an excellent orator, as appears by his speeches at the bar; and a passing wise man. A Colonel of Parliament told me that beyond the seas it is reported of England that it produceth but one wise man in an age, and that the people gaze on him awhile as a monster, then cut off his head. 'So,' said he, 'did they do by Sir Thomas More and the Earl of Strafford.' This story I was telling to the present Earl, his son, who told me (September 1659) that the King of Sweden's Embassador at London did very lately procure there for his master (by his especial command) the pictures of these very same

---

2. This was told me by the Rev. Thos. Stanton, who when a youth resided at that period in the town, and had more than once seen the man who afterwards, as it was said, hastened his death by his sacrilege.

two wise persons I mentioned. His Lordship told me further, that his Lordship's paternal estate was 4 to 5,000*l. per annum*, which he lived to double, but dying in about 80,000*l.* debt, he himself had sold (one-fifth part too cheap) about a moiety of the said estate to pay the aforesaid debts. 20,000*l.* of this debt was incurred by being surety for the King, or by taking up the like sum for his Majesty, at the beginning of the war in Yorkshire.

The Earl of Strafford, upon the scaffold, left as a prime precept to his son, that he should not meddle with Church lands, for they would prove a canker to his estate.

The sad expression which the King made use of to the Earl of Carnwath respecting Strafford is not recorded, but it resembled, no doubt, his utterances on the scaffold Clarendon seems to attribute to this Earl the loss of the Battle of Naseby. He says that when the King was on the point of charging the enemy, the Earl of Carnwath, who rode next to him, on a sudden laid his hand on the King's bridle, and swearing two or three full-mouthed Scotch oaths, said, 'Will you go upon your death in an instant? and, before his Majesty understood what he was about, turned his horse round His followers seeing the movement fled in disorder. (*Hst Rebell,* vol. 2 p 508.) Mr. Blundell would probably meet the second Earl of Strafford at Knowsley, as this nobleman had married Henrietta, daughter of James, Earl of Derby.

The use of stalking-horses is great and notably advantageous in some parts. Horses are easily taught. Some do use to have a painted horse carried upon a frame. But, doubtless, a bust is more easy and not less useful. I know some to have stalked so near to partridges that the birds have pecked at the horses' legs. Let your painted horse or cow have one side of a different colour to the other.

Dotterells in Lincolnshire are taken by candlelight; for whilst they imitate the fowler's gestures, they suffer him to cast his net upon them.

Our posterity will hardly believe the extravagance and damage which we find now in England by the clipping of our silver coin. The present Tuesday, January 11, 1695, I received from my servant Walter Thelwall (who writes this affair after my dictate, and knows the same to be true) the just sum of 10*l.* 18s. for cattle of mine which he sold yesterday at Newbrough fair. Out of this sum I picked out thirteen of the smallest clipt shillings. These thirteen shillings being laid on a pair of scales which were used for the weighing of gold, were then clearly overweighted by five broad shillings chosen at adventure, *viz.* by two Elizabeth shillings and three shillings of Charles I., and I found that these five shillings weighed just one ounce. However, when I had put the thirteen shillings abovesaid to the rest of the same, and weighed altogether the foresaid sum of 10*l.* 18s., I found the whole weight to be very near 26 ounces, and by throwing in an old ninepence it clearly turned the scales. Now, according to this account the said 10*l.* 18s., which ought to have weighed 43 and 3/5 ounces, was no more but 26 ounces, bating an old ninepence.

My landlord at La Fleche, Julian Bionteau, writ and printed a book (which book I have) against the common practice of the doctors at Paris in taking too much blood from their patients. He speaks of horrid abuses in that, and doth bitterly condemn it He entitles himself the King's physician.

Howell, in his *Familiar Letters* (Book 1. Letter 21), refers to this Parisian custom of blood-letting. As the date of this letter is 1622, it would appear that the practice had not abated sixty years later, when Mr. Blundell was at La Fleche:—

At first they let me blood, and I parted with above 50 ounces in less than a fortnight; for phlebotomy is so much practised here, that if one's little finger ache they presently open a vein: and to balance the blood on both sides, they usually let blood on both arms.

Catholics deny the oath, yet keep their allegiance to the King. Others take the oath and fail in allegiance. Mr. Blood was an Irish Protestant, and so great a rebel or plotter, that a great sum (I think 500*l.* at the least) was promised by proclamation to those that could apprehend him. This man did afterwards steal the King's crown in the Tower of London, and was taken in the fact; yet for some supposed discoveries by him made of other traitors, he had his liberty, and, as was said, the King's favour, so that he frequently walked in the court at Whitehall. It may seem that some treasons are too great to be punished, as some services are too great to be requited. There is a great difference between the case of the Pendrells, who being Catholics cannot appear in the court, though they saved the King's life with the hazard of their own, and the case of notorious traitors (*olim*) who are now in favour. Popery is an odd religion. If I mistake not, the proclamation against Blood was in the year 1666, and he stole the crown about three or four years after. His brother-in-law, Lachy, was hanged for rebellion in Ireland. He was a Minister.

Mr. Blundell was not singular in his surprise at the favour experienced by the notorious Colonel Blood Sir R. Burgoyne, writing to Sir Nathaniel Hobarts, February 12, 1671-2, says, 'A fortnight since my Lord Brook told me that Blood had not only his own pardon for all his villainy, but also had procured the like for Desburrough, Kelsey, &c.: certainly, some designs more than ordinary are on foot, that such persons are received into favour.'—(Historical Commissioners' 7th Report, Appendix.)

Sir Josias Child, in his discourse of trade, printed in *octavo*, 1693, assigns one reason of the prosperity of the Hollanders to be their fair dealing in packing up their goods, as herrings, codfish, &c., and ascribes the disrepute and loss to the English by taking the contrary course.

Prologue to a stage play, which I made at the entreaty of some country neighbours who were to act the play—about Christmas 1647:

The bitter storms of war are over-blown,
And joyful peace succeedeth in the place,
The husbandman may now enjoy his own,
And look the armed soldier in the face.
The soldier too doth live an honest life,
Confines himself to quarter and his pay;
And each one, weary with the bloody strife,
Hath sheathed his sword, and now begins to play.
And to a PLAY we do invite you all.
According to the custom of the time;
Though in that art our talent be but small,
Our best endeavours cannot prove a crime.
Excuse us then, who, with a willing heart,
Have ta'en some pains to entertain you here,
And shall we hope (if no man miss his part),
Give cause to think you have not bought it dear.
Then patient sit, with silence, three short hours.
And if you like not then, the fault is ours.
       Nan omnes arbusta juvent

Bare the roots of your trees and make a hole in a principal root, and then put in a pretty quantity of powder, made of such things as you desire your apple should taste of; as of cloves, mace, nutmeg, or such like.

Quaere—if it will not work that effect in other fruit trees, and whether the bole of the tree will not serve to put it in, or whether the bole must be cloven or bored.

Sir George Blundell of Edenderry, King's County, Ireland, Bart His estate is esteemed to be 1,000*l. per annum*. He told me (1662) that he was descended from Blundell of Ince, and that he gives the same coat with a half-moon.

He told me likewise then of one Sir George Blundell of Cardington in Bedfordshire, then lately knighted. The Earl of Aylesbury told me in 1676 that Sir George Blundell was then a D.L. in that county.

There is a Baron of this name, Blundell, living about a mile from Douay, of whom I have often heard as a person exceedingly remarkable for valour in war. I found in the French Heraldry three different families of this name in France, besides an advocate whom I knew at Rouen, *a.d.* 1660. They are all of different families, and their coat armour is not the same with ours. Yet Mr. Thomas Massey told me that he saw a coach in Paris on which were our arms, and that an attendant told him the master's name was Blundell.

The Blundells of Cardington were descended from Thomas, a younger son of William Blundell of Ince Blundell, Esq., who was living 1554. Sir George Blundell, Knt, of this race, married Elizabeth, daughter and heiress of John Gascoigne, Esq., of Cardington, Beds. He was killed at the Isle of Rhe, in 1630, and had received in the early part of that century a grant of land, subsequently called Blundell, in King's County, Ireland. His brother Sir Francis, Secretary of Affairs in Ireland, 1619, was created a Bart in the following year. Sir Montague Blundell, fourth Bart, was advanced in 1720 to the dignities of Baron Edenderry and Viscount Blundell, but through default of male issue, these titles expired in 1756. The Sir George Blundell spoken of as a D.L, lies buried at Cardington, and the inscription on his monument is a curious bit of Latinity. It commences thus: '*Hic jacet corpus Georgii Blundell Militis, Directi successoris et Hæredis Blundellianæ et Gasconianæ familiæ Bedfordiensis. Obiit Nov. 11, 1688.*'

There are two or three families still flourishing in France who bear the name and arms of Blondell.

My neighbour Richard Johnson told me this day (August 18, 1665), in plain terms, that those of his religion did not use baptism by water at all; and that it is not lawful for them to fight in any case; and that one Bennet, in Derbyshire, first called them Quakers.

Mrs. Trask was a kind of primitive Quaker, yet was she called a Sabbatarian. She lived in prison (where she died) a most strict penitential life fifteen years.

One John Blaket (if I mistake not the name) is a great man among the Quakers, and liveth near Sedbergh in Yorkshire.

'This was Justice Bennet of Derby, who was the first that called us Quakers, because I bid them tremble at the word of the Lord.' This was in the year 1650.—(George Fox's *Journal*, ed. Leeds, 1836, vol. 1 p. 132.) Fox's committal for six months to Derby Gaol in 1649 was signed by Gervas Bennet, J. P.— J. E. B.

It were good that all casual manslaughters, as well as murders and executions of felons, were yearly printed in England, upon which many observations might be made of singular use. The Coroner and Clerk of the Crown might much concur to the doing of this.

This summer (1669), a man was overwhelmed with earth in a sandhill at the Grange whilst he was seeking to take rabbits out of a hole; and quickly after, another man perished in Male (but 3 miles off), just in the same manner, in a sandy cop. This I think had hardly happened if he had heard of the other man's chance.

Let there likewise be a history of all trials of felons and duellists, &c., even when the offender comes off with life. But this, alas I would rather encourage offenders by the slack execution of justice.

Honesty is wanting in England, and that want corrupts all commodities and stops the well proceeding of all affairs. Mr. Thomas Clayton, Merchant, told me about the year 1672, when we had war with Holland, that even then he would rather trust Hollanders than Englishmen to negotiate by way of factorage his affairs abroad.

It were good to have steps or seats (as in a cock-pit), for the better sight of public executions and trials, as at Tyburn, Westminster Hall, &c

In April 1660, Mr. Edward Lloyd told me Arbores that his father Mr. Robert Lloyd of Place-ys-asaudd, in Denbighshire (not far from Wrexham), had a tree growing near his house which was seven fathom (measuring by men's arms) round about the bole, which bole was seven yards high to the first bough. But when I seemed not to credit this, he did seriously affirm that he had been assured that it was either five or seven fathom in compass, but that indeed he had never measured it

In Lent, which was in the year 1648-9, just about the equinox, there was a report of the moon rising at an unusual time, and it went a higher or longer course than ordinary. This, they say, was observed by the market men and fishermen, which I little regarded; but one Sunday, when I was at dinner, someone bringing word that the moon appeared out of course, I went down into the orchard, and it being then an exceeding clear day, about 12 o' clock or before, I saw the moon about an hour and a half high to my judgment, and shining with a perfect orb in the east, if I be not mistaken, or rather one point toward the south.

That evening about seven o' clock we went down to the back porch, where standing still, we saw the moon in a full clear orb over the chapel chamber chimney or thereabouts. It appeared higher to our judgement than ever we had seen the sun in the longest day. My cousin Heaton was with me then, and at noon my brother Haggerston. It was observed to go such a like strange course a day or two after. If I be not much mistaken, some did affirm (with such testimony as I then believed it), that the moon was up at least 21 hours together. However, I think the prodigy was very remarkable and the greatest that ever I saw.

The editor has been favoured by the Rev. Sylvester J. Hunter, S. J., with the following observations on this phenomenon:—'If my astronomy is not at fault, I suspect that the phenomenon was akin to that of the harvest moon, which commonly does not attract the same attention at the spring equinox as in the autumn. The harvest moon is much more noticeable in some years than in others, and a rough calculation that I have made seems to show, that 1648-9 would be one of the years , in which it would be most prominent

In these same years the moon, when in the north, would attain a greater height than that of the sun in the longest day, by about five degrees, or ten times her own diameter. And in this we have a remarkable proof of the accuracy of the observations, made as they were by the naked eye. As to the moon being up 21 hours he speaks doubtfully, and with reason: if I am not mistaken, she never can be up for much more than 18 hours in Lancashire. The longest stay above the horizon will occur just in the same year as that in which she attains the greatest light in the heavens, and rises most nearly at the same time for several successive nights.'

A prologue to a sword dance, spoken at Lathom upon Ash Wednesday, 1638:

The common proverb teacheth us to say
'Tis hazardous with sharp-edged tools to play.
Yet we t'increase your honour's pleasures shall,
Adding more triumph to this carnival,
Forget the Muses' Hill, those nymphs, those dames.
And practise with our swords th' Olympic games.
Be but auspicious to our play, while we
This night shall Mars prefer to Mercury.

Mr. Blundell, although already married, was not more than eighteen years of age at this time, and, as he himself confesses, remarkably fond of all youthful amusements. Lathom House, the ancient seat of the Earls of Derby, was then in its glory, soon, alas! to be reduced, by miserable civil broils, to a shapeless ruin. It was the scene of the well-known and memorable defence made by the spirited Countess Charlotte de la Tremouille, who frequently entertained our Cavalier in after years at Knowsley.

The present prince (1659) was born Sept 8, 1621, and is a most bold and vigilant soldier, but immoderate (as they say) in his amours. He sleepeth no more commonly but three hours in the night, and useth to say that the devil rocketh him that sleepeth longer. *Narravit mihi* Gul. Clifton, Feb. 8, 1659.

I do not know in what part of the world dragons are now to be found, nor do I know their shape or size.

This rivals the remarkable chapter on snakes in the *History of Iceland from the Danish of Horrebow*, which is referred to in Boswell's *Life of Johnson.*

Tu pacata vale rore lavata caput.

This verse is the same read backwards. It was made by occasion of a woman dispossessed of the devil by baptism.

Sir Ferdinand Carey, a huge corpulent knight, was shot through his body; the bullet entering at the navel and coming out at his back, killed his man behind him, yet he liveth still and is like to recover.— Mr. Howell's *letter*, 32, sec 3. Yet he hath it from a second hand.

A servant maid, at the siege of Hardin (Harwarden) Castle, was shot in the mouth, and the bullet came out of her fundament, and she recovered the hurt She served Sir William Neale, who affirmed this to be true in my hearing. But the bullet (you must know) came, many days after it was shot, through the common passage.

Choose rather to lend money to your friend (though you borrow it yourself) even upon his single bond, than to enter into bond with him.

There are five Colleges of the Society in England:

1. St Ignatius's College at London, wherein they say are such of the novices as are to be trained in England.

2. St Peter and Paul's College at Norwich.

3. St Xavier's College in North Wales.

4. The College of the Holy Conception in Derbyshire, Leicester, and thereabouts. This college was esteemed the richest of all the foundation thereof, having been no less than 7,000*l.* and the yearly revenue thence arising 625*l.* But 6,100*l.* of that foundation is in great danger to be lost in ill hands. *a.d.* 1660.

5. The College of Bd. Aloysius, including Lancashire, Cheshire, Staffordshire, and no more.

Besides the colleges there are many parts of England called 'Residences,' not belonging to the colleges, as Yorkshire, Cornwall, Northumberland, &c. In 1660 there were 23 fathers in the College of St Aloysius. About Michaelmas 1663, Father Courtney the Provincial came into Lancashire, and received an account or list of 2,500 penitents under those of his order. *Narravit mihi* Ds. Peter Bradshaigh.

Father Edward Courtney, whose real name was Leedes, was the son of Sir Thomas Leedes of Wappingthorne, in Sussex, and had a brother Thomas, likewise of the Society of Jesus. Edward, born 1599, became a student at the English College, Rome, 1618, and entered the novitiate S. J. on August 28, 1 62 1. After his ordination he was employed in various capacities, and must have had a talent for government, as before his death he filled nearly every office in his Province. He was English Provincial, 1660-4, and ended his days at St Omer's College on October 3, 1677. (Foley's *Records*, S. J., vol. 1 p. 251.)

Rev. Peter Bradshaigh was one of three brothers, uncles of Mr. Blundell, who embraced the Society of Jesus. He died April 17, 1676, aged 66.

It is very remarkable that the English in this age have no great talent in writing Latin prose. See my history of the expedition into the Isle of Rhe, writ most pitifully by an English Lord. But that which passes all for barbarous Latin is the work of the *classical* divines, mentioned at large in the history of Presbitery.

The author of the former work was Edward Lord Herbert of Cherbury, of whom Anthony A. Wood writes (vol 3 240): 'Under the tuition of an eminent tutor [he] laid the foundation of that admirable learning whereof he was afterwards a compleat master. The book is entitled, *Expeditio in Ream Insulam,* Authore Edovardo Domino Herbert, Barone de Cherbury in Anglia. . . . *Anno mdcxxx. Quam Publici Juris fecit Timotheus Balduinus, LSD. e Coll. Omn. Anim. Apud Oxon. Socius. Lond. 8vo.* 1656.—J. E B.

It was the saying of Sir Thomas Tildesley his lady told me), that he would follow his business close, to the end that he might the more enjoy his pleasures.

I spent in France a great part of the years 1680 and 1681, and there I found that our catalogue of the new holydays was not then observed; yet sundry days of Saints whose names we scarce know are kept holy there in particular dioceses.

If there be four million of working people in a country who are each able to earn 6d. *per diem*, the work of one day will amount to 100,000*l*. So that the difference of working and not working of the people of a whole nation is no small matter as to civil and political respects. Note the different consequence of industry and idleness by comparing the present state of France, Holland, Flanders, &c., with the present state of Spain and the lazy old Irish. A thousand weighty matters may be considered pro and con. on this occasion.

A.D. 1683. Christmas began on Tuesday, so that we had at that time eight holydays altogether, Sunday being included therein. Immediately before that Christmas, we had six days beginning on Wednesday 19th, whereof five were fasting-days, one holyday, and one Sunday; so that there were at that time fourteen days altogether, which were all of them either holydays or fasting-days. Note that Friday 21st (St Thomas the Apostle) was not only holyday but double fasting-day, to say nothing of the Friday and Saturday following, which were days of abstinence. I was at Paris in July 1680, and found there that the 26th of that month (St. Anne's day) was not kept holyday, neither was the 24th kept as a vigil either by fasting or abstinence. At La Fleche, in Rogation week, I found there was abstinence for five days, but no days fasted, whereas we fast two days in England.

The want of regular Church government in Mr. Blundell's time long prevented any change in these matters; but the fasting-days in England have since been much reduced in number, and are no longer burdensome.

In hac domo quam a vermiculis mutuo accepi, cum fratribus meis, sub spe resurrectionis ad vitam, jaceo Samuel, permissione divinâ Episcopus hujus Insulæ.

Siste lector.

Vide et ride

Palatium Episcopi.

This epitaph was given to me June 18, 1662, by Monsieur Daniel Trioche, Secretary to the Countess of Derby, who saith that it was sent out of the Isle of Man, and that it was found among the Bishop's papers.

This inscription was on a plate in St German's Cathedral, Isle of Man, but was stolen by a tourist, before 1825.—J. E. B.

A pint of ale, a halfpenny in wax, fresh butter one quarter; melt them together. Afterwards (but not before, lest it flame), add some turpentine. And so use it I had this from a shoemaker in Chester, a Quaker. Try it on the boots of your servant When boots are new, fill them with strong wort and tanners' bark bruised. Hang them up for two or three months till all be dried in; then oil them as you please for softness. This (saith Major Gibson) is the best way.

Now in my old age (*ætatis* 59), having spent much time in study for the knowledge of things, I find, with great regret, that I know not so much as what is meant by the common names. of things that are most commonly known and spoken of. And I do persuade myself that the most part of our disputes were ended, if our words were always such as clearly to express our thoughts. How little do Protestants know what we mean by our Church's *infallibility, indulgences* for sin, or *merit* for good works! But let us take more familiar notions: a *day*, a *month*, a *year.* I find in *Miege's French Dictionary* this which follows:—'*Les Babiloniens commencoient le jour au lever du' soleil, les Juifs et les Atheniens le commencoient au coucher, et les Italiens les imitent Les Egyptiens le com-*

mencoient à midi.' As for the beginning, the end, and the just term of a year, the differences in sundry ages and places have been unspeakably great, and caused great confusion.

The most weighty controversy that happened in my time in England before the Judges, was to determine the meaning of the words *twelve months.* The innocent Irishmen had only twelve months allowed them by Act of Parliament to be restored to their lands, after which there was to be no restoration. Upon this, the Court of Claims at Dublin sat one whole year, and making a quick despatch near the end of that term, some hundreds of persons were in the last month of the year restored to their lands. Whereupon their adversaries got the matter to be heard in England, pretending that twelve lunar months was the time allowed But, contrary to men's expectation, the cause was carried by the Irish.

Exempli gratiâ: if a man desire to measure the length of a field or way by pacing over the same, and he finds it hard to remember the several scores or twenties, so that he will drop a pebble into his pocket at the end of each score; which being tedious may be helped by keeping time to the motion of your feet with these or the like words, *viz.*—

Who saw Jack Straw—one.
Who saw Jack Straw—two, &c.

Which being continued to twenty, the whole number is 100.

So one may count at shuttle cock, either with the same words or thus—

Take care, strike fair—one;

or one may say

Take care, strike fair, pit pat, hit that—one;

which being repeated to twenty, makes just nine score.

This thing may be sundry other ways improved to serious uses, notwithstanding the matter may seem to be ridiculous.

An old wine-*tierce* which, being filled with claret, I had formerly bought, was, when I had drawn it out, measured (*me vidente*) with water. It was filled with 131 size—quarts. I mean such quarts, 32 whereof make a Winchester bushel. The quart which I used therein had been measured by my servant James Hoghton with the brazen standard quart at Liverpoole, about the year 1676.

Many persons have money which they desire to put out for lawful interest, &c.; but they are wholly ignorant of the means to do it. Many others would take up money in extreme necessity, and are willing to give security; but they know not where to find money. This hath been the reason the scriveners of London have been employed as brokers for money, with benefit to themselves and commodity to the borrower and lender. This might be practised with much advantage to the country, in each county of England, by the means of some discreet honest person in each town of note, whose known employment it should be either to put out money and take security, or at least to be able to give the names of the borrowers and lenders of such sums as are required to be borrowed and lent This was the judgment of Mr. T. Sel.

The above was writ about the year 1659, since when great practice hath been made in this kind within our neighbourhood, so that now, this present year 1683, it seems so convenient to borrowers and lenders, that I think it is like to continue.

And I believe the like might be practised with great advantage to the country, in other matters: as in buying and selling of land, and even in marriages (if the person employed be discreet and tender of other men's credits). In these he might be used (if you please), no otherwise than as an informer or intelligencer betwixt the parties, and his commission might be so restrained as that he should only tell the circumstances—as the value, price, site, and buildings upon the land: the age, portion, quality, beauty, &c., of such a maid or widow; and the like of such a bachelor or widower as desireth to have a wife.

And when he findeth that these informations are agreeable to the inquirer's desires, he may inform the parties concerned; and telling withal the several qualities of the inquirer, if they do then seem to be grateful to the other, he may name each party to the other, and so leave them to transact their business. This course seemeth to prevent two extremes: the one of wanting the commodity of the thing you desire, by a bashful silence, and the other of becoming necessarily the common chat of the neighbourhood, if you should after publish your desire to buy or sell land, to marry, or the like.

Some such way might be used for the hiring of and servants or 'prentices, and for the utterance of divers wares and commodities.

It would be very expedient if each parish or village might have some place, as the church, smithy, wherein to publish (by papers posted up) the wants either of the buyer or seller, as, such a field to be let, such a servant or such a service to be had, &c. And it seemeth convenient that each man that will sell his horse should tie a mark or sign thereof in the bridle. For, in regard it is often ill taken to ask a gentleman, the price of his horse, many necessary bargains are hindered; as likewise, if a man should now declare his willingness to sell his horse, it would argue some hidden fault, whereas in so general a usage it were not so like to be suspected.

There was a book published at London weekly about the year 1657, which was called (as I remember) *The Publick Advice*. It gave information in very many of these particulars. *Quære*—if it continues still to do so, or the reason that it doth not.

A.D. 1660.—There is an office near the Old Exchange in London, called the office of *Publick Advice*. From thence both printed and private informations of this useful nature are always to be had. But what they print is no more than a leaf or less in a diurnal. I was in this office. The diurnal consisted of sixteen pages quarto in 1689.

I am convinced by reason and my own experience (to say nothing of faith), that it is extreme folly to be transported either with joy or grief in temporal respects. That which hath an end is nothing, saith a great Saint However, it would seem something if it would last some number of years. But we do see desperate and griping sorrows tread upon the heels of the greatest joys. The very day (to the best of my memory and observation) of my own greatest joy did immediately precede the day (in all appearance and probability) of my greatest loss and grief.

Yet, notwithstanding that this loss was no less than my whole estate by incurring delinquency and the mutilation of the strongest limb in my body by a musket shot, it hath proved in the end (as far as human prudence can yet conjecture) the greatest temporal fortune that ever befell me, and that for many reasons, partly known to others, but principally to myself. These changes are no wonder, when we know of far greater happening to whole cities. Today the bells and the bonfires express the violent passions of an overjoyed people, when tomorrow their own reeking blood must extinguish their flaming buildings. That thing for which we do most labour and pray, and for the happening whereof we are even transported with joy, is not seldom our utter destruction, and that speedily.

1665, *May*.—Richard Airey, of London, his bill for Mall [Mary, Mr, Blundell's daughter]:—

For a sky-coloured silk mohair coat   £2 17 0

„ „ coloured stuff coat bought for her	1 3 0
„ „ sky-coloured silk mohair waistcoat	0 17 0
„ „ mixed pink-coloured petticoat of good sarcenet	1 1 0
„ „ suit of knots of pink and silver riband	0 4 6
„ 2 laces	0 0 6

He speaks also of paying 2l. 5s. for two hats of equal price, and 1l. 8s. for a border of hair. Mr. Airey, on the other hand, had sold for him twenty-seven dozen rabbit skins at 4l. 2d. per dozen, coming to 5l. 12s. 6d.

I paid many round sums for clothes for my son Butler (Richard, afterwards Viscount Mountgarret, who had married, in 1661, Mr. Blundell's daughter Emilia). I do remember particularly a stuff suit and coat when he came to me about April 1661—

This I take cost about	£4 5 0
His wedding suit and coat of Spanish cloth, being 2 pair of breeches besides the doublet and the coat, cost about	7 15 0
A velvet coat bought at London, cost	8 0 0
A hat when he was at London 1661	1 2 0
A sword at the same time, about	1 0 0

Besides sundry other things, which partly I do not remember, and partly do forbear to put down.

1667, *May.*—It is agreed betwixt me and John Tildesley that he shall serve me one whole year, from May 2, 1667, for 4l. wages, and for such vails as shall happen in the service; but I am not obliged to give him any further reward for his services, either by old clothes or any other way. (Signed by W. Blundell and John Tildesley.)

Upon the eve (December 7) of the Conception of our Lady, I, being of the sociality with others of my family, proposed to our spiritual director that we might all together say the Rosary upon the said feast day. He said he did very well like it, but could not conveniently be present himself, having but weak health and finding that such exercises did spend him. I told him that he might in such a number of persons answer in silence, and no notice would be taken of it But he said that he found that even the noise of others speaking was often troublesome to him.

In fine, we said the Rosary on the said feast day, and although we had not his company, yet he spent the most part of the afternoon of that holyday in playing at tables and shovel-board in the dining-room and in the hall, and at four of the clock and a half retired to his chamber. This gentleman, was a person of singular virtue and prudence, and one whom I should have chosen before thousands, as well for a companion as for a director. And this I note that I may remember not to have a bitter prejudice against the actions of such men as I like not, when those whom I like so well will do things so contrary to my judgement.

The chaplain whose conduct on this occasion excited the momentary displeasure of Mr. Blundell was, no doubt, the Rev. Francis Waldegrave, S. J. We have already spoken of him in the introductory chapters, and have mentioned the great esteem in which he was held by his patron, who indeed confirms this estimate of him in the foregoing remarks.

The Rosary is still a favourite devotion of the Catholic Church, and sodalities for the daily recital of it have numerous associates. Tables is the same as backgammon, but shovel-board is no longer known as it was formerly played. It seems to have been the forerunner of billiards. An old shovel-board is said to exist at Chartley Hall. It is 31 feet 1 inch long, made up of 260 pieces, 12 or 18 inches long, laid on longer boards underneath, and well jointed.

Those who have made a long sea voyage will be familiar with a description of shovel-board played on deck, which is one of the few diversions possible under such conditions. Flat discs of wood are used, and these are propelled with long-handled spades of corresponding size into divisions chalked out at a suitable distance. On the latter are marked the numerals up to 10, with two forfeits of 10, one at each end. The chief amusement seems to consist in driving your enemy out of the winning numbers and lodging yourself in his place. This is varied by dexterous attempts to land him in the forfeits, and to cover skilfully the approaches, that he may not be afterwards relieved.

It is wonderful to see how notably our countrymen do translate anything out of the Latin, either verse or prose, and yet we shall never meet with an Englishman that either writes or speaks Latin commendably.

Sands' translation of Ovid's *Metamorphoses* is said to bear the bell for a translation in verse. Virgil's *Æneid* hath ever been esteemed a piece too high to be dealt with, with any hope of success in that kind.

Yet hath Ogleby (a fellow that kept a tap house) engaged upon it, and performed it with good applause. May hath done *Lucan* rarely well, and Virgil's *Georgics*.

Sir Humphrey Stapleton [? Robert] hath hit very right of the jog of an English style in his version of *Strada*, yet in sundry places he mistakes the sense of the author. Winterton hath made a most proper piece of English of Drexelius' *Nine Considerations upon Eternity*. But his different opinions in religion hath made him often to mince and conceal the author's sense.

A good lady of my acquaintance was so curious in her attire, as to send out of Lancashire to London her linen to be washed and starched as often as they were fouled; such fine linens, I mean, as were used about her neck and shoulders.

Sir William Petty (in his book of taxes) esteems begging to be the worst way for relief of the poor. Sir Thomas Haggerston told me (this 4th day of August 1665) very much of the abuse of begging in Northumberland, and how gladly himself, Mr. Ralph Clavering and others would reform it, but they are afraid of curses and clamours. That very many Scotch beggars come into those parts, and many that are lusty and able; yet when they have got an alms at the hall, they beg at the houses in the town, and there they get alms too for fear of their curses, although the housekeepers be less able than themselves, as being labouring men, and having no more but a cottage and a yard or garden. That the beggars wherever corn is stirring (as in winnowing, sowing, &c.) do beg, or as it were get by custom a part of the same: and to this end many go about to beg in the time of seeding. That in time of shearing he hath often faulted the reapers for unclean reaping, and that they have frequently answered, 'What shall we leave for the poor ones?' That when he leads his corn many do come to glean in the field at the same time, so that those who should reap for hire do turn gleaners, to his great damage.

An advertisement from the Hospital called Bedlam, printed in the *Gazette* about 24th June 1675, certifies that there is never any licence given nor any plates on the arms to such wanderers as under those colours pass up and down. When I read this, I mentioned one Medcalf, a gentleman, who passed as a Bedlamer. Mr. Tempest and his wife thereupon told me that he was hanged for a murder.

On the 6th July 1673, I caused John Gorsuch to put into the carthouse pit, about six or seven yards north-west of the lime kiln, twelve bottles of claret wine bottled about six weeks since (without sugar), but not kept since that time exactly cool. The cord in which they are threaded is put by a noose upon the head of a stake which is driven in a little below the surface of the water, the head of which is about two yards from the nicks made for a mark on the north-east of an alder tree, which mark is about half a yard from the root of the tree. Note, that the water is very low this dry summer, so that it will be hard in winter to find the cord, as the head of the stake may be probably two or three feet under water.

Cattle bought, 1664:

At Ormschurch, Whitson fair, four stirks and twinters, one for 1*l*. 9s. 4d., two for 3*l*. 3s. 6d., one for 1*l*. 14s 10d.

„ Prescot fair, two stirks, one for 1*l*. 11s. 6d., one for 1*l*. 4s. 6d.

„ Newborough fair, five stirks or twinters, one for 1*l*. 5s. 6d., one for 1*l*. 19s. two for 3*l*., one for 1*l*. 9s. 6d.

It is to be marked that many things which I put down as strange expressions do within a year or two become so familiar that even I myself do wonder why I took notice of them. Which thing may put us in mind how the English language changeth in the age of a man.

About August 1674, Richard Sellings, Esq., told me that he had almost finished the history of the Irish war for the space of about eight or nine years. He showed me a part thereof (*viz*. about 120 very large pages, just at the beginning of the rebellion), which I read over. I do give the greater credit to it, by reason that the said R. B. was a witness to very many things which he writes there. The said R. B. in one of his letters to me speaks of a former narrative of his own in two parts, setting forth the beginning of the commotion in Ireland.

I find the following words in the kingdom's *Intelligencer*, from January 13 to January 20, 1661, p. 28:—

By express command from his Majesty we are to acquaint the reader that a little book named *Boscobel* (being a relation of his Majesty's happy and miraculous escape after the fight at Worcester) hath divers errors and mistakes in it, and therefore not to be admitted as a true and perfect narrative of his sacred Majesty's deliverance.

I am not certain whether the advertisement abovesaid do relate to the first part of *Boscobel*, or to the second, or both. For the author doth profess that he had not so good intelligence for the writing of the second as of the first. And it may be thought that this advertisement may be given to lessen the displeasure which some hot heads have conceived, that Catholics should be looked upon as the King's chief preservers next to God. But the most of the chief circumstances which we read in *Boscobel* are confirmed by Dr. Bate's Latin history, called *Elenchus Motuum*, &c., where you may read sundry more delightful things concerning the King's travels in the west of England, than Mr. Blunt (who writ *Boscobel*) was able to relate, who wanted intelligence of the same.

I was at London constantly for some years last past, where, in the years 1687 and 1688, I chanced to have some conference in Latin with a natural Chinese whom I did sundry times meet with, by reason that he went to the Latin school at the Savoy. He told me that he was a native of Pekin, and that he had been about eight years absent from China. He told me that he judged Pekin to contain about double the number of the inhabitants contained in London, where he had been resident about eight months. I had formerly seen his picture admirably well painted at Windsor Castle. He appeared to be aged more than thirty years, though he pretended (and perhaps very truly) to be but five or six and twenty. He spoke to me imperfectly in Latin, as having learnt the same without any rules.

I do not take him to be a competent judge of the number of people either in Pekin or in London. His stature was low and his complexion very swarthy. His nose was very flat, and his eyes, by reason that his face in that part was also flat, stood outward somewhat oddly, and were very brown; yet his countenance was pleasing and smiling. I did likewise see in London, and had a short and free conference with Father Couplet, a Jesuit that had lived in China about twenty years. He was a native of the Spanish Netherlands, and although he was '*Sexagenario major*,' he was waiting for an opportunity to pass over again to his beloved China, which was so much in his mind that, whether he was waking or sleeping, he was in a manner continually thinking of it I did then hear him hold some short discourse in the Chinese language with that very same Chinese whom I have mentioned above, who came in unto us (when we two were only together) to ask some questions, as it seemed, of the said father.

June 3, 1676.—I saw twenty-six guineas impressed in the space of one minute, measured by my minute-watch. That coin was polished at the very same stroke (or turn) which made the impression. All this was done by one machine fed by one man and turned by three, and only one guinea was impressed at each turn of the said machine or screw. It was in the Tower of London.

The present March 4, 1686-7, I took great notice at Whitehall of that famous large map (lately set out by William Morgan), of the City and Suburbs of London, where the scale of the map is such that every inch of the same represents 300 feet of the town, river, gardens, streets, &c. The circuit is no less than eighteen or nineteen miles. Mr. Morgan, who made the map, told me that he reckoned 1,000 paces to be a mile, which I think is eighty paces less than an English statute mile. I do reckon the gates of London to be as follows: Ludgate, Newgate, Aldersgate, Cripplegate, Moorgate, Postern, Bishopsgate, Aldgate.

In November 1681, I took great notice of that new building, which I found then to be raised above the earth about 10 or 11 yards, according to the guess I made when I looked upon the same. Below the surface of the earth about 14 or 16 feet the foundation seemed to be laid, and all that was hollow like a cellar. If I be not mistaken it was arched all over, even with the top of the earth, so that there is an appearance of a church below as well as above the ground. But there was no manner of building at the west-end of the same, all being left so open that I guessed that the building would be continued much longer towards the west, which way there was then remaining, betwixt the new buildings and the ruins of the outermost part westward of the old burned church, about 80 yards or more.

The east end of this new church was then close built, and the wideness there within the walls was about 41 yards, and the greatest wideness of this church was about 104 yards, whereof 11 yards on the south side and 11 yards on the north side of the same seem to be taken up in porches. At the same time I read a written paper which hung up on a wall or pillar of this new building, mentioning the contributions given towards that work by the several Bishopricks of England, the total of which amounted to 14,000*l.*, whereof London gave 2,844*l.*, Winchester 1,026*l.*, Chester 561*l.* 18s. 6d,, Durham 334*l.*, Canterbury 199*l.* I suppose there is a standing fund or revenue belonging to this same church by which in length of time it may come to be finished. There is or was, as I take it, an allowance given by Parliament out of every ton of coals coming to London.

As I came down from London in June 1676, with Sergeant Rigby, who is a J.P. for Lancashire, he told me plainly once or twice upon occasion given, that the multitude of our penal laws cause them to be ill executed; that he himself was perjured (or forsworn), for not putting the laws in execution against swearers, when he heard and saw their transgressions. I did farther understand clearly by his expression, that he did not in the like case intend to mend his fault

June 27, 1663.—My nephew Selby told me that his wife's grandfather, Thomas Hesketh, Elsq., did in the year 1631 and 1632 (6 and 7 Charles I.) offer to his tenants in Pilling, who had leases in being for 12 years from 7 Charles I, either to seal them new leases upon surrender of the old ones for three lives or for 33 years, *i.e.* for 21 years longer than their term of 12 years. The number of leases in being were about 97, whereof 64 were renewed; all of them but five in 7 Charles I., and those five in 8 Charles I. Of these 64, 49 were taken for three lives and 15 for 33 years. We reckoned by the tenants' books that of these 49 leases five of them did yet retain three lives in being, 24 of them two lives in being, and 19 one life in being. So that it did appear that only one tenement of the 49 (taken about 32 years ago for three lives) had fallen to the lord. On the other hand, the 15 leases taken for 33 years are just upon the point of expiring.

This interesting record shows that the custom of granting leases for lives instead of for a term of years, which was ordinarily practised in the seventeenth century, was greatly to the disadvantage of the landlord Yet it is doubtful if the benefit to the tenant was more than apparent Probably, the custom was injurious both to landlord and tenant. The landlord may be said to have suffered more, for he received a very inadequate rental for his property. It was Mr. Blundell's practice to give an old tenant a lease for three lives at the rate of seven years' purchase. Thus, if a farm was worth annually 10*l.*, he got 70*l.* for the lease with some other trifling allowances, and lost all control over his property for the next thirty, forty, or fifty years, if any of the three lives lasted so long.

There was something paid annually by way of ground rent, but the amount was very small The tenant, on the other hand, having had difficulty in raising the capital required to enter upon the farm, had seldom anything to expend upon his place, which fell into dilapidation often long before the tenancy expired. He had no stimulus to industry, and generally contented himself with an easy and careless management, provided he secured a moderate maintenance for himself Moreover, he or some of those belonging to him might, and often did, render themselves particularly obnoxious to their landlord, whose hands were tied by the lease. *Moore's Rental*, published by the Cheetham Society, and written by Sir Edward Moore, first Baronet of Bank Hall, Mr. Blundell's contemporary and neighbour, contains very severe strictures upon the conduct of his tenants.

It is true that these were mostly leaseholders residing in the adjacent town (Liverpool), whose interests as townsmen would often clash with those of their landlord. Still, the same spirit manifested itself in country places. Mr. Nicholas Blundell, grandson to the Cavalier, frequently complains of the behaviour of certain tenants, and recommends his successor to discard them when their leases expire. The custom of leasing for lives was discontinued upon the Crosby Estate about a century ago, and although it lingered in the neighbourhood for another half-century, it is now almost universally abandoned.

Pilling in the Fylde lies on the borders of Morecambe Bay, and its once extensive moss (reduced gradually by cultivation) is still frequented by large flocks of sea-birds which build there annually. Pilling was a possession of Cockersand Abbey, purchased at the dissolution by John Kitchin, whose daughter conveyed a portion of it to the Daltons, on whose estate of Thurnham lie the ruins of the abbey. These ruins are not extensive, but the chapter-house has been covered in, and is used as a family Mausoleum by the Daltons. The abbey stood at the edge of the sands, through the midst of which the small river Cocker flows towards the sea. Hence its ancient name, but in these days it is commonly called Thurnham Abbey.

The Hall is in the immediate neighbourhood, and is an old rambling manor-house, built at different periods and not without that usual adjunct to ancient Catholic dwellings, a priest's hiding-place. There is more than one place of this kind, and the writer remembers to have noticed that they differ from others that he has seen, in respect that they are entered by the removal of a square stone in the wall This plan of construction was adopted in order that no hollow sound might betray their purpose. The Dalton family is now represented by Sir Gerald Dalton Fitzgerald, Bart.

Barnaby Kitchin, who died July 6, 1603, held the other moiety of Pilling, and married—

1st Ann, daughter of Sir John Aughton, of North Meols, Esq., by whom he had one daughter—

Alice, born 1554 = Hugh Hesketh, natural son of Sir Thomas Hesketh of Rufford, Knight

2nd Alice, widow of William Forshaw, Esq., by whom he had two daughters—

Anne, born 1582 = Thomas Ashton.

Elizabeth, born 1587 = Nathaniel, son and heir of Nicholas Banastre, of Altham, Esq.

In 1649, a partition of Barnaby Kitchin's Pilling estate was made, when Pilling Hall and one-third of the *demesne* fell to Richard, son of Nathaniel Banastre, one-third to Richard, son of Thomas Ashton, and the remaining third to Thomas and Robert, sons of Hugh Hesketh. This Thomas was grandfather to Mrs. Selby, who had likewise inherited North Meols from the Aughtons. This latter township is that on which the modern town of Southport is built At the death of Mrs. Selby, without issue, her estate reverted to her uncle, Robert Hesketh, whose descendant still possesses one moiety of North Meols. The Hornbys, of Poulton, purchased the Banastre and Ashton shares of Pilling in 1678, and the remaining third in 1772. They are now held by E. G. S. Hornby, Esq., of Dalton Hall. (Fishwick's *Garstang*, vol 2 Chetham Society.)

I was told on October 24, 1683, by Mr. Thomas Bootle, that whereas two shillings is always paid in our neighbourhood to the Justice's Clerk for a warrant even in case of felony and of like crimes against the King, that at Manchester there is paid no more than one shilling and sixpence for such warrants. William Norres, who was clerk to Justice Blundell in King James' time, told me oft, that in those days the clerks took not one penny for any such warrant

I did first of all in this my 58th year begin to study French, with design to understand it in a book, and I find it is not hard to do so. It is too late for me to begin with things of this nature, but I have an honest design, though no great hope to effect it.

There should be a north-west passage found, or rather a north-east passage, for the attaining of the Latin tongue. The inseparable difficulties of Latin do arise chiefly from hence, that we pretend to the understanding of Latin which hath been writ in all places and ages for about 2,000 years, whereas we are not able to understand our English Chaucer who lived but 300 years ago. And the several dialects of our own little country used at this day are not understood by any one person. The vulgar tongues are more easy. In September 1677, I knew not so much of French as to understand the meaning of *moi, toi, elle*, or the like most usual words, yet in March next following (having spent in reading French, an hour or two in the interim each day for the most part, and still without the help of a dictionary)

I began to read the first part of the abridgment of the *Holy History*. It was composed by Du Verdier, and consists of 574 pages *octavo*. I read this book twice over in French with much delight, as understanding the story sufficiently well without the help of an English translation. This I did in the space of twenty-six days, spending little time but only after supper, and yet during these twenty-six days I had five fits of an ague. My memory was then very bad, as being dulled with age and cares, yet my knowledge of Latin and English I think did advance me more, by three parts in four, than if I had only understood some one other language or two which had affinity with the French.

I judge that I myself and others of my small bore have in our younger days spent fifteen-fold more labour and time in the study of Latin only, without attaining that degree of knowledge therein which I got as above in French. So that it is not to be doubted, though Latin be very hard, but that it is a ready means to the knowledge of the best modern languages of Europe. I must not conceal that I was helped in reading the French book abovesaid by the knowledge which I had of the story, and although I wanted a dictionary, I had a good French grammar from which I learned much.

Many things have been said well by way of apology for Catholics, and more may be said hereafter as occasion shall serve. In the year 1661, I printed a small book on that subject which I have showed to few, and I think it was never exposed to sale. It is entitled *Quid me perseqiuris?* There are remarkable things in it which may do well now (1678) when the state of things is changed, being put into a better method.

No printed copy of this work has been found, but it is the title Mr. Blundell gave to his treatise on the Penal Laws, referred to in the introductory chapters.

Cherlotta, daughter of the Duke of Trimouil, is now the widow of James Earl of Derby, who was beheaded for his fidelity to the King,

1651, October 15. She was pleased to tell me (December 14, 1659) that she was then one of the five heirs to Madam Mamsel d'Orange, whose estate was 60,000*l. per annum.* There was then a report that that lady was to marry King Charles, which Lady Derby seemed heartily to wish, though it was like to destroy her own expectation. The Duke, her brother, refused (as she said) 100 years' purchase from Richelieu for his Dukedom, but answered that he would part with that and his life together. It may be I did mistake some of these stories by defect of my Lady's English.

It is reported that Sir Kenelm Digby (a person very famous for valour and other great parts) did receive a challenge from a certain young courtier, whose reputation in that kind was yet in question, and his person (by lowness of stature) a little contemptible. But this challenge was flatly refused by Sir K., and when the young spark complained that he had blemished his honour, and therefore did not deal like a gentleman, to deny him a way to clear it. Sir K. replied that he would give it him under his hand, that Sir Kenelm Digby had refused to fight a duel with Mr. A. B. So confidently may a known and valiant spirit slight all the rash contempts of an inferior person.

But when the same Sir Kenelm was provoked in the King's presence (upon occasion of the old business of Scanderoon) by the Venetian Embassador, who told the King it was very strange that his Majesty should slight so much his ancient amity with the most noble state of Europe, for the affection which he bare to a man (meaning Sir K.) whose father was a traitor, his wife a wh——e, and himself a pirate, altho he made not the least reply (as long as the Embassador remained in England) to those great reproaches, yet after, when the quality of his enemy was changed (by his return) to that of a private person. Sir Kenelm posted after him into Italy. There sending him a challenge to Venice (from some neighbouring state), he found the discreet *Magnifico* as silent in Italy as himself had been before in England, and so he returned home.

But how shall a gentleman, refuse a challenge without a note of cowardice, whose valour hath not yet been testified? This let the following story teach you:—

Mr. Langley of Shropshire sent a challenge to Mr. Owen, a gentleman, of the same county, to provoke him, on pretence of an injury, to a single duel. Owen returns a denial, alleging the laws of God and of the nation for so doing, and addeth further that he shall never decline his usual and well-known walks for any fear of Langley, who may find him when he pleaseth with his sword by his side, which he shall not doubt but to manage in his own defence, to the damage of a future assailant Langley hereupon assails him in his walk, but is opposed strongly and in fine disarmed. He sends him after this a second challenge, but receiving the same answer, he assaulteth his adversary again in the former manner and just with the former success. After all this ado, nothing would serve our unfortunate champion but a third adventure, which proving just the same in all kinds of respects with the other two, finding himself condemned, and the other as much extolled by all the country, he was content at length to be quiet *Narravit mihi* Ds. Geo. Fox, January 22, 1659. Mr. Langley lives now in Shrewsbury.

George Lord Digby (now Earl of Bristol) about the year 1649, when he went out of Ireland into France, was met at his landing by the Lord Wilmot, who provoked his Lordship to a single duel upon an old difference in England betwixt the Lord Digby, as Chief of the faction at Court, and the soldiers of fortune patronised by Prince Rupert, and mainly strengthened by the Lords Gerard and Wilmot This challenge was refused by the Lord Digby with much civility and fair words, commiserating the loss of so much English loyal blood as had been spilt in the late war, and lamenting withal the fewness of his Majesty's surviving servants. The Lord Wilmot, interpreting all this mildness to proceed from weakness of courage, did reproach him unworthily with it, but could not for all that wrest his Lordship a jot from his fixed resolution.

At the last he told him the Prince Rupert, esteeming him unworthy to die by his sword, had vowed to shoot him dead at their first meeting. But here the Lord Digby changeth his copy, and that which he would not before accept in defence of his own honour, he offers now to his enemy in defence of another. For charging the Lord Wilmot grievously for having aspersed so basely a person of so great worth and a Prince of the Royal blood of England, he requireth satisfaction with his sword for the Prince's honour. So by the help of his wit changing the state of the quarrel, he is now become Prince Rupert's champion, and to approve himself right worthy of that honour he worsteth the Lord Wilmot in the duel, and is afterwards reconciled to his other great enemies who had intended to have fought him upon the same old quarrel

This encounter between Lords Digby and Wilmot occurred in 1647, as we learn by a letter from Robert Thomer to Sir R. Vemey, dated Paris, in October of that year. 'Lord Digby, O'Neal, and Mr. Digby, son to Sir Kenelm, on Thursday last disarmed the Lord Wilmot, the Lord Wentworth, and his second, to their great dishonour.' (See Collections of Sir William Verney, Bart, in *Historical Commissioners* Appendix to 7th Report)

It is said that there is a certain eel in the sea which is called the whale thrasher, as big as a small mast of a ship, and that there is a confederacy betwixt this eel and the sword fish to destroy the whales. Whereupon the sword fish going under the whale's belly, pricketh the tender parts thereof in such sort as that the whale to avoid the hurt raiseth himself above the water. Then comes the sliding eel upon his back, and having seized fast about his head, she raiseth her tail aloft like a whip and belaboureth his sides and back with continual lashes, until with the assistance of her undermining companion they have effected their design by the death of their unwieldy enemy. Captain Hill (once a pirate at sea, afterwards a lay-brother with the Jesuits) told Mr. Waldgrave (from whom I had the relation, February 8, 1659) that once as he sailed, he saw such an eel for the space of half-an-hour thrashing the sides of a whale in such manner as is aforesaid.

This looks like an early appearance of the sea-serpent

I have observed that in such springs as are neither forward nor backward, our apple trees are fully yet freshly blossomed on May-day, yet have I noted in a very backward year, that very few apple-tree buds have on that day put forth any manner of reddish colour and cast no flower at all. I have noted in my almanac about the year 1669 (as I take it), that on the 3rd of May I could not discern, as I passed closely by the side of the orchard at Haigh, so much as the least red or white upon any apple bud.

A.D. 1679-80, January 30, white violets were plucked in my garden, and daffodils in great number budded and near breaking out, as to the flower. Plenty of tansy about a finger long. On the 1st February many of our apricock buds were red. Some hawthorn leaves were in February as broad as a silver twopence, many were so. On 30th March 1680, very many of my summer russetting apple blossoms were full blown. Our pear trees fully flowered, and in their greatest lustre, March 25, 1680.

Very many barren wives do so strongly fancy themselves to be with child, that they do even send for the midwife as being ready to bring forth, when yet there is no conception. One of my acquaintance fancied herself to be pregnant ten years together. The fanatical wife of a baronet, at such time as her preacher came to give her a visit, said, 'As soon as the voice of your salutation sounded in my ears, the babe leaped in my womb.' Yet was she never with child.

1666, *September 26.*—Winefrid Blundell, writing to a lady of rank who had applied to her for a servant, says, 'I have engaged her for 15s. for a quarter, which is all the time agreed for. I have heard that our country-women are generally esteemed much better servants than I can for the present furnish your Ladyship with, but both the best and indifferent sort are of a humour which must be dealt with (now and then) by giving some little sweet encouragement, and not always by severity. They will commonly for a great fault endure a severe check, but not for every small one, and sometimes they must know it if they do well, &c'

> Mr. Blundell's sister Winefrid, in giving the above advice to her correspondent, evinced a thorough knowledge of the 'humour' of servant-girls from that part of Lancashire, which remains unchanged to this day; the last touch is admirable.

It is well known that this day, 1650, Cromwell won the famous battle of Dunbar, and on the same day, 1651, the great battle of Worcester. On that day, 1658, he ended his own life. The same day, 1662, William Lenthall, Speaker of the Long Parliament, did likewise die. I have heard that Wednesday, as I take it, hath been fatal to the house of Derby. I was born, contracted to my wife, and lamed with a shot upon Saturday, on which day my father died.

The greatest gamblers are those who in public gaming houses, called the offices of insurance, do for a sum of money secure buildings upon the land from fire, and ships upon the sea from water, &c.

> If the writer had lived in these times and seen the accounts of the great insurance companies, he would have retracted this sweeping condemnation. In his day, the few risks of this nature that were taken up were incurred by single individuals, and this certainly wears the appearance of reckless gambling.

Our manner of writing in this age is too exact and wholly turned into points (and witticisms), the continuation of which is impossible. Mr. Gui Miege set forth his great French and English Dictionary, price 30s., about the year 1688. There is in it his English Grammar, which I take to be much better than any I have seen. The word *cozen* is writ twenty-nine different ways.

The book called *Britannia Languens,* p. 131 (note that the pages there for a long way together are false printed), speaking of the poor of England, says that they are increased by computation to near ten times the late number, within the last twenty years, and that their maintenance doth cost the nation 400,000 *l. per annum* constant tax.

In July 1684, I asked a poor woman how many children she had. She answered, 'Six.'

'Here,' said I, 'here is sixpence for them.'

'No, sir,' said she, most simply, 'I will not sell my children.'

A bashful man is not his own master, nor uses his own judgment, but is overawed by the boldness of others, and they that are impudent have a power over him. Bashfulness is sometimes a friend, but more often an evil guardian to youth, betraying it, contrary to its own desire and inclination, to the worst of men, who hurry it to evil actions and places. How many men have lost their estates, honour, and lives, because they were ashamed to distrust A man invites you to game, drink, rob, or to be bound for him. This foolish modesty is to be cast off. Deny him. An impudent flatterer comes to eat upon you; he begs a horse, a ring, or garment of you. Give to the deserver; respect not him that begs. Some are so bashful as not to send for a good physician, nor employ a good lawyer, because they are acquainted with a worse. Begin betimes to break this fault, and in small matters to assert your own liberty; deny to debauch, deny to lend money, or to admire everyone you hear praised; be constant, and be not overcome by importunity which is a part of impudence, needful (perhaps) to them that know not otherwise how to live.

Some men ask pardon where there is no offence, but when it is commanded by God and reason, they will rather die than do it.

In August 1662, there happened a hailstorm in these west parts of

MANCHESTER EARLY REGISTERS

	Baptisms	Burials		Baptisms	Burials
1663	158	212	1671	163	182
1664	254	172	1672	209	307
1665	174	282	1673	191	213
1666	205	176	1674	166	285
1667	174	212	1675	164	231
1668	192	242	1676	174	242
1669	187	230	1677	206	224
1670	194	143	1678	—	210

Lancashire, whereby many fields of good corn were quite destroyed in an instant. Some parts of Sefton parish (especially the Lunt), some parts of Halsall, Aughton, and Ormskirk parishes, did suffer very much damage. Pigeons were killed thereby, fruit spoiled, and the boughs of trees cloven and slit with the hailstones. In February 1661, there was a short storm of wind, which exceeded (as some affirm) all that have been known in these parts. Sundry buildings and some orchards in Cheshire were quite overturned. And the damage to ships in Liverpool was such, as the like (in no proportion) could ever be remembered.

Mr. Humphrey Bagarley lent me a MS. of this expedition, writ by an eye-witness, wherein I find this. That Prince Rupert and his brother Prince Maurice began this voyage from Helvoet-sluys *a.d.* 1648, in January. He returned to Nantes in March 1652-3. He had many sad disasters, but made no considerable fight in the whole voyage, which was most of it spent in and about the West Indies. Prince Maurice was lost in the night, driven upon a rock (as was supposed) by Ireland. Prince Rupert's ship, towards the end of the year 1652, was sunk by a leak, wherein perished 333 persons, who forced him to save his life by the help of a small pleasure boat The story of that is very long and tragical. Prince Rupert was wounded with an arrow in Affrick. They took some prizes, but not many. This relation is not well penned, nor is it at all exact in the chief particulars.

Her letter to my sister Frances, dated March 23 (it came into my hands, May 1674), tells that she was at the writing of it in as great a depth of misery and grief of heart as ever she was since her dear husband and children left her. That her house and lands were fallen into my lord's hands for want of payment of rent That she cannot get money to pay the rent, but is at suit for 10*l*., which is owing to her, but that the officers cannot give her justice till an officer come from the old Bishop who banished her. That the officers have given her a letter to him (who is at London), but that she knows not well how to get it thither. That she is tabled with her daughter Ratclif at a market town, fifteen miles from her own house, but her son Ratclif having come to some loss by her, she finds a change in some things.

That her daughter Cannel's husband aims to get her lands, who asked in the face of the Court why they suffered her to live there? and who would live in a house with a papist? They were bloody, and he would not live with any of them. He swore the peace against her, and that he was afraid she would burn his house upon him, and so she was ordered to put in sureties or go to prison. That her health is worse and worse each day, and that her grief is great for want of the Sacraments. She intends to come over to her daughter Jane (if Jane's husband be content) for one year.

This unfortunate gentlewoman, was a daughter of Thomas Hesketh of Meols, Esq., and had married Deemster Cannel of the Isle of Man, from whence she writes this pitiful letter. She was related to Mr. Blundell through the Norris's of Speke, her grandmother, wife of Mr. Molineux of the Wood, being sister to Edward Norris, Esq. We find from his book of accounts that Mr. Blundell frequently extended his charity to her and her impoverished family. She seems to have had a daughter settled at Crosby, and no fewer than five of her children became Religious abroad.

October 1, 1677.—My son made a large firkin, two parts and more of orange apples, the rest were large sour apples. The liquor was strained through a cloth and stood two days in a large vessel, then was it drawn into a firkin and stopped up.

October 5th and 6th,—I made three firkins of cider—one of orange apples, one of Harrison's apples, and one of grove apples. All these were turned immediately into the firkins. The two first were stopped up the second day, the last stopped up the first day. Some small vent was left in all. The second had far more pills and uncleanness in it than the rest I put some wheat into the first and second when I made them up. We had generally near a third part of liquor proportionable to the measure of the apples. The grove apples, which made the last firkin, were got about eighteen hours before they were pressed The rest were plucked or shaken some days before. The five firkins contained, I think, one hogshead.

A list of the names of Popish Recusants of the greatest quality in the county of Lancs. to be banished by Act of Parliament, held October 1680:—

Caryll Lord Viscount Molyneux.
Wm. Molyneux, Esq.
Sir William Gerard, Bart.
Sir Chas. Anderton, Bart.
Wm. Molyneux of Croxteth, Esq.
Richd. Sherburne of Stonyhurst, Esq.
Ricd. Walmesley of Dunkenhalgh, Esq.

Edmd. Trafford of Trafford, Esq.
Edmd. Tildesley of the Lodge, Esq.
Thos. Tildesley his son.
Ralph Tildesley.
Humphrey Trafford.
Robt Dalton of Thurnham, Esq.
Hugh Dicconson of Wrightington, Esq.
Hy. Blundell of Ince Blundell, Esq.
John Harrington of Huyton, Esq.
Wm. Blundell of Crosby, Esq.
Richd. Butler of Rawcliffe, Esq.
Wm. Hesketh of Singleton, Esq.
Thos. Stanley of Eccleston, Esq.
John Brockholes of Claughton, Esq.
Robt Molyneux of the Wood, Esq.
Sir Rowland Bellasis, Bart.
Richd. Towneley of Towneley, Esq.
S. Langton of Abraham, Esq.
— Eccleston of Eccleston, Esq.
— Scarisbrick of Scarisbrick, Esq.
Thos. Culcheth of Culcheth, Esq.
Thos. Braithwaite of L'pool, Esq.
Richd Chorley of Chorley, Esq.
Richd. Grimshaw of Clayton, Esq.
Richd Sherburne of Stonyhurst, gent..
Wm. Standish of Wigan, gent..
Wm. Blundell, Jr. of Crosby, gent..
Wm. Dicconson of Wrightington, gent..
Alexr. Standish of Standish, gent..
Richd. Gerard of Ince, gent..
Chrisr. Anderton of Wigan, gent..
George Carus of Whittington, gent..
Thos. Lydiate of Lydiate, gent.,
Wm. Wolfall of Huyton and Roby, gent..
Edmd. Stanley of Aughton, gent..
Thos. Stanley of Aughton, gent.
Thos. Worthington, Senr. of Wigan, gent.
Chas. Harris of Bowland, gent.
Cuthbt Hesketh of Goosenargh, gent.
Edmd. Threlfall of Goosenargh, gent.

Thos. Gooden of Pendlebury, gent.
Edmd. Gooden of Little Bolton, gent.
Jas. Duckett of Ashton, gent.
Christr. Hayes of Bulk, gent.
Richd. Massy of Ashton (q. Rixton), gent.
George Leybourne of Nateby, gent.
Hy. Gerard of Bamfurlong, gent.
Wm. Anderton of Euxton, gent.
Edmd. Standish of Worthington, gent.
Peregrine Tasburgh of Ormskirk, gent.
Geo. Westby of Up. Rawcliife, gent.
Josh. Bryer of Lathom, gent.
Bernard Westby of Manor, gent.
Wm. Money of Dunkenhalgh, gent.
Geo. Culcheth of Towneley, gent.
Thos. Knype of Dalton, gent.
Wm. Fazakerley of Liverpool, gent.

This list was sent by Mr. John Gelibrond to Mr. Blundell, and he says that it is imperfect in names and places, but is a true copy of the list given by Lord Ancram to Sir Roger Bradshaigh.

1624, *October 19.*—A speeche of a bargain with Nichs. Hewett Brikeman for the making of eight schore thousand breekes:—

The claye must be feighed, upon my master's charges and a horse and carte fownde during the tyme of moulding; a moulding boarde and three whyte barrows; a bearing barrow and a burbette to keep water.

He must have 2s. 9d. for a thowsand breeke. The breeke must be 10 in. long, 5 in. broade, and 2½ in. thicke, which cometh to the sum of 22*l*. The payment of that he would have at three tymes *viz.*, at the carting (which must be as soon as my master can make ready for it) the sum of 5*l*. 10s.; at the moulding, 11*l*., and at the burning 5*l*. 10s. Towards the burning there must be provided twenty tunne of coale and sixty tunne of slacke, ten loade of woode and three of turfe. He must have two beds found him, and housing fitting to lay his bed and dressing meat, and a cow grass during the tyme of moulding, which will be about Whitsuntide; the tyme of burning must be abowte St James' tide (July 25).

Although this memorandum is before the time of the Cavalier, it is inserted on account of its interest, as regards the price of building material early in the seventeenth century. It points also to the period when large additions were made to Crosby Hall, and when probably the older portions of the house were demolished.

I fee'd an attorney (Mr. Samuel Andrews) after my conviction at the Assizes, and thus he writ to me August 26, 1673:—

I have enquired in the Crown Office at Lancaster, and am informed by the clerks there that you are not in any danger of conviction till the next assizes at soonest The course being, that such presentments as were brought in at the last assizes are at the next drawn up into a formal bill and found by Grand Inquest, and at the latter end of that assize (if prosecution be intended against them) their names are read up and a proclamation made, that unless they conform before the then next assizes, or in the mean time render their bodies to the Sheriff (this seems grounded upon two several statutes, *viz.*, 29 Eliz. cap. 5. and 3 James, cap. 4) they will be convict So that I conceive (supposing a vigorous prosecution be intended, which I hope is not), there can be no conviction against you until next summer assizes, unless the Justices of the Peace at their Quarter Sessions proceed against you, which the statute of 3 James, cap. 4 directs.

The Lord Scudamore caused a marble altar table to be taken from Abbey Dore in Herefordshire, and brought to his own house, Holme. In the carriage whereof one of his servants had his leg broken and another was killed outright The table or stone was used in his house for the pressing of cheeses. But the cheeses that were pressed therewith did run blood, whereupon it was removed to the laundry for the linens to be washed and batted upon it. Then again it was observed that a continual noise of batting upon the said stone was heard in the night, whereupon the stone was taken by the command of the said lord to the place from whence he had taken it

This happened about seven or eight or ten years ago and was told to me by Mr. Stanton, November 7, 1660. He heard the relation from one Mr. Scudamore, a priest, for whom the Lord Scudamore had sent to advise with him concerning the fore-mentioned prodigies. Mr. Stanton did likewise hear the son of the said lord, when he told the same story to other persons.

There was a stone cross standing at Whalley on the side of a bowling green which was found one day when the bowlers were come to play to be thrown down upon the green; and in regard it lay in their way, they desired to have it removed off the green. Whereupon an able strong man that was present reared up the stele or shaft of the said cross upon one end; and because it was too heavy to be otherwise removed by a single person, he wrested it from edge to edge (keeping the higher end all the while in his arms), intending in that manner to have removed it off the green.

But it pleased God that while the man was labouring hard to effect his purpose, he fell down flat upon his back, and the stone falling upon his breast killed him outright, so that he uttered never a word. The news of this strange accident coming to a house in the neighbourhood, a certain man who heard the relation cried out immediately, that some sudden death would undoubtedly betide himself, because (said he), that same man and myself did, this very last night, privately pull down the cross that hath now killed him.

This relation I had from William Norris of Blackrod, gentleman, January 3, 1660, who told me that he had it from Mr. Richard Craven of Dinkley, about thirty years since; who told him that he himself was an eye-witness when the man was killed.

Whittaker in his *History of Whalley* makes no mention of the latter remarkable circumstance.

When the King of Morocco expressed his wonder to the Embassador sent from King Charles of England, that so mighty a prince as his master was entitled so poorly; the Embassador returned answer that many of his titles were left out for brevity sake, for besides the dominion of Great Britain, his master was likewise King of Northumberland, Cumberland, and Westmoreland, and of many other places no less considerable; which answer did abundantly satisfy.

In the use of excessive gaming my passions have been very great and many—*viz.* hope, fear, joy, sadness, &c., but above all anger. And I do believe that my passions have been more frequent and violent about this one thing, than upon any one other occasion, hitherto, in the course of my life. Yet see the folly of this. The sense of those things at gaming which troubled or rejoiced me so much, was commonly so inconstant and short, that within one hour or two (especially at tables, and at all other games of dice), I had quite forgot the occasions of my several passions. And now at this present all those things which have formerly troubled me so much do seem no more to concern me than if they had been only dreams. I am therefore persuaded that if I had now the courage to leave the superfluous things of this world (which trouble and solicit me so much), I should within a short time be no more concerned in the want of them than I am now concerned in those desires and passions which I have had long since at play and which are now all forgotten.

The many great virtues and high abilities in sundry kinds of my dear brother Richard have been told unto me by divers persons who have lived long in his company, some of whom were present at his death. These were Mr. Thomas Bradshaigh, Mr. Kempe, Mr. Christopher Bradshaigh, Mr. Edwards, Mr. Walgrave, Mr. Cotton, and sundry others. His learning and judgement were so great that the Italians would point him out in the streets with these words, 'There goeth the great English Wit' He lived at Rome but about three years at the most, yet he had learnt the Italian language; he spake Greek so perfectly that he frequently repaired to the natural Greeks in Rome to hold discourse in their own language. He wrote a pretty book in Latin (which is now in my hands), concerning the nature of meteors, and another small book in English, wherein he did epitomise the chief part of Sir Kenelm Digby's book of Bodies.

His nature was lively and cheerful, and exceeding sociable and grateful He was very exemplary in his life and conversation, insomuch that I have been credibly informed that the remarkable passages of his life are collected and read frequently in the college where he lived and died, for the example of others. One of the above-named persons, who was his dear friend and chamber-fellow in the college, did inform me that he hath sundry times invited him, especially upon the eves of some notable feasts, to retire into their chambers, where they have offered to God certain devotions and sharp disciplines for the good of their native country. Sundry of the persons above mentioned appeared so extremely affected to his memory, that I have heard them make long and feeling discourses of many of these particulars, and of other notable things concerning his life and death.

Mr. Henry Long, who came this year, 1666, from Rome, told me that to this day there is a great memory even among the Italians at Rome of my brother Richard, and that he hath heard sundry of them much extol his great abilities. He told me with what great applause my said brother did make his public defension of Philosophy in the Roman College, and that the famous divine and philosopher, Father Geteen, did dispute against him. This Mr. Long told me, December 16, 1666.

Richard Blundell, born 1625-6, entered the English College, Rome, September 7, 1645. At that time he made the following answers to the usual interrogatories:—'My name is Richard, youngest son of Nicholas Blundell and Jane Bradshaw, who on account of divers persecutions for the orthodox faith fled from her native country of Lancashire into Cheshire, and there brought me into the world her eleventh child; but ten days after my birth sent me back to her own home to be nursed, and there I lived to my thirteenth year under various tutors, both Catholic and Protestant, but with little fruit My present condition is not unlike that of my country, that is, miserable.

Only in this I consider myself happy, that, snatched away from all the troubles of my friends, I am so fortunately landed at this port of happiness. But notwithstanding that my parents were oppressed by the multitude of their children, they have provided for each one an annual pension for their respectable maintenance. My father, son of William Blundell, Esq., was born, or at least suckled, in prison, where his parents lay for a long time on account of their faith. He, when a youth, married Jane, the eldest daughter of Roger Bradshaw, Esq., the fruit of which marriage was thirteen children, of whom six only are now alive who, left orphans, mourn over the premature deaths of their parents. All my relations to a man, as far as I know, are and always were Catholics. Of these four uncles are priests, two sisters and three (paternal) aunts, nuns. Besides these I have many other connections.

When I was thirteen years old, I went to St Omer's College,' &c He died at the English College, of fever, on August 7, 1649. On his deathbed he was received into the Society of Jesus, having long had the desire of entering it In fact, his fever was occasioned, as his intimate friend and schoolfellow Father Waldegrave declared, by his great travel through the streets of Rome during the heat of summer to obtain by the interest of certain cardinals a dispensation from his college oath. An interesting memoir of this pious youth, containing many edifying particulars, will be found in Brother Foley's *Records S. J.* vol. 1. It was written by Father George Gray, and is addressed to Father Richard Bradshaigh, his uncle. A copy of this document is amongst the *Crosby Papers*.

It must be remembered that the term English *Wit*, as applied to

R. Blundell, would then have a much wider signification than it has at the present day.

On Thursday, August 11, 1664, the Earls of Castlehaven and Arran (whereof the first was about fifty years of age or very near it), in St James' Park, upon a wager laid with the King, killed a fat strong buck by running on foot, having each a knife in his hand. They had six hours to perform it, but they did it in two and a half. They were a good while before they could unherd him. Then they run him till, being extremely hot, he took the water in a pond where they threw stones at him, and toiled, and drove him so to a side, till they killed him with their knives. This was told me by a gentleman that was present when the buck was killed, and the thing is very true.

James Touchet, second son of Mervyn Touchet, Baron Audley and Earl of Castlehaven, executed on Tower Hill for infamous crimes, had a new patent of his father's titles in 1634. Was general of the Irish army which acted against Cromwell and the Parliament After the subjugation of Ireland, he retired to France, but returned to England when the King came back. Was restored in 1678 to all the honours forfeited by his father, and died October 11, 1684. His brother succeeded to his titles, but the Earldom expired in 1777. The Barony of Audley, being a barony in fee, has descended through the last Earl's sister to the present Lord Audley.

Lord Richard Butler, second son of James, first Duke of Ormond, was created Earl of Arran in 1662. Became a Peer of England under the title of Baron Butler of Weston, 1673. He distinguished himself in the naval engagement of that year, and later on, in 1682, he did good service in Ireland He died in 1685 without male issue, though he had been twice married.

The Fathers do accustom themselves to public disciplines in their colleges on the eves of great feasts. *Narravit mihi unus ex illis.* The same party told me that when the Swede was expected in Lithuania, the Fathers in Vilna, whereof he was one, did take a bloody discipline each day for a whole month to avert the displeasure of God

I told Father Richard Banister (who had been Provincial the year before), that one great cause of the disaffection of some Englishmen to the Jesuits in England was the false apprehension of the greatness of their number in this province. To which he answered that he knew for certain that there were not in England at that time 150 Jesuits, and said, if an account were taken, he would be content to die, &c, if the number were so many 1661.

Sir Edward Widdrington showed me a picture of a Frenchman who, he said, had killed twenty-two men in single duel, and was finally slain himself in such a combat

Baron Limbeck, a Burgundian (yet living, 1660) had eight brothers slain in duels. He fought a famous combat, as one of the six subjects of Spain, against the like number of French who were under the Prince of Condé. They fought upon post horses to prevent inequality of management Two of the French were slain, and the Spaniards got the day. *Narravit mihi* Mr. Jo. Molineux, Februaiy 16, 1660.

Baron Botavil was a most desperate, implacable duellist He was beheaded for this in Place Royale, having killed divers men even upon mere shadows of affronts.—*Idem narravit*

Lewis XI., King of France, had granted a pardon four or five times to one who had killed so many men in duels. He asked his Confessor whether he might lawfully pardon him anymore, the like occasion being then happened. The Confessor replied that the King might do it as well then as he had done it the first time. For the murderer had only killed one single man, the King (who had pardoned that) killed all the rest.

The story is very famous of the fleet which was sent by Cromwell to subdue this island about the year 1655, where as they marched through the woods to surprise St Domingo, a great part of the army was routed and destroyed by one troop of about fifty horsemen. After which repulse the remainder of the army went and took Jamaica. In the year 1673, I was told by owner William Williamson of Liverpool that he was at Hispaniola at the same time, and upon Blaster day he saw the English army mustered there, and that the muster-master, being his friend, told him that the army mustered was 9,774, of which number 1,200 were seamen and no more.

In or about the year 1673 there happened in one family in Salford, within the space of twenty-four hours, these several births following, *viz.*: the wife of the house was delivered of a son, a cow of a calf, a sow of fifteen pigs, a bitch of sixteen whelps, a cat of four kittens, and a hen hatched fourteen eggs. All this I took in writing from Mr. Samuel Andrews, and he professed that he had it credibly affirmed to him by persons in the same neighbourhood.

September 2, 1666, a fire began in London, and in four or five days burned the greater part of the city. Mr. Thomas Massey in his letter to me from thence, October 9, 1666, saith that of 410 acres within the city, the which hath been measured, there are 335 burnt and 64 out of the city.

The London Gazette, ending April 30, 1666, tells us of Colonel John Rathbone and seven more old rebels, found guilty at the Old Bailey for plotting the King's death and surprisal of the Tower, &c. The 2nd and 3rd September was pitched on for the attempt, as being found by *Lilly's Almanack*, and a scheme erected for the purpose, to be a lucky day, and a planet then ruling which prognosticated the downfall of the monarchy.

I saw a great brass gun mounted over the cliff at Dover Castle, *a.d.* 1660. It was (I take it) both in repute and appearance about 24 feet long, made in Utrecht about 200 years before. It seemed to carry a ball of less than 12 pounds. I have been in a castle, besieged at the same time by the enemy and battered with a shot of 18 pounds at near distance, which made but a small dint in the stone walls thereof (*viz.* little more than the concave side of a large deep saucer) at every single shot However, by repeated shots, the same or the very like cannons did make a large breach (which I saw) in the like walls elsewhere. I have seen the gates of a town bored with many such shots, but not broken or split I stood by the cannonier when with an iron gun under eight feet long, with a ball (as I guessed) of seven or eight pounds at the most, he cleared a road from the enemy's ships, which he sundry times hit and harmed at a long mile's distance; and finally drove them away.

Yet I looked sundry times at the levelling of his cannon, and found it to be mounted, when he made the best shots, much above the hull of the ship even to the main-yard, so that the gun could carry the bullet point blank nothing near so far. One of these, removing full a quarter of a mile further from the danger, did afterwards shoot a random shot, armed with strong pikes, into the town from whence our cannon played, which shot came in through the back door of my house, where breaking through the door near the bottom, grazed on the floor, and raising itself again brake in pieces the pottage pot which was then actually in the hands of my maid servant, who was making the same clean.

The maid received no harm, but one of the pikes was broken close off at the globe of the bullet, which was done, as I think, by the grazing, but we found it not I think the round ball of this was about eight pound in weight It flew near a mile and a half before it came to my

107

house, which being armed (and consequently much hindered) by the pike or pikes abovesaid, was, as it seemed to me, a wonderful distance. I do think it probable that the gun of 28 pound, first above named, might, being mounted to its best height, send forth a random bullet five miles.

In my younger days I thought that the names of the poor husband-men in our township did sound poorly, and to signify something contemptible even in the very sound. But I have lately observed my error and the cheats which custom puts upon us; whereas I do rather now find that many of those names are of great fame and esteem, *viz.*—

Marrow	Sir Wm, Marrow, Mayor of London, 34 Hen.VI. A valiant colonel slain in the King's service, 1644.
Barton	A famous Scotch commander, called Sir Andrew Barton.
Harrison	The late powerful rebel and regicide.
Williamson	Sir Joseph, a late Plenipotentiary and Secretary, 1676.
Ryce	A name in Wales most famous in our annals as princes or kings.
Griffith	Famous in the very same respect
Howard	The chief name of English nobility.
Bullen	The name of an English Queen.
Hatton	The now Lord Hatton.
Ferrers	Anciently Earls of Derby
Stock	Said to be the name of the Emperors of the House of Austria.

Quibble, pun, punnet, pundigrion, of which fifteen will not make up one single jest I find these words in Counsellor Manners' last legacy, printed 16761

St Ignatius advised the Provincials and other great officers in the Society of Jesus to be very attentive to the great and public affairs belonging to them, but not to meddle much in smaller matters. He said it was fitter that they should (fail to) correct others who erred in such small things than to lay themselves open by their own errors (which will be sure to happen oft if they meddle in small matters) to the censure or reprehension of inferior officers. And I think this is good advice even in worldly affairs.

April 8, 1665.—Colonel Daniel, who had been a soldier for the Parliament and Commonwealth from about the beginning of the war and in many great employments, told me that during the whole time of his service on that side, which continued till the King came in, *a.d.* 1660, he never knew of any officers in their armies that ever fought in a single duel saving a corporal and a drummer. The corporal, having killed the drummer, was presently hanged at Edinborough, two regiments being drawn up for that purpose. I hope it will not be denied that these armies consisted of valiant men.

I think it less damage to Christianity if we conceal a hundred true miracles, than if we publish one false one.

June 25, 1666.—I dined in the Castle at Dublin at the Lord Lieutenant's table. There were, besides the Duke and Duchess (Ormond), sixteen persons: we sat with our hats on. The first course had seventeen dishes, the second seventeen dishes, the third fifteen dishes, most of them choice sweetmeats. I had formerly dined there in the year 1662, and there was an excellent concert of instruments, the table being furnished much after the same manner as is above said. And I was told that it was his daily state and custom.

This present January 12, 1663, Major John Beversham told me that he was present at the Old Bailey when a minister (one Wilson, as I remember) was arraigned for having thirteen wives, and he was saved by his book, when another was hanged (for two wives) not being able to read. *Quære*, whether the book may be given in that case.

Although the life of man be most uncertain, yet do I not doubt at all but a far greater number of people grow up to old age than are commonly reported to do so. As a small instance of which I have observed that, within my memory (who am now this present year, 1660, forty years of age), no fewer than forty-three or forty-four persons at the least are counted of the inhabitants of Little Crosby, betwixt the Hall and the hill, who have lived about sixty years, and yet the number of houses are but twenty or thereabouts.

Beat turrs (or old green gorse) in a tray till the pricks be rebated; a beast or horse will eat them, and do as well as with hay. This I was told by Mr. Whittle of Kilkenny, an old soldier of Cromwell's.

Feed sheep in the house with beans, ground round, and bran (with some oats if you will). Give them plenty of water and hay, and keep them warm. They will feed exceedingly fat in fourteen days. This is the practice in Flanders, where I learnt it I suppose the winter is the chief time for this.

I did once make trial of this, but it did not succeed well. Yet it is most certainly and successfully practised beyond the sea, as I was told at St Omers by F. John Cary, the minister of the English College, 1660.

The Duke of Buckingham, being asked by my Lady Castlemaine what religion he was of, answered that he had not faith enough to be a Presbyterian, nor good works enough to be a Papist, and therefore he was an honest old Protestant without faith or good works. Mr. Anderton of Lostock told me this, August 11, 1669.

It is a great damage in England, that it is held a shame for a man to do the offices of a woman in housewifery, as washing, milking, making cheese, butter, &c. In Flanders and Holland men do these things even much better than women, and very frequently. Here in England, seeing men are the best cooks, brewers, bakers and midwives, why should it be held a shame to milk, &c? The want of this causeth many men to marry fondly or to do worse, seeing they cannot (by reason of bad custom), keep house without a woman.

It is now quite customary for men to milk, but they neither wash nor make butter; cheese is no longer made in that part of Lancashire.

Keep rather too few than one too many, feed them well, and pay them with the most.

Adam Jovius, who writeth, thirteenth century, in the continuance of Baronius' Annals, speaking of the steeple at Argentine (Strasburg), *a.d.* 1277, saith it is 574 feet The tower at St Stephen's Church, Vienna, he affirms to be 480 feet high, and St Paul's, in London (*e terrâ*), 534: Our Lady's at Antwerp, 466. I did ascend the square steeple at Durham, *a.d.* 1634, and I counted the steps to be between sixteen and seventeen score, which are more than the steps of St Paul's in London, there being between fifteen and sixteen score to the top of the square steeple which I ascended in 1638.

Yet there were at Durham upon the same church two spires at the west end (besides two less spires at the east end), which were leaded on the outside and were much higher than the square. But one of them being fallen of late years, I hear that the other is taken down (1664). In 1660, I counted the steps of the steeple of St Martin's Church at Ipres to be 342, containing more than six inches a piece. Upon this steeple is a spire, which I did ascend by twenty-five larger steps. I ascended St John's steeple at Gant (1660), by 426 steps of seven inches at the least. Upon the square top of this there is a tower to be ascended by thirty steps more, but I did not ascend that.

I counted the steps of Nôtre Dame in Paris to be 250, so far as I could well ascend, for the height was much more, these 250 reaching even with the top of the church.

On July 8, 1666, I ascended St Patrick's steeple in Dublin by 176 steps of an unequal height, which I take to be (at a medium) 7¾ inches.

He that has too much of a good fellow, has too little of a good Christian.

The improvement of land by marl, where timber did lately grow, is well known to be exceeding great Sir William Gerard told me (March 11, 1662), that Mr. Leigh, having marled sundry acres where Haydock wood stood, has farmed the same for 4*l*. 10s. and for 5*l*. the acre yearly for the term of ten years. Sir William Gerard told me at the same time, that he himself hath two acres of such improved wood land, which hath yielded him 120 bushels of barley yearly upon each acre. He told me likewise then, that he had land which hath at some times yielded 140 bushels by the acre

I have a book which is entitled *Opusculum de regimine rusticorum*. It seems to be a notable piece. It is said that if you put seed corn into a sack which hath lately been filled with meal, the meal not being well dusted out, that the said seed when sown will produce pitiful dwindling corn. *Uredinem Contrahit* This was told me by Hamlet Massey, who noted it out of *Kerkerous* Sympathies.

'Tis surely a far less deplorable spectacle to see a gentleman spoiled of his fortune by his conscience than his luxury, and to behold him under the stroke of the headsman, than under those more infamous executioners, his lust or intemperance. Shall those, who have not so much Christian patience as to bear the slightest reproach for God, have yet so much unchristian stupidity as to endure the greatest in opposition to Him? Those that consume all on hawks, hounds, and horses, seem to make the same menace to their estates which Goliath did to David: *I will give thee to the fowls of the air, and to the beasts of the field.*

Sir Vivian Molyneux told me of two verses written over the gate of the Savoy at London; which are (as I remember), these—

King Henry the Seventh, to his worship and honour,
Builded this hospital, poor people to succour.

Sir Vivian Molyneux, born November 1, 1595, was fourth son

of Sir Richard Molyneux, who was created Bart in 1611, the first year of such creations, and was brother to Richard, the first Viscount Molyneux. Anthony-a-Wood says of him: 'He travelled into several foreign countries, was at Rome where (tho' puritanically educated under the tuition of Sam Radcliffe of Brazen-nose College, Oxford), he changed his religion, returned a well-bred man, was knighted, and in the grand rebellion suffered for the royal cause. He translated from Spanish into English *A treatise of the difference between the Temporal and Eternal*, London, 1672, October, wrote originally by G. Eusebius Nieremberg, S. J.' (Fasti 1 346). He was admitted amongst the students of the English College, Rome, as a 'convictor' or boarder, on September 29, 161 7, under the name of Thomas Leigh.—J. E B.

The best cure for a flux of blood is suppositories made of the fat of hung bacon, put up betwixt every stool till you find the effect, which will be complete in two days. If the bacon be reasted, it is rather better than otherwise. This was told me by my old kind friend Mr. Price, the Protestant Bishop of Kildare, who had good experience of it

I take flattery not to be that common and harmless faculty of good language and plausible address, but a diabolical art of holding intelligence with natural corruption and accommodating itself to our vices whatsoever they be.

She was the wife of Judge P. of Wales, a woman of an incomparable wit, but fondly besotted of her children. When her eldest son was in the cradle, she would not permit either geese, hogs, or any such like things to be kept about the house, lest their noise should wake the child. The magpies were persecuted for that reason with a gun up and down the *demesne.* Her indulgence in other things was ridiculously suited, to this. Witness her standing with the child to delight him with the creaking of an old gate, whilst they lost the sermon at the church to which they were going. When this son of hers was sent to the University, he had a maid along with him to attend him.

After, when the mother lay desperately sick, the gratitude of the children appeared. For her sons (otherwise immeasurably disrespectful), drank up in contempt the ale that was brewed for their mother, and ranted so loud in the next room to hers, that she sent to require their silence. Whereupon they doubled their noise, with shouts and horns, and dogs and horses, brought for that end into a ground chamber where they were, by trampling and howling to fright away their mother's soul. She died, indeed, soon after, and even at the last gasp confessed her fond indulgence to have been the cause of her own greatest grief and her children's wickedness.

Since her death they do frequently make mention of her in this manner, 'That w——e, my mother.' When the Judge, their father, lay upon his deathbed (where.upon he had lain as a languishing man for many months), this his eldest son would reproach him with these words: 'Oh thou old wicked rogue, now do despair and the pains of hell seize on thy cursed soul for such and such faults in thy younger days.' These things I heard from Mr. George Fo. and Mrs. P. a Welsh woman, 1659. And no doubt much more no less horrid might be learned of others. And other things I have heard since, October 6, 1660.

In a letter to Laurence Ireland, dated November 22, 1667, Mr. Blundell gives the following account of the miserable end of the eldest of these unnatural children:—

> Mr. P. of Flintshire, the great heir of the Judge of that name, lost his life by the same excess, concerning whom alone I could write a history, which might fright all the parents in the world from being too fond of their children.

John Bradshaw, the President who condemned King Charles I., was the younger son of one Bradshaw, called Goodman of Cheshire. Mr. Raphael Hollinshead told me that, being a boy at the school, he made certain English rhymes in contention (as it were) with his brother, some of which ran thus—

> *Harry thou art, and thou must to the plough and cart,*
> *But I am John, that honour must attend upon.*

John Bradshaw the Regicide was the youngest son of Henry Bradshaw, Esq., of Marple Hall, County Cheshire, lour miles from Stockport The property is still held by a descendant in the female line. The verses said to have been scratched by the President, when a boy, upon a tombstone, are elsewhere differently given, but the above version, resting as it does on the authority of a Cheshire man, a relative and namesake of the famous Chronicler, is probably correct

1663.—Lords esteemed to be Catholics who are Peers of the Realm:

Marquises—Winchester, Worcester, Dorchester.

Earls—Bristol, Cardigan, Shrewsbury, Norwich, Rivers.

Lords—Andover, Abergavenny, Arundel of Wardour, Teynham, Langdale, Stourton, Wentworth, Barkley, Montague, Carrington, Powis, Crofts, Bellasis, Vaux, Audley (Earl of Castlehaven), Petre, Stafford.

Catholic Lords not Peers of the Realm—

Dunbar, Molineux, Fairfax, Baltimore, Lumley.

In this list Mr. Blundell seems to have omitted some Irish and Scotch Peers who were Catholics, and on the other hand, to have represented as Catholics some English Peers who were not really so. Taking the list as it stands, we find only five of the above peerages held by Catholic descendants. For the sake of comparison we give a complete list of Catholic Peers at the present time (1880):—

Duke—Norfolk.

Marquises—Bute, Ripon.

Earls—Denbigh, Newburgh, Westmeath, Fingal, Granard, Ashbumham, Kenmare, Orford, Gainsborough.

Viscounts—Gormanston, Netterville, Taaffe, Southwell

Barons—Mowbray and Stourton, Camoys, Beaumont, Vaux, Petre, Arundel of Wardour, Dormer, Stafford, Clifford, Ashford, Herries, Lovat, Louth, French, Bellew, De Freyne, Howard of Glossop, Acton, O' Hagan, Emly, Gerard, Braye.

Of these, twenty-nine only are Peers of the Realm, against twenty-five in the preceding list It will be noticed how very little remains of the old element in the present Catholic peerage after the lapse of two centuries. No fewer than twelve of the peers above enumerated are converts to the Catholic faith. When the comparative small number of peers in 1663 is taken into account, it will be seen that a much larger proportion of peers was Catholic at that period than at the present day. At the same time it must be remembered that from the time of James II. to the end of the reign of George IV. (a period of 150 years), no Catholic received the distinction of a peerage, although the creations during that period were very numerous. Lingard gives the list of Catholic Peers excluded from the House of Lords by the Bill of 1678 as follows:—

Duke—Norfolk.

Marquis—Worcester.

Earls—Shrewsbury, Berkshire, Portland, Cardigan, Powis.

Viscounts—Montague, and Stafford

Barons—Mowbray, Audley, Stourton, Petre, Arundel, Hunsdon, Belasyse, Langdale, Teynham, Carrington, Widdrington, Gerard of Bromley, Clifford

The Rhemes Testament is bad English. I heard that Sir Toby Mat-

BUGLE NOTES FOR THE HUNT

To call the companie in the morninge.

The strake to the feeilde is seven.

When the hounds be uncupled—the seeke.

When the hounds doe hunt a game unknowne.

When the hounds have found the game—the rechaite.

The strake of eight to drawe from the covert.

The yearthinge of a fox if hee bee coverable.

If he be not coverable—the call away.

The death of a fox in feild or covert.

The calls for a keeper in parke or forest.

The death of a bucke with bowe or grayhound.

The death of bucke in parke or forrest.

The prise of a harte rial with the rechaite.

The strake of nine to call home the companie.

The strake of five for the tarrears.

The recuile is from parte to parte, and curicall three repeated.

The long rechaite.

thew, reading the title page, *The New Testament, &c., faithfully translated into English,* said it was a lie, for it was not English.

John Scott.

Sir R. Bradshaigh.

This seems to have been inserted in *Hodge-podge* by Sir Roger Bradshaigh. John Scott was his huntsman.

1664, *May* 7.—The wainscot of my dining room being finished, we measured the same, and found it, without the chimney comer, to be 109 yards 2 feet And the lining of the great door cheeks were, although plain work, accounted as wainscot. The plane tier and the crest were reckoned (measuring not perpendicular but slope-wise) to 7 inches high or broad And the cusitooses (besides the rail on which they stand) were measured at 2 inches high. So that the whole work was 11 feet 11 inches high. My bargain was to have all the panels cloven timber except the frize and the lowest course. But yet there were fifteen or twenty panellings of sawed wood, contrary to bargain. I was to pay 3s. 7d. a yard for all, and if I liked the work, 2d. more. The work I did like and paid for—

	£	s.	d.
109 yards 2 feet	17	6	0
The man with whom I bargained, made the pilasters upon his own account, for which I gave him 4s., which 4s. he gave to the labourer, an honest workman, who made all with the help of a boy or two in short time	0	4	0
I gave this labourer at several times 8s. and to his son 3s.	0	11	0
All the nails which were used cost me about	0	3	0

I had a mason three days to make holes for the wood to be put, unto which we pinned it. The joiner and his boy were working seven days in putting up the wainscot I only gave them meat I take this wainscot to be the cheapest great work which I have done about my house, and I think it was the only great thing in all my expenseful work which did fall short, in charge, of my expectation.

Mr. Loveday's letters are esteemed by many to be most quaint and ingenious, but it seems to me as if they were of that number, which Ben Jonson saith go a-begging to be understood. The expressions, indeed, are nothing vulgar, but the sense is as plain as may be. For an example of which I do propose, that one of the choice epistles be translated out of that new-fashioned English phrase into plain honest English, and I think it will then look like a plucked peacock. And the like may be done to show the worthless gaudiness of many other writings.

A good character adds much to a well-indited letter, but the faults of an ill-indited letter are much hid by a character which is not easily read. My physician [Dr. Worthington of Wigan—Ed] wrote unto me most material prescriptions in time of my great danger by sickness. I showed these unto three most expert readers, and neither they nor I could read it, or understand the main points of the letter. I told the writer how ill he had done therein. He answered that the letter was so plainly written, that there was never a boy In Wigan school unto whom the same was not legible.

Captain Tarleton shot a right good musket, with a charge and a half of powder, at a full bag of wool (about twenty stone). He stood about nine yards off it, and shot quite through it and next an inch and a half into a door behind it He told me this, and showed me the hole in the door. And he said that he saw one shoot a musket, at thirty yards distance, at a bag of cotton (which is very hard and close). He shot not through it, but the cotton appeared thrust out by the bullet, like a finger, on the other side.

The verse *Alexandrine* consists of twelve or thirteen syllables. This I take to be the way of our old English poets, and particularly in the old translation of *Virgil*, where the second book begins thus—

They whisted all, and fixt with eyes attentive did behold
Where Lord Æneas from high bench thus he told

Thomas Phaer translated *Virgil a.d.* 1555, being moved thereunto for the defence of his country's language, which he had heard discommended. What a silly piece of English this is may be judged by the reader.

R. Willes writes a preface to Peter Martir's *Decades of the West Indies* translated by R. Eden, printed in London, 1577. Willes says, 'Many of his English words cannot be excused in my opinion for smelling too much of the Latin, as, ponderous, antiques, despicable, obsequious, homicide, destructive, prodigious, &c' These words are now common (1690).

Jealousy is a bad daughter born of a good house.

Let the married couple, when they consult together upon occasion of differences with others, carry themselves justly, lest by teaching each other how to wrong a third person, they be instructed, as conscious of their own mutual knowledges, to be unjust to themselves.

It is accounted a piece of ill-breeding to see a man go abroad with his own wife. (*Ladies' Calling.* pt 2. page 30). I suppose those who brought up these rules are not to seek what use to make of them.

When I was at Paris in the month of August and September 1681, I received there from Sir John Warner a catalogue of the names of the English Jesuits, the total number whereof in all places, living or supposed to be living 23rd May 1681, was just 280, *viz.*, Fathers 174 (69 professed), and brothers 106. Of this number there were then at Liege 16 fathers and 59 brothers, students, &c.; in all 75. In England there were 109, of whom four were lay brothers. The rest were at St Omers, Ghent, Watten, Spain, &c.

The Rev. Sir John Warner of Parham, Suffolk, Bart, had a romantic history. He married in 1659 Miss Trevor Hanmer, daughter of Sir Thomas Hanmer of Hanmer, Flintshire, Bart, and had this title conferred on himself in 1660 for his loyal and faithful services. Lady Warner and Elizabeth Warner, a sister of Sir John's, became converts to the Catholic faith in 1664. Sir John being inclined the same way consulted Dr. Buck, who had been his grandfather's chaplain, and afterwards called on the Archbishop of Canterbury (Dr. Sheldon). The latter handed him over to Dr. Dolbin, Dean of Westminster, who told him that it was a mere *punctilio* the Pope stood upon, which hindered the union of the two churches. Sir John Warner, not being satisfied, ended his doubts by entering the Catholic Church.

He and his Lady then agreed to part for the purpose of embracing a religious life. Sir John, after providing for his two children, settled his estate on his next brother Frauds, and entered the Novitiate, S.J., at Watten, under the name of Clare. Here he 'divided the commons,' to use Mr. Blundell's expression, with Laurence Ireland of Lydiate, Esq., who had lately taken the very same step, and who wrote to his friend about this time, a full account of the conversion of Sir John Warner.

In 1667, his brother Francis came over to see him, and having been in the mean time converted, felt the same longing for a religious life. Having visited Nieuport, where there was a colony of Carthusians, he admired their strict way of life and resolved to embrace it In his eagerness to return to England, to settle his affairs before carrying out this design, he urged the captain of the vessel on which he had taken his passage to set sail, although the weather was threatening.

Overcome by his promises, the ship was put to sea, and had scarcely left the port when she encountered a terrible gale and became a complete wreck. Francis Warner was drowned within sight of the monastery where he had hoped to pass his days, and was interred as one of their brethren by the Carthusian monks. Sir John Warner, hearing of the sad occurrence, and having his estate once more fallen to him, was obliged to undertake a journey to London, where he found a second brother Edmund, on whose not unwilling shoulders he laid his burthen.

After his ordination Sir John spent most of his life abroad, but was in England in the office of Provincial, S. J., from 1689 to 1693. He died at Watten in 1705. Lady Warner died a Poor Clare at Gravelines in 1670, and her two daughters ended their days as Benedictine Nuns at Dunkirk. The Cavalier's grand-son, Nicholas Blundell, relates that Sir John Warner had in his younger days been passionately fond of hawking, and that once, when he happened to be at Dunkirk, a tame hawk which had been caught was brought to him. On examining it Sir John discovered by certain secret marks that it was his own hawk which had flown out of Suffolk. The life of Lady Warner of Parham was published in London in 1692. (See Foley's *Records*, S. J. vol. 2) Laurence Ireland adds to the above particulars, that the estate which Sir John Warner resigned was of the value of 800*l. per annum*, and that he was twenty-six years of age when he made this sacrifice.

Peter Blundell of Tiverton, clothier, erected a fair free school in that town, and allowed it a competent maintenance and lodgings for a master and usher. He bestowed two scholarships and two (fellowships on Sidney College, Cambridge, providing Tiverton scholars should be elected therein. 'Tis thought he died about 1596. In the Paris *Gazette*, January 26, 1686, I found this:—

> *January 22.* '*Le sieur Blondell, Maréchal des Camps et Armées du Roy, Professeur Royal des Mathématiques, de l'Académie Royale des Sciences, et ci-devant Maistre des Mathématiques de Monseigneur le Dauphin, mourut ici après une longue maladie. Il avait été Envoyé du Roy à Constantinople, et il avait fait pour le service de sa Majestie divers voyages en Levant, en Afrique, en Amérique et en plusieurs cours de l'Europe. Il s'étoit acquitté de tous ces différents emplois avec une grande capacité*' This man hath published many learned writings.

I found at London a good number of Blundells, *viz.*: a considerable merchant at his house near London Stone. One Richard Blundell, an ingenious young man and surgeon, lived near Bishopsgate Street, westward from it and in some close buildings. There was then an At-torney of good note who frequented the coffee-houses in and about Gerard Street Another attorney of good parts (yet somewhat blemished by good fellowship), in one of the Inns below Holborn Bar, who had a brother of the same name, living in or very near Bloomsbury Market He has the repute of a very ingenious man, and is said to keep at the joiners' trade about eighteen or twenty servants. Mr. Thomas Morton, silkman, told me, about the year 1687, that one Blundell in the city, a plain, clownish man, had gained an estate by weaving laces, of above 1,000*l. per annum*. I think he told me that the weaver was lately dead, and that the son was a very well-bred and genteel person.

I have writing, which came under the Privy Seal of King Henry II., where my antecessor N. B. is written Nicholas Blondell, Esq.

A.D. 1681.—There are in Paris three Academies, in all which the learner's expense is equal—*viz*, 1,300 *livres* for his diet, exercise, and lodging; for a Governor's diet and lodging, 600 *livres*; for a servant's diet and lodging, 300 *livres*. The six masters (if you use them), each of them a *louis d'or* or one *pistole* at your entrance—*viz*. for dancing, fencing, geography, mathematics, pike and musket, and when first you ride the ring. Thirty *sols per mensem* for switches, and as much for music. Some few half-crowns a year to other officers. It is a question whether besides all this you be not charged to pay for the furniture of your chamber. I rather think you are not All this is besides apparell for yourself and servants. If you will lodge in the town, you may exercise riding in the Academy at four *pistoles per mensem*, but no other exercise. Those in the Academy may stay as little a while as they please, and the advance wilt be refunded. The expense of Academies out of Paris amounts to a full third part less, the charge for diet, exercise, and lodging being but 800 *francs*.

I read in the great English Chronicle at Croxteth, September 10, 1660, of great punishments that happened to those that had a chief hand in the subversion of the forty monasteries, granted by Pope Clement VII. to Cardinal Wolsey. Of those five men which were chiefly employed by the Cardinal about it, two fought with each other: one of them was killed and the other hanged for it. A third drowned himself Another, that was a bishop in Ireland, became sadly lamed, and the fifth, that was formerly a rich man, died a beggar. The Pope suffered by the loss of Rome, &c, and the King and Cardinal as we know.

I have heard of a part of England (either Norfolk or Northampton, as I take it), wherein it is observed by a Protestant writer of note, that within a small compass or tract of land there lived about twenty gentlemen, consisting all or in part of religious lands. About as many lived in the same tract whose estates had no part of any such lands. It was noted that, whereas there was but one or two of this second sort that had come to ruin or any notable decay since Henry VIII., there were but one or two of the first sort that had 'skaped from such ruin. I believe Mr. Edwards, *alias* Anderton, can say something to this business.

The horrid judgments upon sequestrators, committee men and farmers of Catholic estates, have been remarkable. *Quære*, of Mr. Chorley and his daughters' disastrous ends. And note those incomparable disasters upon Mr. Moore's family, since Edward Moore, about the year 1632, fell dead upon the road. He was a great persecutor, &c.

Spelman is the writer of note referred to above.

Soon cry, soon dry. See how mourning and tears are commended at funerals, as it were for fashion's sake and to satisfy others.

A curious person who spends two much time in reading, may be said to be ignorant of almost nothing, his own misery and weakness only excepted. If we ask him for whom he labours, he will tell you, 'I read to please myself.' This upon the whole is no more than to please a roving fancy, and it is very well for him if he do not regret it when repentance comes too late. A man may be too covetous of knowledge as well as of coin, and whether he stands possessed of the one or the other without making advantage of them for himself and his neighbour, it is like to cost him dear when the account is made.

In his *Observator*, No. 3, February 19, 1684-5, in answer to Trimmer, who taxes him with meddling too much about Oates' miscarriage, he says: 'I entered upon this commission by the order of his late sacred Majesty of ever blessed memory. I continued my proceedings upon it by the same Royal and repeated commands, and if it had not been for some previous deliberations in what manner to proceed and which causes to pitch upon out of the choice of eleven or twelve, this matter had been brought to an issue time enough for the late King to have seen this wretched creature brought to public shame and justice. . . . I must avow further that his Majesty was pleased to declare this scrutiny to be a point highly incumbent on his Royal justice. Thus I began, thus I proceeded, and by the grace of God thus I resolve to continue, till I see this point brought to a conclusion. Having the honour of his present Majesty's commission, also to prosecute the orders and intentions of the late King.'

I saw (in 1658) an old hollow oak close by the road betwixt London and Tunbridge, wherein (as I was then assured) 140 boys were placed, who all came swarming out of it unexpectedly to entertain King James with admiration, as he passed that way on hunting.

Mr. Ireland of Lydiate told me, that he saw an oak that grows in the forest of Delamere, the bole of which is affirmed to be in circumference 14 yards. Mr. Henry Stanley told me at the same instant that the said oak was measured to be in circumference about the bole 14 yards 1 foot This they told me October 2, 1663.

When I was about nine years old, my grandfather Blundell showed me the oak in the north corner of the new orchard, and making me to clip it about, I found that my finger ends did overreach each other some little, less than an inch I take it. He told me, that he did plant that tree when it was like a small twig which he showed me (less than ordinary riding rod). And now this present December 18, 1663, I being in the 44th year of my age, I measured the same tree again, clipping it in my arms as high as I could well reach, standing on the west side, and I found it to be 9 inches (within less than one straw's breadth) more than I could fathom. My grandfather was born 1560.

Mr. Samuel Aspinwall, a zealous puritan of a moral conversation, talking with me this day (February 13, 1663) as he hath often done, professed that if he did not think the Pope were Anti-Christ, he would turn Papist. 'For if he be not so,' saith he, 'we cannot excuse ourselves from schism.'

The same old beggar whom I have mentioned before used to beg in a rhetorical bold way at the races on Crosby marsh, and he would flatter the noble gentlemen, and tell aloud what gallant houses they kept His importunity there was insufferable. I did there once see a gentleman cast a shilling unto him, saying, 'A pox o' God take thee!' The boldest wandering beggars (and a Bedlam one, Medcalf, above all others) ever speeded the best at these races, whilst the truly poor Widows and orphans who lived in the parish found little effect there of their modest low way of begging. Tom Arnold told me that he saw at night near that place thirty or forty of these wandering beggars at Rogerson's (a paltry alehouse), spending the money they had gotten at the race.

April 21, 1676.—This day my servants did shear eight wethers unwashed, and weighed (*me ipso vidente*) the fleeces of the same, the weight of which was fully sixty pounds, whereof five pounds was foul-knotted wool. One of these eight fleeces, without any knotted wool, weighed eight pounds fully. These were Irish sheep, part of forty-six which I had bought for 23*l.* the last June, and I did shear the same afterwards (1675), so that these last fleeces wanted much of a year's growth. Note that I had sold twenty choice sheep out of the forty-six aforesaid, and afterwards ten choice sheep, so that six or seven of the abovesaid eight sheep were as it were the refuse of the forty-six. After the wool aforesaid had been washed and dried it weighed (as my wife told me) but forty-five pounds.

It think it is probable that the false pronunciation of many words hath first arisen through a childish error in reading. For example, the word 'through' is but one syllable, and yet it is now commonly pronounced, especially by the nicer sort, as if it were of two syllables. The word 'ask' is called by many 'axe' by a mistake (I conceive) in reading. 'Massacre' (I take it) is called 'massacar' by the like mistake. But custom in this is a law. I have heard sundry gentlewomen, who were good readers of English, pronounce the word 'anxiety' as if it had been writ 'anexety.' And who can doubt but if that word were very commonly mistaken in the same manner, it might in the end exchange its own essence? We may add the words 'sure' and 'sugar,' which are commonly pronounced 'shure' and 'shuggar.'

We may observe that many Englishmen, who are great scholars and have spent their time abroad, are very defective and oftentimes ridiculous (although they will hardly believe it) in their English tongue. I heard one of these in a sermon repeat the name of a certain precious stone (unto the rare virtues of which he did piously allude) no fewer than twenty times. And yet the name of this stone did sound as filthily in our language, as any word whatsoever in the English tongue. What strange apprehensions would the ruder sort of people frame hereupon?

An amusing incident of this nature happened a few years ago in a neighbouring town. A youth had been sent to Louvaine from a country district in Ireland to study for the Priesthood. Here he soon acquired the language of his new companions, and made good progress in his studies. In due time he was ordained Priest, and came home a well educated and polished man. On landing in England he was asked to preach to a mixed congregation of English and Irish. He had no difficulty in preparing an excellent discourse, but found that he had no language wherewith to clothe his ideas excepting that of his boyhood. As may well be imagined, his thoroughly Irish manner and the droll expressions which he used had an irresistibly comic effect

Women may pretend a little to govern because men have governed so ill, as plausibly as some have reformed the Church upon the like pretence.

Concerning the great tun of Heidelberg mentioned by Ben Jonson and by other English poets, I did enquire of a German whom I met in France and of a Frenchman who travelled in our company, and one of them affirmed that it did contain 300 wain-loads of wine, which was no less, said the other, than 2,800 French hogsheads or *dolia*. Both of these gentlemen had seen the said tun and they were very sober men.

King Charles II. in his flight from Worcester, 1651, was cast by his nobles (by the Earl of Derby) upon the care and fidelity of Richard Pendrel, a poor Catholic in leathern breeches. And Catholics were many of them the sole instruments of his safety at the first brunt.

Boil galls in wine, and with a sponge wipe over the letters. They will presently be seen when they are once wet, and be well coloured as they were at first Aquafortis in a feather (or a sponge) held near to the letters will exhale the ink to it John Wilson saith that one Mr. Denby, a stationer at Warrington, useth it

This was the wife of Philip III., who was a singular great friend to the Jesuits. It chanced that one of that order in Spain had committed some kind of fault, which came immediately to the King's ear. Whereupon the King, going in all haste to the Queen, related the story, and asked (by way of reproach) what she could say now in excuse of the Jesuits. The Queen returned this sudden and witty reply: 'Sir, I can nothing say in defence of those fathers but this—that (without all question) the belt that sounds so loud with so small a touch must needs be of an excellent temper.' *Narravit mihi*, Pater Richd. Banester, Provs. Ord. in Angliâ, 1660.

I do not remember that any capital crime, but this of duels, is frequently and publicly defended by persons otherwise discreet and sober. The women (or young girls) do urge on the men by crying that down for cowardice, which God and the laws command. And this the giglets do, because it is not the mode in the romances for gentlemen to refuse a challenge. I knew a youth in the fourteenth year of his age, with whom I had great means to be acquainted; but I found him reserved and unwilling to talk (though I tried him in sundry ways and on many subjects), until I chanced to speak of the point of honour and duels. You cannot believe how far he was transported with this discourse.

To show how deeply he was possessed with it at that age, he gave me a spontaneous account of the most remarkable actions of that nature in the country where he lived, and seemed able to give a list both of the swordsmen and the cowards. This I conceived was occasioned by the discourse which he heard from his father, who was ever a great deal too forward in the mistaken points of honour. How far did boys and girls who were martyred in the primitive Church exceed these swashbucklers in valour! There were no parasites or pot companions to extoll them; they were wounded on all hands as well by words as by blows.

The young man referred to was no doubt one of his grandsons, a son of Viscount Mountgarret, who had married Mr. Blundell's eldest daughter Emilia.

See a story in the fifteenth book of Davila, his *French Civil Wars*, where the Sieur de Coquein Villiar, one of the King's servants, gave a box on the ear to Monsieur de Bonivet in the King's ante-chamber; for which Coquein Villiar acknowledged his fault and offered to ask his pardon, refusing a challenge which Bonivet sent unto him, and keeping himself indoors to avoid the duel. At last, being forced to fight, he killed Bonivet and had the King's pardon and favour. This is noted as well for the worthy satisfaction offered for striking a man where he durst not defend himself, as for the King's great moderation in pardoning a gentleman who, being surprised with the apprehension of losing his own honour, forgets his duty to his sovereign, and doth yet upon that occasion afterwards show both great submission and valour.

Take a kite and a carrion crow, and tie them down in the stubble with sufficient liberty, and they will fight and cry in a strange manner; upon which there will come immediately great flocks of crows from all parts, which striking freely at the kite will many of them be taken in the lime twig which must be placed round in the stubble for that reason. Remember that you tie up one foot of your kite to make the battle more equal. You may easily take a kite with a pigeon and lime. The dun horny kite is thought to be the best

Set many lime twigs in a tree, growing in a wood, the boughs many of the smallest being first cut off. Then betake yourself to a bower under the tree, a good while after sunset There, with an owl-call made with a hazel, you may call a world of birds about you, pyes, jays, thrushes, &c, which will hop up and down, and many of them be taken with the twigs. Your dog or yourself may fetch them in. October is the best time for this sport

If you take a quick and lively magpie, and lay her on the ground upon her back in such sort that her wings be fastened to the earth, the stir and noise she will make will call many other magpies about her which lighting upon her (as it were to succour or relieve her), she will hold the first that comes fast with her claws, till you may come and take her. This you may pin down by the other in like manner, and so you may do until you have taken a great number of those birds. The best time for this is when they pair.

Take waterfowl with hooks baited with the lites of a beast, which is a flesh that will swim. The above experiment with a magpie has been tried successfully by Mr. Thomas Stanton, from whom I had it.

This course, as it is now used upon the marshes of Great and Little Crosby, was stooped out by me W. B., *a.d.* 1654, at the request of Richard Lord Molyneux. I did not then, nor have I yet measured it (1663). Only I caused my man to pace over the first mile of the old course of Liverpool (which standeth partly even with a part of Crosby course), and I find that from the stone where the first mile ends to anenst Crosby stoop, is contained 35 rods of 8 yards. To anenst the stoop in the Gorse, 125, and to the ending stones, 237 and 3 yards. This mile (and the whole course of Liverpoole), which seemeth not to agree with the measure in use, was set out by my father. From the end of this mile to the plat, 27 rods. From the plat to the starting pole on the Morehouse marsh, 1 16 rods and 4 yards. But note that these measures are not to be relied on till further trial.

In or about the year 1683, I procured a great change in this course, *viz.* that the starting place (which was also the end of the course) having been formerly on the Morehouse marsh, it was then changed to that pole or comer of the said course which stands on Great Crosby marsh, about 30 yards from the sandy fence or doles which separate the marsh from the holme. This is now (1686-7) both the beginning and the end of the course.

See his *Discoveries* where he speaks of the envy towards an able writer who shall be better understood in another age. He showeth his abilities to be such, as if he hath given a character of himself (page l00). Ben Jonson's head is put up for a sign in London and sundry places.

The above passage has been generally supposed to refer to Shakespeare, of whose writings Mr. Blundell appears to have known little. (See Introductory Chapters).

Drunkards and other sensual persons may be considered, in reference to the number of sober and virtuous men, as wolves are considered with sheep. Wolves are produced in multitudes, five or six at a litter. Sheep, but one by one. Wolves destroy sheep. Sheep destroy no wolves. Sheep in great multitudes do yield their lives and blood, and suffer themselves to be shorn and even exenterated without the least resistance, for man's behoof. Whereas wolves, by all dexterous arts of force and craft, avoid the sight of man, are rarely entrapped, and doing much mischief to the world, do very seldom pay for it with the loss of their lives. Then how comes it to pass, that the number of wolves increases not to be infinitely more than the number of sheep? which we see to be much otherwise. It is answered truly that wolves, however they join oft in mischief, do frequently kill and devour each other, and by that sole means do disburthen the world in a great ' measure of their mischief. The application of these things is very obvious.

Lerpoole had three Lord Mayors not four years since,
Then an honest tradesman, and now a prince.

These three lords were the Earl of Derby, Lord Colchester, and Lord Strange. The townsman was Mr. Bicsteth, Dr. Richmond is called a prince by reason of his noble way of living. This was writ 1673.

Dr. Richmond resided at Thornton Hall in the immediate neighbourhood of Crosby. The property is still held by the family, and its present representative has his residence near the old mansion.

1664.—I concluded to pay 1*l.* 5s. the thousand for hewing' and filling, and to brew three bushels of malt into small beer for hewers and fillers, and two bushels for strong beer for all the workmen. The carters were to have 2s. 6d, per day and no meat for their horses. The whole sum of loads I do account to be 5,180, and the workmen do account the loads to be 5,200.

	£	s.	d.
After which account I have paid them	6	10	0
And I do account for carts hired	6	0	0
And for my own carts at 2s. 6d, per day	1	12	0
For fourteen days' spreading with two men	1	9	8
For a water-bearer at jd, for fourteen days	0	8	9

Total	16 0 5

I do moreover conjecture that the feying
of the pit cost about   2 4 7
My wife sent the workmen 5s. when their own
small beer was ending, and bade them choose whether
they would have that or else a supply of small beer till
the end of the work. They chose the latter, and I believe
all our beer given by bargain or otherwise from first to
last was worth 1*l*. 2s., which with a little tobacco, &c.,
and a poor accidental dinner on Saturday when they had
ended, may be accounted   1 5 0

So that the total charge was   £19 10 0

I guess the land to be somewhat considerably less than four acres. The hewing and filling, at 1*l*. 5s. per thousand, cost one farthing per load. The men had about 16s. as I take it in gifts from my friends.

It is no small victory for reason to overcome the senses. And it may appear the greater, if we do well consider how long the senses have domineered in us (during our whole infancy and childhood) with little or no opposition at all of our reason. Let me judge of the far different powers of sense and reason by this one example. Upon the first or second sight of the skull of a dear friend of mine who died many years before, my reason hath been so convinced concerning the vanity of wit, beauty, and other worldly blessings (whereof my dear friend had enjoyed a great share), that I have very seldom been more disposed to goodness and more adverse to vanity than at that time.

And yet, upon the frequent renewing of the same object, I have looked upon it at the last as if I had only looked on a painted skull. But now on the other side, where sense hath the sway, I must needs remember that I have viewed the faces of some living persons, which upon the first sight have made no greater an impression of sensuality in my thoughts than if it had been no more but a painted thing upon a sign post; and yet the often renewing of the same objects hath so much discomposed me in the end, that if grace had not come to save me, my reason had been fooled, and all had been utterly lost

I have found by experience that my great jealousy of my wordly reputation hath much disturbed my mind, endangered my soul, and hath rather hindered than promoted what I aimed at For my honour can never receive a notable blemish until I dishonour my Maker.

Worldly honour is a shadow, that flies when you follow it, and follows you when you fly it

See the *Intelligencer*, Monday, April 11, 1664, p. 234.—'Barbados, February 16. In the latitude 2·50 south, 900 leagues eastward of this island, a great fish struck the ship under the starboard side, and passing under it touched the rudder and threw the man from the helm; and when she came on the other side, heaved a great sea into the ship. At her first stroke she ran her horn (or fin) through the sheathing, a three-inch plank, through the timber into the ceiling, and there brake it short off. So that a piece of 12 inches long and 1½ c. weight was left in the hole. If the horn had not been broken in the hole the vessel had been lost; for that stoppage notwithstanding, the water came in so fast, that it kept a pump employed. Since the ship came in here it hath been careened, the piece taken out of the bulge, and the hole stopped. The horn is like an elephant's tooth, but more ponderous.'

Mr. Roger l'Estrange, in his letter to me on occasion of this story (which I had touched upon in some of my letters to him), writes thus: 'As to the disproportionate (and indeed incredible) weight of the fish bone, I delivered it as a wonder, but not without an express direction of conformity to the relation sent to his Royal Highness, however mistaken.'

The weight assigned to the horn is of course an absurd error. Nearly a century later we find the following record of a similar event, taken from the narrative of the crew of a ship from St Eustatia to Edinboro': 'In our passage from the Main hither, June 16, 1754, in lat. 15° long. 61°, we were struck by a sword-fish, or sea-unicorn, on our starboard bow, which ran his horn through our outside plank (a timber of 10 inches thick) and ceiling into the hold, broke his horn off, and left it in the hold 10 inches. We reckon that the horn went through 14½ inches of solid oak.' (Nichol's *Literary Illustrations*, vol. 3 p. 800.)

Mr. Howell's *Letter* 78, vol. 2 *a.d.* 1646, saith 'We have multitudes of witches among us, for in Essex and Suffolk there were about 200 indited within these two years, and about one half of them executed: more I may say than ever this island bred since the creation.' He saith that 'never a cross is left to fright the devil away.'

The cruelties of the Irish against the English are in everybody's mouth, and set forth in printed pageants sold in London. Some cruelties on the contrary part are these that follow.

An English parson that lived in Ireland told me that one of his own coat, born in Wirral in Cheshire and beneficed in Ireland, killed with his own hands one Sunday morning fifty-three of his own parishioners, most or all of them (as I remember) women and children. This was told me at Chester, *a.d.* 1644, in the hearing of Mr. Ralph Bridoke, chaplain to the Earl of Derby.

Colonel Washington told of great cruelties committed by the soldiers against the Irish; among other things, that he saw one take an infant upon his pike and toss it up in the air.

Captain Robert Bramwel told me he was in danger of his life from his own party for covering a young gentlewoman with his cloak who had been stripped by them; they afterwards dashed out her brains.

One Captain Phillipson (as I take it), one of the English officers, told me that about 100 or 200 of unarmed Irish, that climbed up to the top of trees to avoid the soldiers, were all killed with shot from below, and that a child of two years old was barbarously (and oddly) murdered in the same place.

Archdeacon Pryce told me that Major Monce hanged a gentlewoman, only because she looked (as he was pleased to phrase it) like an Irish lady.

The *Politician's Catechism* relateth briefly other sad particulars of this nature. Few of the populous country of Fingal left alive; all perished by fire and sword, being innocent people and having nothing Irish-like in them but the Catholic religion. The army killed man, woman, and child in the county of Wicklow. A gentlewoman, big with child, was hanged on the arch of a bridge. Mr. Comain, who never bare arms, was roasted there alive by Captain Gines. They murdered all that came in their way from within two miles of Dublin. Mrs. Eustace of Cradockston in the county of Kildare (sister to Sir William Talbot), of 80 years of age, after she had entertained with victuals, was murdered by the Protestant officers, with another old gentlewoman and a girl of eight years of age.

Mr. Cauley of Westmeath, showing his protection, was killed with a shot, the protection being laid on his breast to try if it were proof. Mr. Thomas Talbot, a great servitor in Queen Elizabeth's wars in Ireland, aged 90 years, was murdered tho' he had a protection. From 700 to 800 women, children, and labourers were murdered in one day in the King's land within seven miles of Dublin. And yet it may be a question whether those great transplantations to Connaught and to America exceed not all that hath been said.

Concerning the *Royal Sovereign*, see Howell's *Ep.* 33. sec. 6. Her length, 127 feet; her greatest breadth within the planks, 46·6; her depth from the breadth, 19 feet 4 inches. The charge of building, 80.000*l*. Her burthen, 1,636, which was the year in which she was built.

I saw this ship in 1660 lying in a dock at Chatham. I saw her dry to the keel and I did judge her to be about those very dimensions which Mr. Howell speaks of but not altogether so wide. This I can add, that her firm flat side in the port holes was 17 inches thick as near as may be.

A country song remembering the harmless mirth of Lancashire in peaceable times (1641). Tune, 'Roger o' Coverley':

Robin and Ralph and Willy
Took Susan and Ginnet and Cisly;
And Roger and Richard and Geordy
Took Mary and Peggy and Margery;
And danced a hornpipe merrily:
Tired out the bagpipe and fiddle
With dancing the hornpipe and didle.

But Gilbert and Thomas and Harry,
Whose sweethearts were Nell, Nan and Marie,
Took sides against Giles, James, and Richard,
Whose wenches were Joan, Jane, and Bridget
The wager was for a wheat cake.
They danced till their bones did ache
That Gilbert and Nanny and Nellie
Did sweat themselves into a jelly.

The lads of Chowbent were there.
And had brought their dogs to the bear,
But they had no time to play,
They danced away the day;
For thither then they had brought Knex
To play Chowbent hornpipe, that Nick's,
Tommy's and Geffrey's shoon
Were worn quite through with the tune.

The lads of Latham did dance
Their Lord Strange hornpipe, which once
Was held to have been the best.
And far to exceed all the rest
But now they do hold it too sober,

And therefore will needs give it over.
They call on their piper then jovially,
'Play us brave Roger o' Coverley.'

The Meols men danced their Cop,
And about the may-pole did hop,
Till their shoes were so full of sand.
That they could no longer stand.
The Formby trotter supplied,
Who, though that his breeches were wide,
Yet would he ne'er give it o'er
Till the piper was ready to snore.

But Gilbert and Susan and Nanny,
With Tom and Dick, Cisly, and many,
Tripped and skipped full merrily.
The music now sounding out cheerily.
Dick booted, Nel flouted, he shouted
'Tak't thee James Pyper of Formby;
Tak't thee, tak't thee, tak't thee,
Tak't thee James Pyper of Formby.'

At length it was time to go,
And Susan did hear the cock crow.
The maids might go make up their fires.
Or else be chid by their sires.
Next holyday, they'll ha' their fill
At Johnson's o' th' Talke of the hill,
Where Bell shall be brought to play.
Alack, how I long for that day!

The second part, to the tune of the 'Upstroke':

That day it was past
On Tuesday last.
And you might have seen there,
If you had been there,
The lasses and louts
With smirkings and shouts.
Such did I ne'er hear on.
Good Lord, they would fear one.
For still they cried merrily,
'Hey for Crosby!
Hey Sefton! hey Thornton!

Hey for Netherton!'
Till hoarse they whopped
Being weary they stopped.
Then cakes and prunes stewed
Were greedily chewed.
Of ale that was good
They poured down a flood.
And being got giddy,
Then stepped forth Neddy,
And swore by his fakins,
That he would go dance again;
Aye, by the makins
Then hand in hand they went,
Cheerily, cheerily;
Calling on their Bell,
Merrily, merrily.
All sport was forsaken
To see loose legs shaken.
But Rowland and Nelly,
With Susan and Billy,
Got all the glory.
That is in the story.
And those that are sager.
Say they won the wager;
For whilst there was any day.
They would ne'er get away.

Mr. Blundell seems to have had some misgivings in leaving on record this lively sketch of the frolic and pastimes of his earlier days. In the margin he has written '*Ne reminiscaris, Domine, delicta juventutis meæ*—Remember not, O Lord, the sins of my youth.' We gather from the context, that he is pourtraying some of the festivities connected with the rearing of the May-pole. By King Charles' warrant, October 18, 1633, it was enacted that 'for his good people's lawful recreation, after the end of Divine Service, his good people be not disturbed, letted, or discouraged from any lawful recreation: such as dancing, either men or women; archery for men, leaping, vaulting, or any other such harmless recreations; nor from having of May Games, Whitson ales, and Morris dances, and the setting up of May-poles, and other sports therewith used,' &c. In 1644, May-poles, described as a heathenish vanity, were ordered by the Commonwealth to be destroyed throughout the Kingdom.

After the restoration they were again permitted to be erected, and the custom held its ground almost to our own time. Within the last half century, May-poles and the festivities connected with them have gradually become things of the past; but memorials of them, and traditions of their sites, are still abundant The gathering round the May-pole of Crosby must have been very large, as it comprised the youth not only of the neighbouring villages, Formby, Sefton, Netherton, and Thornton, but also of the more remote ones, Meols and Lathom. The first ceremony was decking the pole with flowers, and this was done by the fair hands of the village maidens. To this custom Herrick alludes; for the May-pole figures in those loose and flowing numbers with which at this very period he was beguiling the tedium of his solitary life at Dean Prior:

The May-pole is up
Now give me the cup;
I'll drink to the garlands around it;
But first unto those
Whose hands did compose
The glory of flowers that crowned it

Then the rearing took place; and the pole was fixed in its position amidst the tumultuous cheers of the assembled crowd. A general dance round the newly-erected pole followed, and in this everybody took part, joining hand to hand. At Crosby, the squire himself who, though already married, was then but twenty-one, would certainly be present to witness, if not to participate in the dance.

The lords of castles, mannors, townes and towers,
Rejoic'd when they beheld the fanners flourish;
And would come down unto the summer bowers,
To see the country-gallants dance the Morrice.

(Pasquil's *Palinodia*, 1634.)

Mr. Blundell has recorded his love of dancing, but the fatal accident he met with in the eventful year which followed these festivities, put an end to his capacity for such amusements. The dancing on these occasions was kept up with great spirit, assisted by the piper's melody. In those days almost every township had its piper or fiddler, for the two instruments in vogue were the bagpipes and fiddle. Some of these pipers were no mean proficients on their instruments. Thomas Knex, of Chowbent, was a noted piper, and he must have received a special invitation to join this gathering. The lads of Chowbent, which is thirty miles from Crosby, would hardly have made so long a journey unless they had come in the train of their celebrated player. The Cavalier's grandson, Nicholas Blundell, has the following entry in his diary, regarding Anderton, the piper:—

'1707, *January 31.*—I sold my horse Buck to William Anderton for one day's playing of the pipes *per annum*, as long as he lives in Lancashire, and for 25s. to be paid by parcels as he can get it; if the horse prove ill, I promise to bate him 5s.'

The Chowbent lads had brought their dogs to the bear, as the barbarous sport of bear-baiting usually formed part of the May-pole festivities. There was generally a bear-garden in each township; that at Lydiate was let in 1682 at 3*l. per annum*. The bears were chiefly itinerant, and there must have been a large supply for the whole of England. To this pastime we may suppose that the lads from Chowbent were specially addicted; for we have been accustomed to associate with that spot ideas and customs not the most refined. But it is fair to remind our readers that Chowbent has recently undergone the purification of railway official baptism, and has begun a new life in the character of mild-mannered Atherton.

The dancers contended for prizes, but these were of a Spartan simplicity of character, 'the prize it was a wheat-cake.' The winners were apparently those who could remain longest upon their legs, and the lusty lads and country lasses must have taxed the patience of the spectators, to say nothing of the pipers, by their powers of endurance. Cakes, stewed prunes, and ale was the fare provided, and no doubt much of the last was consumed, but Mr. Blundell does not speak of any excess. Prunes were then largely imported into Liverpool and much used in the country districts around it Mr. Nicholas Blundell, the diarist, records that Mr. Houghton, a merchant of Liverpool, told him that he had once imported eight casks of prunes, from which he expected no small profit.

He warehoused them carefully, but on examining them a few months later, he found to his dismay that the rats had got into the casks, and had eaten every kernel out of the prunes. Talk-ont'hill (Tulketh Hill), formerly outside Preston, is now absorbed in that town. This was the scene of the second festive gathering commemorated by Mr. Blundell in another metre—the whole forming an amusing and spirited description of May-pole festivities in the year of Grace 1641.

The Scots are severe in keeping the Sunday holyday. They do not permit a barber or a bottle of wine to come into a gentleman's lodging through the streets. My son William tells me that he heard Mr. Alexander Rigby (who was newly come thence to Haigh in November 1669), relate this following story. The Earl of Athole's brother had his wine taken by the guards, who drank it off as it was coming through the streets to his chamber. Whereupon he sent a bottle partly filled with poison and partly with sack, which the guards took and drank, and were sundry of them grievously sick, whereof one lay in great danger of death when the said Mr. Rigby (who was then a companion of the said Earl's brother, when the deed was done), came out of the kingdom.

The peasants about Rome do come on Sundays to hear Mass in the city, from whence after noon they carry their weekly bread home which they do buy in the city. This was told me by Mr. Edward Anderton, March 1669-70. He told me further that workmen did publicly expose themselves there on a Sunday in the streets or market, where it is the custom to hire them for the following week.

Nine persons may enter at a door or sit at a table 362,700 times, and each of those times with a different precedence. I mean in such sort as that all of them shall never be twice in the same order, which may be well expressed by these nine figures, 123456789, which may be varied 362,700 times.

Twelve (e.g. the twelve bells in Bow Church, which I have seen and counted) may be varied with different changes 478,764,000 times.

Consider the life of some virtuous poor souls—Bridget Stock, for example. She is disabled to work, hath nothing whereby to subsist, being neither a beggar from door to door, nor relieved by a tax on the parish. Some little work she can do to earn perhaps a penny a day, and that but sometimes. A raging sore leg hath long tormented her, the bone is almost bare for a long way. She sells her best clothes to buy salve for this, and alas! to little purpose. Now, in the winter, she keeps no other fire (or at the most exceeding little), but to melt her salve. Her windy, cold house is very small and uncomfortable, and she lives in a poor town, where the relief they bring her is very scant. She is born of good friends, is fair and young, and a virtuous patient soul. The sixth part of one extravagant madam's useless ribbons would relieve twenty such maids as these, and yet one of these maids is worth 10,000 of those madams.

It was the saying of a widower who had children, when he was asked why he did not marry again, '*Liberorum causâ duxeram uxorem; liberorum causâ rursus non duxi.*' Colloquium senile. 240. [I married a wife for the sake of children; for the sake of my children I have not married again].

A man must be twenty or thirty years in raising a fortune; the business is hardly done till he be growing up to sixty; when he is an old man he begins to build a fine house, and just when he finishes it, he drops away.

1681.—After my master, W. B. Esq., had been long ill of a violent cold. Dr. Worthington came first unto him on January 8. He staid two nights and received for his pains 1*l*. 10s. He brought along with him, and left with my master, a kind of syrup or consistence in a small earthen pot; this he called Lohoch. He brought also ten pills, with a bottle of spirits somewhat bigger than one's thumb, and a paper of lozenges, with French barley and several ingredients for the making the water thereof. On the 11th day he sent a glister, with a large pint bottle of a cordial julep, and a small bottle of syrups to be sucked up with a liquorice stick, also some small quantity of sal-prunella.

On the 21st day he sent by way of Liverpoole a bottle containing, as we guess, five or six ounces of syrups, also another bottle less by more than half than the former, containing the oil of sweet almonds, together with ten pills. His letter of instructions, which came then, mentions some spirits and sugared oil which were not delivered. The doctor was with my master the second time on January 17, and received for his pains 15s. This is writ by me Walter Thelwall, by my master's order. Note, that the spirits and sugared oil were brought to my master by Mr. Thomas Worthington on January 24, and were both of them to be taken together mixed with barley water and other beverage.

The elder Lady Bradshaigh sent my master a bottle containing, as we guess, about one ounce of balsam, which in her letter she calls (if we read it aright) balsam of sulphur. Her ladyship there saith that it is an approved cure for a cough; that she had it from Sir Peter Brooks that it had cured him of a most violent cough, and that the Lady Ossory had sent it to him. That it must be taken morning and night, three or four drops naked and alone in a spoon, that it must be a little warmed before it will drop at all, by reason it is thick and clammy.

Copy of Dr. Worthington's Bill.

For Mrs Blundell, sen.

	£	s.	d.
1681, Oct 24— Spirits	0	4	6
An ointment	0	1	4
For Mr. Blundell, sen.			
1681, Jan. 8— Spirits	0	4	6
Ten pills	0	2	0
A Lohoch	0	2	0
Lozenges	0	4	0
Jujubes and sebertines	0	0	8
French barley	0	1	0
Ingredients	0	1	6
Syrups	0	3	0
A cordial julep	0	10	6
A glister	0	2	6
1681, Jan. 11— Syrups	0	3	0
White powder	0	0	4
Five pills	0	1	3
The oiled sugar	0	7	0
Syrups	0	5	6
Oil of sweet almonds	0	1	8
Spirits of ptisanne	0	7	6
For a messenger	0	1	6

£3 5 3

My master's opinion of these several things in particular is here to be inserted for farther use, *viz.*, That the *spirits* first named, of which twenty-six drops were put into one small cup of barley water and beer or into barley water alone, had no apparent effect, although he doth not much doubt but the secret effect might be good. That the like might be said of the *pills* mentioned in two places; although it seemed that they did somewhat assuage his cough, which was extremely violent. The *Lohock*, a liquor like a syrup, did apparently bring up phlegm, and was well liked. The *lozenges* were pleasant, and did sometimes stop the cough. *Barley Water* with the ingredients was cooling and pleasant.

Syrups, twice mentioned, although of much different prices, seemed to be the same. They seemed to stop the cough, and bring up phlegm. The *cordial juleps* of which there was a large pint bottle, was pleasant, but the effect not apparent. The *glister* extraordinarily effective and good. *White powder*, supposed to be sal-prunella, assuaged thirst The *oiled sugar* with the *spirits of ptisanne*, besides the extreme dearness, were almost wholly useless in regard that the patient, being much on the mending hand when they were sent unto him, drunk little barley water, and these were only to be infused in that beverage. He sent back to the doctor about seven-eighths of the oiled sugar, and yet he paid for the whole. The *oil of sweet almonds*, of which seven or eight drops were taken in a bolus of white sugar candy, frequently helped the breast, made very sore by coughing.

> Dr. Thomas Worthington lived at Wigan, and some mention of him occurs in *Lydiate Hall and its Associations*, where it is recorded (page 125) that he was obliged to sell his goods and fly from that town at the time of the ferment which followed the pretended discoveries of Titus Oates. As he is found attending Mr. Blundell in 1681, he must have soon returned, and his death is mentioned by Mr. Nicholas Blundell as having occurred on November 27, 1 701. He reached the age of 83, and his son Francis, called by Mr. Nicholas Blundell, Dr. Fanny Worthington, continued the practice of medicine in Wigan, and is frequently mentioned both in the Tyldesley and Blundell *Diaries*.

September 12, 1666.—I did engage with my cousin Henry Blundell of Ince Blundell, Esq., to join 40*l*. with him as an adventure to the Barbadoes in the good ship called the *Antelope* of Liverpoole, and he undertook at the same time to Dr. Richmond to become a merchant for that voyage for one-fourth part of the said ship to Barbadoes and back to Liverpoole, for which he is to pay 3*l*. per ton thither and 6*l*. back. Dr. Richmond said that 80*l*. would be sufficient for him and me to venture for the fourth part of the said ship.

September 15.—I delivered 40*l*. to my son to bring for that purpose to my cozen Blundell or to John Laithwaite (Mr. H. Blundell's steward).

October 11.—I received from my sister Winefrid 5*l*. as one-eighth part of my adventure abovesaid, and she is for that to have one-eighth part of my profit, paying for the tonnage, according as I do myself, over and above this 5*l*.

The *Antelope* went from Leverpoole, Monday, September 15, towards Barbadoes, 1666.

1667, *August 19.*—The *Antelope* returned to Leverpoole from the Barbadoes.

1667, *November 1.*—I received upon account 83*l*. 6*s*., and the next day 2*s*, 6*d*, more from my cozen Blundell. And there yet remains to be accounted for one butt of sugar, besides 1,3000 lbs. weight of sugar left at Barbadoes.

1671, *July 7.*—This day I call to mind that I did receive betwixt 3*l*. and 4*l*. more than is mentioned above, *viz.*, for the odd parcel of sugar late mentioned, and I cleared all with my sister.

Our excess and curiosity in victuals, furniture and apparell, &c, are often destructive to ourselves and to the Commonwealth. What wonders were wrought by the Spartans and other ancient nations, who avoided all excess of this kind. There is one that observeth (and seemeth in a sort of demonstrate), what a vast advantage would arise to this nation if all would observe abstinence from flesh on those days on which the Catholic Church commandeth it And it is not to be doubted but the money which would yearly be saved (if all the nation would agree to regard no other thing but warmness and other useful conveniences in their habits), might keep in continual pay a considerable army. And this besides providing competently for the necessities of such as otherwise would be like to perish, because their superfluous handicrafts would now be unuseful.

King James and King Charles I. proclaimed a licence to the people to use sundry recreations upon Sundays, and particularly the sport of dancing after evening prayer. In April 1660, I saw the Dukes of York and Gloucester, with their sister the Princess of Orange, play a long time at ninepins upon a Sunday, whilst the King their brother looked on. It was at Breda.

Mr. Langhorne, in his letter to me of September 5, 1668, speaking of his long silence, saith, 'Friendship is a marriage of two affections, and if either party fail sometimes in their duty (as of late I have done), yet it is no real disobligation, so far as to justify the other in a failure of what is just in him to practise.'

I do hereby strictly charge and conjure my heir, and so far as lawfully I may (who have all my estate now in fee simple) I do obleege him hereby in strict justice, that (notwithstanding what he may find written in any book of mine) he do regard the heir of John Howard according as he regardeth or ought to regard his ancient tenants. And I do farther desire my heir to show sometimes unto the said John and his children some marks of particular favour, which may be known to be chiefly done in memory and gratitude for the long and faithful service of his uncle Edward Denton, performed to my grandfather and myself. Witness of what I have here required and desired—my hand—William Blundell, June 15, 1663.

The pits where lead is digged, in Derbyshire, are called grooves. I was informed by many there, that these pits are extremely narrow, viz., not one yard square, and yet forty fathom deep, and some of them more. The price of lead at the mill (as Wm. Harrison, who deals much therein, told me, 1668) is now at 10/. lox. a fodder, which is very cheap. About the year 1663 it was more than 15*l*. A fodder is eight-horse load (as he saith), each load being 21 stone and a half, of 15 to the stone, each pound being 18 ounces. This seems to be a great horse load, but the account is very confused. I was told as for certain, that anybody might get lead anywhere in another man's ground where the same is known to be, allowing the owner of the land a thirteenth part This is in the Peak of Derbyshire.

On May 1, 1673, Sir Thomas Clifton made a relation to me at Scarisbrick to this effect, *viz.*, 'On Monday se'night my wife, told me that she had dreamed that herself and her cousin Scarisbrick and his brother Thomas were all of them laid out in white as if they were dead.' Sir Thomas did then express in many words, what trouble of mind he had to hear so speedily after the death of my cousin Thomas Scarisbrick, which happened on April 23 (but two days after we had heard of my lady's dream), and then again to hear of my cousin Scarisbrick's death, which happened on the 29th of the same, at whose burial on May 1, he made this relation to me:

All this above I wrote on May 2, 1673, and this I shall add, that my cousin Scarisbrick was in health when my Lady told that dream: and I think it is true that my Lady did not then know anything of my cousin Thomas his sickness, which had been but a day or two. If my Lady (who I think is now in health) die within a short time, I shall not doubt but the matter was revealed unto her by a special favour from God; otherwise I shall not well know how to interpret the dream or rely on the relation.

The recorded pedigrees of the Clifton family do not give the date of Lady Clifton's death, but it is highly probable that if it had taken place within a short time, Mr. Blundell would have added a note to this effect She was Bridget, daughter of Sir Edward Hussey, Knt of Honington, co. Lincoln, and second wife to Sir Thomas, who had been created Bart, 1660. Dying in 1694 without male issue, the title expired while the estates descended to his nephew. Thomas Scarisbrick, Priest, S.J., had resided with the Cliftons at Lytham, and seems to have been on a visit to Scarisbrick when he caught a fever of which both he and his elder brother died. James Scarisbrick, of Scarisbrick, Esq., had married Frances fifth daughter of Robert Blundell, of Ince Blundell, Esq., by whom he left a young family. She survived her husband 47 years.

In June 1695 I caused my man, Walter Thelwall, with the help of another person, to measure the Crosby course exactly with a chain, and this was the result, each rood being 24 feet:

	Roods	yds
From the chair or starting place to the sea-post	82	4
From the sea-post to the left-hand post	81	0
From the left-hand post to the plat	122	0
From the plat to the post on the Morehouse marsh	118	0
	403	4

The total, ridden twice over to make the course complete, amounts to 807 roods.

That which followeth is a copy of my letter to Mr. Henry Howard (*alias* Ireland), and his answer thereunto was written on the back of my said letter:—

To Mr. Henry Howard at Chester, October 7, 1654.—I beseech you, do me the great favour to give me your opinion in the cases of conscience following:

1. What doth the claim of the heir of a deceased tenant (commonly called tenant right) amount to in Lancashire after his father's lease is expired? If you be not acquainted with the

ground of their claim, I will give it you as best I can. The land-lords in that county have generally admitted the heirs of former tenants not only before another, but at a much lower rate than any other; so that where a stranger will pay ten years' value at the least for a lease of three lives, the heir of the former tenant shall have the same for six years' value. Very good landlords will take but the half from the heir that a stranger will give him; some will take less than the one half. There are some again (but not many) that turn them quite off without any regard to the claim. These last are railed upon and cursed, and many of the former cannot 'scape it We know no law to cause these favours, nor anything but the custom of our country, to use our tenants kindly, which is variable according to the landlords' humour, affection, &c.

2. In case the landlord be bound in conscience to bate some-thing considerable to the late tenant's heir, of that which a stranger will give, and a stranger bids 100*l.* fine, and the lord will let a deserving tenant take it for 50*l.*, and yet make a tenant in the like case that he thinks undeserving to pay 60*l.* or 65*l.*, or else go without it, is there any injury in that? By *undeserving* I understand all great misdemeanours, or notable disrespect to his landlord for which the landlord would punish him.

3. The landlord supposeth that when a stranger will give 100*l.* he may safely take 60*l.* of the heirs to preceding tenants. But yet he resolveth to take but 50*l.* or less of all such tenants as shall please him, and of those that shall displease him to take 60*l.* Is not the supposition true, and the resolution of the landlord law-ful, provided he do it for example's sake and not for revenge ?

A resolution of the cases expressed.

1. I say that by the laws of England, as they have been expound-ed by divers judges in open court, there is no tenant-right at all remaining when their leases are fully expired. The reason and ground for this is, because the land being the lord's the tenant can claim no more right than that the lord of the land did grant by the bargain expressed in his lease; therefore, when his lease is fully expired, the former bargain is wholly ended, and conse-quently there remains no tenant-right at all.

2. I say in answer to the first case, that there is a probable opin-ion commonly received by the best divines in England, that

what is law betwixt party and party as concerning the right of private persons without any penalty for religion or delinquency, is also good and lawful in conscience. Wherefore, as by the laws of England there is no tenant-right at all when the lease is fully expired, so by this probable opinion there is no obligation of conscience for the landlord to give or grant anything for tenant-right after the tenant's lease is fully expired.

3. I answer concerning the same first case, that the custom of the country begets no tenant-right, nor brings any obligation at all upon the landlord to give, grant, or allow anything at all for it The reason for this is, that the most that can be said for the custom is, that there has been formerly and peradventure there may still remain an opinion amongst many, that there is some such tenant-right brought in by custom, and, to grant unto these as much as can be required, that this their opinion should be allowed for probable and still in practice amongst many.

Yet, notwithstanding, should all this be granted, being as much as any can say for that side, it is without all doubt most certain that the opposite opinion that denies any such tenant-right brought in by custom is at the least probable, as hath been sufficiently proved. Wherefore it is lawful not only by the laws of England, but also in conscience, for any landlord to choose and follow whichever opinion he shall like the best For it is a certain principle amongst divines, that in all cases where there are two opposite opinions and both probable, it is lawful in conscience for any one in particular to follow which opinion he will, and if any therefore shall curse or clamour against him, it is for no fault he has committed, but a bad effect of their own malicious mind.

Now, to come to the second case. First, I say in that opinion of such as will hold landlord bound in conscience to bate something considerable to the late tenant's heir of that which a stranger will give, it is no wrong or injury at all to make an undeserving tenant to pay 60*l*. or 65*l*. or to go without it, as the second case relates. For the opinion that makes for tenant-right brought in by custom does not prescribe in particular what the landlord is bound to do, but leaves landlords to their own discretion, which teacheth more is in reason fitting to be done for one well deserving or that has not given any cause of offence, than for any undeserving man such as your case describes. Secondly, I say to this second case, that by the other opinion which admits no tenant-right after the lease is fully expired, that of an undeserving tenant you may take what you will more than you would of another, so you do not exceed the just price that strangers would give for it, and that you do not do it out of any anger or ill will towards him, but for any good motives of virtue, to teach him and others by example how to perform their duty.

By this that hath been already said, you may gather a full answer to all the rest you have writ. For seeing there is a probable opinion that admits of no tenant-right at all after the lease is fully expired, whatsoever you shall bate to any tenant of that a stranger would give, is a favour which you may show more or less as you shall see cause for it—(Hen. Ho., October 11, 1654.)

> It is difficult to identify this Henry Howard *alias* Ireland Sir Thomas Haggerston, second Bart of Haggerston, Northumberland, had two sons, Henry and John, who became Jesuits and were known by the *alias* of Howard, their mother being Margaret, daughter of Sir Francis Howard of Corby. These, however, belonged to the next generation, and the Henry Haggerston of the earlier period, a brother-in- law of Mr. Blundell's, was a married layman who had borne some part in the Civil War on behalf of the King. Of the Ireland family of Lydiate, Alexander, born 1604, became a priest and entered the Society of Jesus in 1640. In 1632 a younger brother, Thomas, in answer to interrogatories on entering the English College, Rome, declares that he has two brothers, priests, one a secular (Alexander), and the other a Jesuit, but gives no names. This may possibly be the missing brother, but it is more likely, from Mr. Blundell's usual mode of writing, that the real name of the casuist was Howard
>
> In solving the question, prominence is given to the doctrine of probabilism, which was then in great repute. Concina, in his *Delia Storia del Probabilismo'* (Lucca, 1743, vol. 1 p. 18), says that Barto Medina, a Dominican, first broached this doctrine, *a.d.* 1577, in a work on the Summa of St Thomas. It did not attract much attention till 1620, when a book of P. Milhard advocating it was

prohibited by the Sorbonne. This gave rise to wider discussions, and these opinions, growing into favour, were taken up in the Jesuit schools. Sanchez, Layman, Garasse, and especially Diana, who is called the *Lamp of Probabilism*, became the chief exponents of this doctrine. Mr. Blundell's correspondent, in his reply, seems to have regarded more the requirements of justice than those of custom or charity. He has perhaps not allowed sufficient weight to obligations arising from a custom then clearly established by long and umversal usage. It has been already remarked that the practice of granting leases for three lives has of late years been generally abandoned. Whatever Mr. Blundell may have thought of his correspondent's opinion, he continued to the end of his life to follow his accustomed plan of favouring old tenants by requiring from them only a six or seven years' fine, while exacting from a stranger one of ten or twelve years. At the same time he would doubtless use his liberty in the extreme case of very undeserving tenants.

Father Warner, the Provincial of the English Jesuits, told me in 1681 of a late professed Atheist, who was (as I take it) well known to him, that wished he had lost an arm on condition that he could have firm Christian faith.

The merry tale told by Jo. Molineux of the drunken frolics betwixt the Lord Goring and Admiral Opdam. Opdam having been pressed to sacrifice some garments of better value than the rest of the drinkers had, to the health of the King, took the like advantage of Goring, and caused him to burn a cloth of gold doublet on the like occasion. Which affront was retorted on Opdam, when Goring caused a foetid tooth to be plucked out of his own head, to the honour of the party they drank to, and Opdam (for shame) was constrained to second the frolic with a sound tooth.

George Lord Goring, the Royalist general, possessed undoubted courage, but his life was vicious. Having gained his pardon and lost his estate, he retired in the time of the interregnum to the little Court of Charles II., and his manners were perfectly adapted to it when it rose to the height of frolic and debauchery (Granger's *Biography*). He was created Earl of Norwich in 1645, having married Lady Ann Denney, sister and ultimately co-heir of her brother Edward, who had received that Earldom in 1626, and had died without issue. He died suddenly in 1662. No doubt the meetings with Admiral Opdam would take place at the King's Court abroad. This Dutch Admiral had the reputation of being a skilful and brave commander. He met with his death in the famous naval engagement of June 1, 1665, which covered with laurels the unfortunate James II., then Admiral of the English fleet It is said that Opdam was forced by the peremptory orders of his Government to give battle, although much against his own judgement Sir Charles Sedley is elsewhere described as the hero of the above story.

To prevent quarrels and jostles in the streets, it were not amiss that all that have the wall on their right hand might go next to the wall. This would cause almost all persons to pass one way, *i.e.* all on one side of the street to go one way and the rest another way. It is the custom in Italy (especially where enemies do meet) to play for the precedence at a game, which in Latin is called *micare digitis*!

It were good that the miscarriage of a business should not be a bettering of the reward of him that miscarries it Why should the nurses of sick persons (especially in London) have all that they find upon them when they die? Doth it not make them to desire they may die? Lawyers and their clerks get the more money if they make the deeds superfluously long; the inconvenience of which is unspeakable in two respects.

I found once the tails of my cattle cut almost to the rump. The cowman did this, who had the hair for a fee.

We pay the tithe of corn in kind. Hay we compound for. In 1662 I paid for the tithe hay of my *demesne* at Crosby, 17s. In 1663, 16s. For many years together during the Usurpation, I paid 13s. and 13s. 4d. But about the year 1639, we paid little less than 40s. for the Hall and the Town. Wool is paid in kind. For hemp, 1s. the bushel seeding; for flax, 1s. *ditto*. If it do appear that we have ten calves, of which by rearing, selling, or killing, we have had any profit, we must pay for tithe 20s. If we have seven calves or upwards, we pay as much as for ten calves, only we have to receive back for every calf short of ten 1s. For five calves we pay 10s., and for fewer 1s. for each calf.

I paid, 1664, for one lamb, 2s, 6d.; for hay, 16s,; for half a calf, 10s. But that year I had more than twelve kine, and commonly, when I had ten or twelve kine, I came off with half a calf. For christening and churching, 4d.; for weddings published in the church, 1s. 8d., and for their marriage; for marrying by the parson with a licence and not asked in the church, 6s.

Smoke, 1d. Garden, ½d. Windmill, 1s. For eggs at Easter, twelve eggs are paid or 2d.; 1d. for the master, as much for the dame, and but one halfpenny for each other person at all. Receiving at Easter: clerk's wages, 1d.; one colt, 1d. Leys for the repairs of the church, everybody in the town pays 2d.

The Lord Gerard of Brandon told me in the hearing of my nephew Selby, Hy. Banister and others, May 18, 1663, that the late King had 900 servants, whereof no more than twenty-seven engaged with him in the late war. He said there were very few lawyers that adhered to the King, and spoke ill as to the same thing of the nobility in general that were made before the war. He said at the same time, that the King's cause was truly and constantly maintained by the English gentry.

> Thomas Selby, Esq., of Biddlestone, Northumberland, owed much to the care and good counsel of his uncle. He met with an early death on December 6, 1666. Mr. Henry Banister, of Bank, came to a melancholy end, being slain at the races at Delamere (Sir Philip Egerton's) in April 1665. His murderer Colket, or Colcoth, was hanged at Chester for the crime. A diary of Roger Low, mercer, of Ashton–in–Makerfield, has this entry:
>
> > '1665, *April 3.*—Mr. Banister de Banke came through Ashton, being slain at the forest of Delamere, being accompanied by a store of gentry.' He was son of Henry Banister of Bank, Esq. (*ob.* 1641), married to Dorothy, daughter of Roger Nowell of Read, who survived him. They had no children. (*Local Gleanings*, vol. 1) Mr. Blundell says in a letter to Lawrence Ireland that it was a drunken quarrel.

August 22, 1664.—At the Swan, in the Strand, near Charing Cross, I saw (for 6d.) John Dodes, as I understood him, a Hollander, born at Schonhaven. All I could do, standing flat on my heels, was to reach with the point of my long finger to the very top or middle part of his head. His shoes were full three inches, as I take it, high on the heel. I could not reach with my head to his armpit by a full handfull. His wife was there, a woman of a middle or rather of a mean stature. He had had two children, both of whom were dead. I asked him for one

Gerrard, his neighbour, whom I had heard, as I told him, to be higher than himself. He did not deny it, but said that the man was crook-shouldered or deformed.

This John said he was himself twenty-eight years old, and that he was grown the breadth of his thumb since the age of twenty-seven. He was a handsome straight man in appearance, but he wore an Indian gown. He said he had been in Turkey (I saw him in a turban), and that he had been in Paris, where he received at the first half-a-crown of all that saw him, and that he took less and less.

The weekly news-book called the *Intelligencer*, printed Monday, July 25, 1664, tells us of an overgrown elephant sent by the Persian to the Great Turk, and how a lion was turned to him, which after they had gazed awhile did assail the elephant The elephant did forthwith throw him up with his proboscis, with the bruise of which the lion being astonished was trodden or crushed to death by the said elephant This is confirmed by many who say that the lion is dead.

An excessive multitude of laws is the destruction of justice. When they can hardly all be read by one man, they are not possible to be remembered or comprehended. And if rigid penal laws do abound in a great measure, they settle an arbitrary power: for whereas the rigour is too great to be put into frequent execution, it must necessarily come to this, that the magistrate must punish or release offenders according to his own pleasure. *Quære*, whether for the very same reason a multitude of pious laws and universal customs in the Church (I mean such as are painful or costly) do not, after some time, undoubtedly occasion the like effect; the prelates being forced either to dispense, or connive at the breaking of the same. And hereby may probably have risen the slender regard which is given in many places to holy-days and fasting-days.

I have thought sometimes that it might have good success, if one should collect the whole proceedings, charges, writings, and troubles, which have belonged to some particular suits of small concernment Then to publish in print a relation of the same with the hard terms of the law (*Justitia civilis*), not forgetting the abbreviations, the Latin, the French, and the strange hands. This may be useful to deter people from suits, and to induce them to submit to arbitration. The best examples for that purpose may be taken out of our Chanceryes, where all is done upon record; and I would have the bill printed with the answer thereunto, as likewise the reply and rejoinder, and let it be mentioned what sheets they contained.

Articles for Races at Crosby, drawn up by W. B. at the request of Hon. W. Molyneux, to be run on 1st Monday in August 1682, and yearly afterwards:—

1. It is articled and agreed upon, that a piece of silver plate, or plate consisting of sundry pieces of silver, shall be then exposed upon the stoop, commonly called the chair, where the horse course on Crosby Marsh doth usually begin and end, and that the said plate shall be given to such horse, mare or gelding, as by the observance of these articles shall win the same.

2. Horse to be brought to the ground ten days before the race, aired and trained there, housed and fed within a mile and a half of the course. Name of horse and person who intends to put him in to be given two days before the horse comes to the ground, to a qualified person or subscriber of 20s.

3. Every person bringing a horse to deposit 40s. as a stake eight days before the race, which stake or stakes either to be given to a second horse, or held for another race next year, as the subscribers may judge, 40s. subscribers to the plate exempted. No subscriber to bring more than one horse.

4. Horses to be drawn out on the race-day at two p.m., and weigh with rider and accoutrements ten stone.

5. And whereas the limits of the said course, by reason of long discontinuance, are unknown to many persons, every rider in the race shall leave the three first stoops, which stand upon the marsh belonging to Great Crosby and next to the town so called, all of them on his right hand, but the fourth and last stoop standing on the said marsh to be left on the left hand of the rider, at whose choice it shall be to leave the distance post and the post or chair, at the end, either on the one hand or the other.

6. That the horse which shall first end the first course or heat by returning back to the starting post, and by carrying his rider thither with his full weight or within a pound thereof, before any horse be come back to the distance post which stands upon the same ground, about twelve score yards from the end, shall win the plate. But if no such thing happen, a second heat to be run at the end of half an hour with horses not distanced. Again, after another half-hour, a third heat if necessary.

7. In case the plate be not gained in three heats, the horse coming in first in two, and within the distance in the one he loses, shall have the plate. If two different horses win the first and second, the winner

of third shall take it

8. Riders not submitting to the rules to be excluded from winning. A cloth or flag to be placed at the top of the ending post, to be let fall immediately the first horse comes to the end.

9. If only one horse come, he must take the plate after galloping over the course. Riders and horses to be weighed afresh after each heat, and before he enter the scales, a flagon of beer to be given to each rider if he require it

10. Three gentlemen to be chosen by the majority of subscribers, for umpires in case of dispute.

The foregoing rules have been somewhat condensed, but they contain all essential particulars. There is frequent mention of Crosby races, from 1702 to 1728, in the *Diary* of Nicholas Blundell, Esq.

Chatsworth in Derbyshire, within the Peak, is the Earl of Devonshire's house, most stately and noble. I take the pile to be about 100 yards square on the outside. It is built about a court My lord told me that it cost in building 80,000*l.*, and that the less of his two houses at Hardwick cost 30,000*l.* Chatsworth was built about the year 1573, and the little house abovesaid about 1597, both of them, and also Oldcotes (which was sold by his lordship to the Earl of Kingston), were built by Elizabeth, Countess of Shrewsbury.

The great chamber at the less house at Hardwick is 26 of my long paces in length, and 12 wide. That and the gallery (which, is, as my lord saith, accounted to be 60 yards long, though he thinks It is but 57) are, as my lord saith, 30 feet high. But the gallery seemed to me to want about a large foot (as I judged by the four heights of the windows) of 30 feet in height, and I take the hall to be as high as the gallery. The gallery is over the hall, which makes a most stately high pile, exceedingly full of windows.

The new gallery at the Duke of Newcastle's house, called Bolsover, is in length (as his Grace's architect told me) 72 yards, 22½ feet wide, and about the same height In the great chamber there is almost 29 of my large paces long, and almost 12 wide, and half a foot higher than the gallery.

My Lord of Devonshire told me Sir Benjamin Rydicar did write these verses on Chatsworth:—

A woman thus composed much love would win,
Hard of access, fair without, fair within.

But these verses or rhymes, written in large gold letters over the dining-room chimney, I am sure are bald ones:—

Truly to serve in sight, duly by day or night,
My Prince with all my might, such is my nature right

Many other worse rhymes, and most ridiculously spelt, are written there in large gold letters. In the drawing chamber at Hardwick, where a stag (or two stags) supports a coat of arms over the chimney, are these verses writ (as my lord told me) by Lady Arabella, who was cousin to King James:—

Sanguine, cornu, corde, oculo, pede cervicis et aure
Nobilis; at claro pondere nobilior.

A great help to the cymbal nets for bringing in of larks about your net, is a gigg of feathers standing a distance off, which twirleth swiftly round on the least breath of wind. When the sun doth not shine, a fox tail pulled up within the compass of your net will make the larks strike at it as if it were a weasel.

Dress lime-twigs by the fire; anoint your hands and your twigs a little with goose-grease, or any such like thing; cleanse your hands with bran, &c.

You may take a hawk by turning out a bird with a most slender limed twig; lime the bird's back, and that alone will entangle the hawk.

When you hear a pheasant crow, turn out near to him a housecock, which will answer the crowing of the pheasant, and thereupon they will meet and fight, so that you may take the pheasant with your hand.

My Lord Langdale (the first) bred up his children in much awe and fear. His eldest son, being then a father of many children, did observe him (even till my lord's death) with a childish awe. And though this son was a man of a high spirit, yet finding it to be, as he thought, ungrateful to his father, he durst not give him nor procure anyone to give him notice in his last sickness of the apparent signs of his death, so that my lord (who did not expect death) died without the help of a priest His son, who lived in the house and durst scarce visit him in his sickness, did not so much as adventure to pray by his bedside till my lord was in his last pangs and not able to observe what he did. One of the family told me this, that was present at his death.

Sir Richard Houghton's daughter did fly from her parents and married a poor minister. The bustle she made to be got away was apparent to the servants, but no one durst speak a word, for my lady her mother, who had made her daughter the idol of the family, would never endure to hear anything said against her.

Praise your children openly, reprehend them secretly.

Sir Marmaduke Langdale, the famous Royalist leader, was created Baron Langdale of Holme, County York, in 1658. The austerity of his manner is spoken of by others. Lloyd describes him as a lean mortified man, so that his enemies called him the ghost They had some reason for this, considering that he haunted them so much. He is highly commended by Clarendon, and is said to have spent 160,000*l*. in the King's service. He died at his seat, Holme, in Yorkshire, on August 5, 1661. His son Marmaduke, second Lord Langdale, was Governor of Hull for James II., and Mr. Blundell says that he was offered the command of a troop of horse, which he declined The Barony became extinct in 1777 by the death of Marmaduke, fifth Lord Langdale, whose sister Mary had married Charles Philip, sixteenth Lord Stourton.

Their third son, the Honourable Charles Stourton, assumed in 1815 the surname of Langdale only, in compliance with the will of Philip Langdale of Houghton, county York, Esq., to whose estates he succeeded. His honourable and religious character is well remembered, and on his death-bed he was admitted at his earnest desire into the Society of Jesus, putting on the habit of a lay-brother. The Cavalier's grandson, Nicholas Blundell, of Crosby, Esq., married in 1703 Frances, second daughter of Marmaduke, third Lord Langdale.

Sir Richard Hoghton, third Baronet of Hoghton, county Lancaster, was M.P. for his native county, and died February 1677-8. He had married Sarah, daughter of Philip, first Earl of Chesterfield, who survived him till 1698. This will be the lady referred to.

The casuists say it is not lawful to sell anything above such or such a degree of dearness. *Quære* then, whether it be lawful to buy above such or such a degree of cheapness. If one may buy as cheap as he can, and yet may not sell as dear as he can, how comes this judgement to pass in favour of money? For he that giveth the money is called the buyer; he that giveth any other thing (I mean by such contract) is called the seller; whereas my horse doth buy for me my neighbour's money, as well as my neighbour's money doth buy my horse for him.

Cato counselled those that were to take a farm, to have a great regard what neighbours it had, and Themistocles, being to sell a certain manor, caused the cryers to proclaim that it had good neighbours.

A friend of mine, a person, of great virtue, who used to spend eight or nine hours each day in prayer and meditation, made a long relation to me, how valiantly his son had lately behaved himself in the acceptance of a duel. He made little complaint against him, only (when I said so) confessed it was unlawful, yet it seemed very apparent that he took a kind of glory in his son's supposed gallantry. So much doth false honour deceive even virtuous men. For this same person was at that very time continuing in a long and great displeasure against a younger son of his own for having married below his quality, although the portion was really more than his own fortunes deserved. So that it seems, if sins be fashionable sins, we cannot blame them. We would not go to hell unless honour calls us. Nay, we should be content to go to Heaven, if it were not against our credit to receive an affront

The tyrannical decimation of Cromwell is yet in fresh memory. It was once conceived to be so firmly established, that a friend of mine took my 6d. to give me 10s. when the decimation should cease. This he did soon after perform. The decimation was laid upon us in the year 1655, and taken off about two years later. Sir Wm. Petty, in his book of taxes, proposes a way for the saving of 500,000*l. per annum* of the Church revenues of England, which being allotted for the publick charge, the care of souls may, notwithstanding, be taken sufficiently by encouragement for the remaining revenue.

1646.—My Lord of Derby took the custom of some mills from Deemster Christian, and the Calf of Man from Dick Stevenson, and after that Stevenson and Will Christian feasted his Lordship: on which was made this epigram—

Will did invite his guests; they eat their fill;
He gave them bread that robbed his father's mill;
But was not Dick the madder man by half,
To give him veal that stole away his calf?

1664, *May 23.*—Laurence Ireland, Esq., being that very day aged thirty years, and left by the late death of his wife a jolly, healthful widower with two daughters and no son, told me as we were coming from Holywell, that he would not marry again, although by that marriage he should know that all the people of England would become

Catholics. That day I took leave of him, who was then on his journey towards the other side of the sea with intention to undertake a religious life.

Laurence Ireland of Lydiate, the last squire of his race, after the death of his wife, became a Jesuit, and died of consumption at York, June 30, 1673. He was an intimate friend and neighbour of Mr. Blundell, and entrusted his two young children to the care of his lady, to whom he writes afterwards in terms of grateful acknowledgment for the care bestowed upon them. He settled his estate of Lydiate Manor, &c, on his elder daughter Margaret, who married Sir Charles Anderton, second Baronet of Lostock, and had a numerous issue. The second daughter, Katharine, became a Nun O.S.B. at Dunkirk, where she died February 4, 1740. (See *Lydiate Hall and its Associations*.)

A.D, 1660.—About the end of June, I met with a young Polander at Dieppe, with whom I had much free and pleasant company for sundry days at the same inn. He was newly landed from his own country. He spoke Latin most readily, and learnt it (as he said) at seven years of age by conversing with his father and a tutor. He appeared to be little or no less than twenty-four years of age, yet he told me he was born November 10, 1641, so that he had not then attained to the twentieth year of his age. If that was true, he was almost prodigiously learned for one of that age. Sure I am he gave me great occasion of humility. I could scarcely mention anything, even out of those Latin books which I had studied and pored on with endless repetitions, but he had it almost by heart; or else knew the substance thereof much better than myself.

Especially Barclay's *Argenis*, the historical part of which I had read over no fewer than eight times. The like of *Quintus Curtius*, &c. I never met with an Englishman that seemed to know the tenth part of what he knew and repeated to me of Owen, our English epigrammatist Seneca the philosopher was his *vade mecum*, and he seemed to have sucked all the marrow out of that book. He wrote his name thus in my table-book, *Stanislaus de Ratiborko Morstin*. He said he was nephew to that Morstin whose name we often read in the news-book as Secretary to the King of Poland. He wrote in my book sundry epigrams, one of which is as follows:—

In Reginam Poloniæ nomine, non re, Bonam.

Qui tibi cunque Bonæ sacris dum tingeris undis

Extract from a letter of William Blundell to Mr. Scarisbrick at St Omers Collie, April 29, 1655:—

Hugh Worthington, your tenant, hath found a few days since, in the ground about his house, divers scores of most ancient Roman pieces, many of them pure silver, others (supposed once to be gold) prove now but brass: these about half-a-crown in weight, those but sixpence. The faces and inscriptions upon the silver coin are clearly apparent, and very neatly cut; the character is the same now used, or with little difference. One of these bears the face of Vespasian, with his name and title (Caesar) stamped at large upon the verge. On the other side is a woman, despoiled of all her dresses, in a sedentary and pensive posture, and the inscription upon the ring, Judæa You have in others S P Q R in a wreath of laurel, the Roman eagle displayed, the altars and instruments of sacrifice, with the faces of sundry of the first twelve Caesars, no less discernible than the stamps of our modem coin. Thus, sir, you may see that your learned Worship's poor tenants, without the trouble of Livy, Tacitus, Suetonius, or any other of those crabbed companions, are as conversant with the noble old heroes as yourself.

We have here an odd opinion, that the finding of iron is lucky, but of silver extremely unfortunate.

James Scarisbrick of Scarisbrick, county Lancashire, was first cousin to the writer, their mothers being two sisters, daughters of Roger Bradshaigh of the Haigh, Esq. Mr. Scarisbrick succeeded his father Edward in the estate in 1653, at the age of eighteen, and had returned to St Omers to finish his studies. He died of fever April 1673, and was the subject of the remarkable dream of Lady Clifton, related in another place, and told Mr. Blundell by Sir Thomas Clifton on the day of the funeral, May 1, 1673.

December 18, 1663.—Jack Hesketh, starting at the usual place of Crosby course, and running by Lightheeles stubb (left on the left hand) to Crosby pole, and turning back the very same way, came to the start again in twelve minutes and two-thirds of a minute, as near as I could hit it by the help of a half-quarter and a half-minute glass. The horse was the Earl of Derby's, matched to run for 100*l*. January 11 following, with a gray gelding to carry 15 stone 9 lbs., and the horse

12 stone 9 lbs. The rider abovesaid weighed, when he gave the heat, 12 stone 10½ lbs.; he was shamefully beaten. My blind stallion did run, by the same glasses, upon the sea sands (which were then heavy), running off and on, and turning in a compass of about 25 yards in diameter, just 5 miles and 82 roods. Each rood is 24 feet, and each mile 220 roods, which is after the measure of 320 statute perch to a mile, each perch or rod consisting of 16½ feet. He ran this space of ground in fifteen minutes time, wanting about the sixth part of one minute, and no more.

The news-book, August 24, 1665, tells how 'it hath pleased God to move the hearts of some citizens of London, &c. to consider of the great necessities of the poor of the out-parishes of this city, by reason of the dreadful visitation of the pestilence, and they have remitted the disposal of their charity to the Right Honourable Sir John' Laurence, Lord Mayor of London.' Then he tells us the just sum is 6l., and names twenty-five benefactors, beginning John Wiat, &c. This I note as a ridiculous charity to be so published.

John Widowes, the churchwarden of Winwick, when he opened the poor man's box which stands in the church, called upon the parson, Mr. Sherlock (a very charitable man) to be present at the opening of it, and withal said to him, 'Sir, if here be any brass money you ought to make it good.'

'Who, I?' said Mr. Sherlock, 'I pray, sir, your reason.'

'Marry, sir,' replied Widowes, 'there is never a man but yourself that ever puts money into it, and therefore you ought to make it good if any be amiss.'

My aunt Massey used sometimes to give a peck or bushel of corn to several particular persons of the poorest sort Once, when she had given a measure to a poor woman, the woman held her sack open after the corn was put in, and said, 'I hope, good Mrs., you will give me now some charity or overmeasure, according as others do after a measure of corn sold.'

I knew an old wandering beggar, by name Hesketh, of whom I have credibly heard this talc. He understood one time that a company of young gallants (most or all of them Catholics) were passing through Downholland, towards Scarisbrick. It was in the times of usurpation, and in the summer season. The man, being very old, had his grandson to attend him, whom he commanded to go aside; then he threw himself into a puddle, and wallowed therein. The gallants, coming to the place, asked him what he was. He replied, 'I will never deny myself to be a Catholic, and because I am so, your comrades the troopers that went before you have beaten and used me thus; and now I do expect you will kill me outright.'

Hereupon the soft-hearted gallants made a contribution of twelve or fourteen shillings. Which when he had got, and the gentlemen passed away, he called to his boy and said, 'Here is a trick to help you when you grow to be old'

Rev. Richard Sherlock, D.D., born 1612, was presented to the rectory of Winwick by Charles, Earl of Derby, and died June 16, 1689. He had the reputation of a pious, humble, and charitable man. The epitaph dictated by himself may still be seen in the chancel of that ancient church. It concludes with these words, '*Sal infatuatum conculcate;*' (Tread underfoot the worthless salt) Dr. Sherlock's niece married Bishop Wilson.

The Masseys of Rixton Hall, near Warrington, were an ancient family, which became extinct in the male line about the middle of last century. The preceding anecdote regarding Dr. Sherlock would probably come to Mr. Blundell's knowledge through his relatives at Rixton.

The golden mean is the best measure for all things; and the hitting of this aright is the greatest wisdom. I fear my countrymen are not guilty of too much wit upon this account We love all in excess. Our modes are now excessive little, then excessive large; excessive broad and excessive narrow; excessive long and excessive short; extremely rich and extremely plain. The breeding of our children is and hath been faulty in the contrary extremes. The manners of wives for the most part are strangely changed. Once a velvet gown would have passed from mother to daughter for two or three generations, and they knew no more of London but only the name. Now they know the streets as well as the porters of the town; and they pay not for their gowns and silk stockings till there be half-a-dozen on the score.

A while ago the best parts of the nation were given by pious souls into churchmen's hands, and a law was made to restrain these excessive gifts. Then presently comes a zeal which holds it a Christian work to destroy the Church and the churchmen. And because there was or seemed to be an excess before in some religious duties, the fonts were pulled down and the churches turned to stables.

Mr. Richard Bellings in his letter to me, January 10, 1674, saith,

'I must say this for my nation, that next the Spaniard it is the laziest generation.'

In August 1676, many great causes were brought into the Court to be tried, I being then at Lancaster, where I saw wretched mean persons most commonly (yea, almost wholly) upon the juries. Of these sundry were bum-bailiffs, as Tom Tilsley, Edward Atkinson, &c, whereof the latter was by far the best like man in the whole twelve. Sundry of these men served on twenty or thirty juries, and each had 4*l.* a piece in each cause. One John Brewer (who wants an eye) being then often sworn on the jury, a gentlewoman, who stood next me (daughter to Mr. Rigby, Clerk of the Crown) told me that the said Brewer had two brothers who were drudges at her father's house and natural fools, and that the said John was little better; all which Mr. Rigby confirmed to me about two days after. Yet I saw this Brewer, and others that appeared as simple and as poor as he, sworn on the jury for the trial of Mrs. Anderton's estate in Lydiate, Melling, &c. which I take to be worth 10,000*l.* and more. Of which jury young Mr. Preston of Holker was the first, but no other like a gentleman, except one, Crowder. In this cause the plaintiff was non-suited.

> The Mrs. Anderton, who had to defend her title to her estate under the disadvantages spoken of, was Margaret Ireland, who had married Mr., afterwards Sir Charles Anderton, second Baronet of Lostock. Her father, Laurence Ireland, on leaving the world in 1664, had settled his estates upon her. After his death in 1673, they were claimed by his cousin Francis Ireland, who pleaded a settlement made by the grandfather in favour of the male line. Although this deed was recited at the Inquisition P. M., it was proved never to have been executed, so that the opposition fell to the ground. Lady Anderton enjoyed her estates till her death in 1720, when her bequest of them became the occasion of some curious proceedings. (See *Lydiate Hall and its Associations*.)

I am now (1676) eight or nine years older than Cato Uticencis was at the time of his death, yet I never drew blood by giving a blow to a servant. But Cato, the very next night before his designed and much-famed death, blooded his own hand by striking his servant even for a faithful and loving act. Yet Cato was very patient, and I am a passionate wretch. We are not to judge of men by one act or circumstance.

Edvardi Scarisbrick, Armigeri, Lancastriensis,

Quod reliquum, hic situm est
(&c) *Obiit* November 7, 1652.

The above is engraven upon a square marble, which I procured to be set in the church of St Andrew in Holborn, together with his coat of arms. You may find it over his grave, upon the left hand as you enter at the little south gate.

There are nine eulogistic lines, in one of which the deceased is described as dear 'to God, to the Angels, and to Stanley' (Deo, Angelis et Stanlaeo), a curious climax, the conception of Rev. Samuel Rutter, Chaplain to the Earl of Derby and afterwards Bishop of Sodor and Man, who composed this inscription. A friend who kindly undertook to look for it in the present church informs the writer that the ancient monuments are put together in an ante-chapel under the tower. He says that the room is so dark and the monuments placed at such a height, that it is difficult to see, and impossible to decipher any inscription.

The church standing in 1652 escaped the fire, but did not escape the destroying hand of Christopher Wren, by whom it was rebuilt in 1686. Hare (*Walks in London*, vol. 2. p. 193) calls it a bad likeness of St James', Piccadilly. Its associations are not without interest Richard Savage, the Poet, was baptised there, and it was the burial place of the unfortunate Chatterton, Stillingfleet was its Rector in 1665, and later on, Dr. Sacheverel, whose name became the 'shibboleth' of a party. He died Rector in 1724, and lies buried in the chancel.

A former Edward Scarisbrick had been receiver general for Henry, Earl of Derby, and was one of the gentlemen-ushers who attended the burial of his father Edward, Earl of Derby, in that remarkable display of funeral pageantry which the town of Ormskirk witnessed on December 4, 1574. The full details may be found in Collins' Peerage, which says that the place assigned by the Heralds to Edward Scarisbrick was to accompany the chariot which conveyed the body itself:

Then the chariot, wherein the body lay, was covered with black velvet garnished with *escutcheons*, drawn by four horses, trapped with black, and on each horse was placed four *escutcheons* and a *shaffron* of his arms, and also on each horse sat a page in a black coat, and a hood on his head; on the fore-seat of the said chariot sat a gentleman, usher in his gown, and his hood on his head, and a white rod in his hand' (vol. 2 p. 76).

This Edward Scarisbrick, having lost his only son Alexander, left the property to his nearest heir-male, Thomas Scarisbrick of Borwick, in Furness, whose son Henry died in 1608. The latter was succeeded by his son Edward, the person commemorated by Mr. Blundell, whose uncle he was by marriage with Frances, daughter of Roger Bradshaigh of Haigh, near Wigan, Esq. The last in the male line of this ancient race was the late Charles Scarisbrick, Esq., who died unmarried in 1860, leaving large possessions, inherited and acquired. The manors of Scarisbrick, Halsall and Downholland, fell to his eldest sister, Ann, widow of Sir Thomas Windsor Hunloke, of Wingerworth, Derbyshire, Bart, who assumed the name of Scarisbrick. At her death in 1872, she was succeeded by her only surviving daughter, Eliza Margaret, married to Leon Biandos, Marquis de Castèja. This lady is since dead without issue, and the Marquis now enjoys the estate.

I do not remember any frost in England so long and so violent as that which happened in the year 1683-4, concerning which I shall here insert some words out of Mr. Michael Rock's letter, dated at London, January 29, 1683, and directed to Edmund Butler, Esq., at Crosby, *viz.*:—

We have but little news about town; that which gives most occasion of discourse is the extremity of the weather, and our great river Thames being frozen over. The like was never seen, it being almost every day covered over with people; several booths—nay, several thousands of booths are built on it, and coaches and carts go as frequently on it almost as in the streets. The common passage from the city to Whitehall and Westminster is on the Thames, it being the shorter cut. We had yesterday a bull baited on the Thames. In fine, it looks like a vast common, and not a river. Every day for this month past, it seemed as if there were a fair upon it, all things being sold there in booths, of which there are several great lanes between the bridge and Westminster, besides what are all along up the river and below the bridge. The like was never seen by any man now living. All trade and commerce is ruined by this weather, for no posts can come or go. There is now due from Ireland thirteen packets, and five or six from other parts.

On August 26, 1674, 1 was told at Dublin by one Mr. Carney (who lived, as I take it, at his own house, the Holy Lamb, in High Street), that he had seen the crosier staff of St. Patrick, which he saith is kept by Donogh, *alias* Denis Carney, of Ballidough, in the county of Tipperary. Alford speaks of this staff, *tome* 1, p. 539.

There died in the compass of about one year four of our chiefest Lancashire colonels of the Parliament party, *viz.*, Ashton, Dodding, More, and Rigby. Of which the last was thought, as his nephew told me, to be certainly poisoned.

There died within the compass of seven weeks, 1656, Lieutenant Colonel Aspinwall, Colonel Holcroft, and Colonel Egerton, of which the last did poison himself by mistake. There died also a few months before, Jo. Atherton, Esq., High Sheriff of the county, who had been a captain for the Parliament. Since the Great Committee for Sequestration was changed, there have been five new Commissioners, four whereof, to wit. Holt, Cunliffe, Massey, Aspinwall, are all of them dead, and had the same precedence in death as they had in their severity. Mr. Pigot, indeed, who had left the place, and was esteemed the most moderate of them all, is yet alive.

The judgement that hath been shown upon sequestrators hath been very observable, and no less upon those that have intruded to other men's estates. Witness Mr. Ambrose, Ellison, Richardson, the man that expired in so horrid a manner on the edge of Yorkshire, that other that was killed with a tile, and the man that left the employment upon the breaking of his leg. These were all sequestrators, but inquire further.

For intruders, there was Mr. Chorley, his daughter, and others of his family that died in a horrid manner. Then Norris, Whittson, Latham. I have heard it confidently reported that Peter Ambrose (that worst sequestrator of all others) died of phthisis, being a prisoner to the State, because he could not make his accounts.

Colonel Ralph Ashton, Major-General, and M.P. for Lancashire, was of the Middleton branch of that family. He is said to have died 1652, aged forty-five. Colonel George Dodding was son of Miles Dodding, of Conishead Priory, Lancashire, Esq., and had commanded one of the Lancashire regiments during the civil war. Colonel John Holcroft was of Holcroft, Lancashire, and defended Lancaster Castle against the Royalists in 1643. He was buried at Newchurch, in Winwick parish, on April 22,

1656. His daughter Mary married Colonel Blood

Colonel Peter Egerton, of Shaw, near Flixton, commanded the Parliamentary forces at the siege of Latham House. From the Flixton register he appears to have died May 22, 1656. In Newcome's Autobiography, November 1657, we find the following reference to his death:—

> This induces to remembrance another sad story that was notoriously known not many years since of Colonel Egerton of the Shaw, here in Lancashire, who used to take flower of brimstone for some distemper he had, and he sent the maid into the closet, and she mingled it with milk, and he drunk it, and it proved mercury; and by this woful mistake he was poisoned, and died within a few hours.' John Atherton of Atherton, Esq., died January 17, and was buried at Atherton January 24, 1655-6. In his funeral sermon, delivered by J. Livesey, minister of the Gospel at Atherton, he is extolled as one who in his youth was counted worthy of command in a valiant, victorious army.

Alexander Norris, of Bolton, was treasurer of the Parliamentary Committee for Lancashire, in 1645. On April 1, 1643, Nicholas and Robert Cunliffe are both in the list of Lancashire sequestrators; the former is said to be of Hollinge Peter Holt's name appears in 1649, and that of William Ambrose at an earlier date. George Piggott was a Commissioner in 1650; Edward Aspinall and Ra Massey, in 1654.—J. E. B.

Colonel John More was son and heir of Edward More, of Bank Hall, near Liverpool, Esq., who fell down dead in the street (as Mr. Blundell records) about 1632. To Colonel More was entrusted the defence of Liverpool when besieged by Prince Rupert He conducted a force into Ireland at the time of Cromwell's expedition, and died at Dublin on his return in 1650. He was MP. for Liverpool, and one of those members who signed the warrant for the King's death.

There were three Colonels Rigby of the name of Alexander, all active partisans in the civil war. The one referred to was of Middleton, and originally bred to the law. Entering the army, he became one of its foremost leaders, and is styled by Lady Derby 'that inveterate rebel' He was MP. for Wigan in the Long Parliament, and made a Baron of the Exchequer in 1649. He died the following year at Croydon, while on the circuit, of an infectious disorder, to which both his companion Judge Yates, and the Sheriff of the County fell victims. His son Alexander was also a Lieutenant Colonel for the Parliament, and is mentioned by Mr. Blundell as having related to Mr. William Blundell, when they met at Haigh, an anecdote already givea The third. Colonel Alexander Rigby, was of the Burgh family, and on the side of the King. It was his son, Alexander Rigby, of Layton, who, when Sheriff of Lancashire in 1677, erected the monument to Sir Thomas Tildesley, which may still be seen on the battle field, near Wigan, where that gallant hero fell.

Mr. Blundell has the following notice at the end of an obituary for 1679: 'Evan Heaton, of Billinge, an old sequestrator, drowned in a pit as he came frqm Wigan, in the way from which he had drunk at two ale-houses.'

I heard the Countess of Derby say, *a.d.* 1644, Minaxia. that since miracles ceased in the Church, she thought there had not been a more wonderful thing than the preservation of Latham House. It was then newly relieved from a long siege in which her Ladyship had made a most noble resistance.

It has been asserted by some writers that Mr. Blundell himself took part in this memorable defence. This is clearly a mistake; as the wound which he received at the assault on Lancaster, March 18, 1642-3, was of so severe a nature as to render him totally incapable of any further active military service. Charlotte, Countess of Derby, died at Knowsley on March 22, 1663.

Observe a flock of stares (or shepsters) when they are ready to lodge themselves in a dovecote or some thicket, and you shall see how they will fly up and down together a long time in a great and thick knot If you do then turn out a quick stare with a limed thread of near three yards long, she will straight fly to the rest, and flocking among them she will infallibly bring down entangled with her thread one or two (at the least) and perhaps five or six of those birds; and this you may do often with the like success. But take heed that the thread be not limed too near the bird. This experiment has been tried successfully by Mr. Thomas Stanton, from whom I had it.

He told me of a merry conceited experiment (which I rather take to be a mere speculation) of catching wild ducks. If you go into the water up to the neck, with a pumpion put over your head, and whilst the ducks come to eat the seeds which must be stuck upon the outsides of the pumpion, you may take them by the legs, and pluck them quietly one after another under the water.

He told me likewise of an odd ridiculous way of catching herons, which I forbear to relate. October 29, 1660.

About the year 1648 or '49, I sowed cherry stones upon a garden bed finely wrought for that purpose. There came up no cherry tree at all, but in place thereof a pretty crop of ash plants, sundry of which were planted afterwards in the parsnip yard or dovecote croft, as we now call it I do not doubt at all but that they were really produced of the stone of cherries, for no seeds of ashes were sown on that bed that I do know or suspect. And I do presume that the stones grew of such a tree as had been grafted in the stock of a cherry. For the seed of fruit will produce a tree agreeable to the stock or root from whence it came.

The following are the latest notes written by Mr. Blundell, and were compiled in answer to an application from some London booksellers for any remarkable facts suitable for a new edition of Camden's *Britannia*. They were addressed in 1693, a portion of them to Mr. Abel Swall, Bookseller, at the Unicorn, at the Westend of St Paul's, London, and the remainder to Mr. Timothy Childe, Bookseller.

I find the township of Altcar &c in Lancashire to have the privilege to be free from taxes, at the least from such as are laid for the behoof of the county.

Mr. Camden speaks of fishes caught by the diggers within the earth. He calls the place Femeby, but the name is certainly Formby. I. have lived above sixty years in the neighbourhood, yet I can by no inquiry hear of any such thing. True it is that the unctuous matter he speaks of there is greatly remarkable. A chemist in our neighbourhood reports that he has extracted from it, being first congealed into a turf, an oil extraordinary sovereign for paralytic distempers, &c.

Mineral waters or spaws are now abounding everywhere in the kingdom. We have one of these in the Earl of Derby's ground near Lathom Park, Lancashire. The want of convenient lodging makes it less frequented, and I had not mentioned it but that it hath done some notable cures, and one to my certain knowledge the greatest and the quickest that ever I knew to be done by any such water.

I think you ought to inform yourself of that most wonderful mine of solid salt lately discovered in Cheshire. A lump of the same was given me by Sir J. P. and I can scarcely distinguish it from alum except only by the taste. It is said to be about forty foot thick, and certainly all the rich salt springs in the Wiches mentioned by Mr. Camden deirive their perpetual flow from this or from such like.

The buildings and people of Leverpoole, our next post town, are certainly more than doubly augmented and the customs eight or ten-fold increased within twenty-eight years last past.

That heroic and loyal act of Sherlotta Countess of Derby in her personal and successful defence of Latham House against a potent and long siege in 1644 may deserve an entire history. It is true that that ancient house afler a second siege was laid almost flat in the dust, and so was the head of James, that loyal Earl of Derby, cut off at Bolton in Lancashire October 15, 1651, by the rebels' prevailing power.

A mine of lead in Whittle, near Chorley, Lancashire, lately found and wrought with good success in the land of Sir Ric. Standish, I take to be the first lead mine that has been wrought in this country.

Near to the same place is a plentiful quarry of mill-stones not less fit to be noted than that which is mentioned by Camden in the *Peak*.

Mines in Furness and elsewhere which produce iron-ore. I have seen one of them long since, but I know not how they succeed. I think they were not known in Camden's time.

There are plentiful and profitable mines of an extraordinary canel-coal wrought now and long in the grounds of Sir R[oger] B[radshaigh] of Haigh, near Wigan. Besides the splendid flame it yields in burning, we have often seen this coal framed and curiously polished into the appearance of black marble and into the forms of large candlesticks, sugar-boxes, spoons and many other knacks to garnish as it were a cupboard with a kind of sable plate. These things have been a very acceptable present to our friends at London and to others beyond the seas,

Mr. Camden speaks of the prodigious floating of certain fatal blocks as predicting the death of the heirs of the family of the Breertons. I never heard the thing contradicted, saving that in a long discourse which an ancient lady of that house made of that subject to Sherlotta Countess of Derby, I heard her say that she did not give much credit to it Yet she seemed to ground her disbelief too much upon one late imposture proved upon the boatmen of the place who had drawn much people together and gotten some money from them by playing a knavish trick. The truth of the main matter may be worth the search.

In 1646 I observed in the Isle of Man that a person who desired to commence a suit brought a small piece of slate or thin stone to the Governor, whereon he wrote his name or mark with a stile or such like matter and gave it back to the plaintiff. He was then pleased to tell me that this being delivered to the defendant imported as much as a summons under a penalty to appear in the Court. This story may be pleasant enough to an Englishman that spends so much money in his proceedings at law.

It may be noted upon the city of Northampton that from the ancient rotten buildings of wood and clay it has now become the handsomest little town in the kingdom, and not unlike to the fine buildings in Holland.

Dublin is strangely beautified with building on new ground and also with several bridges. The bowling-green is highly pleasant, convenient, and large. There I have seen eight companies or sets of bowlers playing all at a time; and the Lord Lieutenant himself being one, it is not to be thought he would suffer the ground to be cloyed.

The reason why the city of Kilkenny in Ireland is commonly said to have *water without mud, air without fog, and fire without smoke*, is taken from the limpidness of the river, the dryness of the seat, and from that admirable hot-pit coal which is hardly ever seen to blaze or smoke. The castle peereth aloft delicately just over the river.

The following obituaries which Mr. Blundell has added to collections of his letters, may be useful in fixing dates and particulars of the deaths of remarkable persons:—

1672-3.

Mr. Moore dyed June 17. Mr. Thomas Moore dyed June 21. Mrs. Peters, of Greenfield. Mr. William Anderton. Elin Shepard. Ginet Hil. Mr. Fenwick Moore dyed June 28. Edmond Hulm. Captain Asmal, of Amerston. Lady Howard, of Corby. Mr. John Gerard and his only chyld. Catherine Bridge. My niece Clenel. Mr. Plumpton Attumey. Mr. Thomas Blundel, of I nee. Mr. Haskene, of Haskene, and (a few weeks after) his brother. Mr. Samuel Aspinwill. Mr. Raphael Hollinshead. Mr. John Vincent, alias Kanes. Mrs. Elinor Eccleston. Mrs. Catherine Shakerley. About eighty men drowned on Formby shore in a ship, September 22 or 23. Mrs. Elizabeth Ogles. Sir Cicil Traford. Mr. Sayers drowned a hunting at ye Breck, November 25. The Earle of Derby dyed at Knowsley of a dropsie, on December 21, 1672. Alderman Brownlow, of Leverpool, a young man who had been maicr ye year before. Mrs. Townley, of Townley, a mother of many young children.

At Leverpoole dead in a few dayes three young men of note, Alderman Brownlow, Mr. Robert Breers, merchant, and Mr. Formby, newly marryed. The Duke of Richmond sodainly. Sir George Midleton. Mr. Farrington, of Werden. Mr. Marshal, of Prescot. Mr. Charles Walmsley, of Selby. Sarracol (Sorocold) of—, reported to be worth 26,000*l*. Richard Adam. Mr. Thomas Scarisbrick. The Lady Haggerston. The Roman Empres. James Scarisbrick, Esq. Young Mrs. Preston, of Howker (Holker). Young Mrs. Nowel, of Read. Lady Mountgaret dyed in February or March.

The Lady Shakerley. Somerset Oldfield, of Oldfield, Esq. dyed sodainly; so did Mr. Francis Hollinshead. The Lady Preston. Mr. Plowden, of Plowden. Mrs. More, of Bank Hall. Mr. James Anderton, of Lostock, was slain in the year 1672, in parting som persons that fought My sister Haggerston, June 22, 1673, and her onely daughter at ye same hour. Mr. Laurence Ireland, June 30, 1673. Mrs. Stanley, of Eccleston, dyed in chyldbed. Sir William Stanley, September 24, 1673. Mr. Gerard P.

In the margin these notes are inserted:—

Mrs. Brigit Savage maryed. Lady Stanley distracted. Mr. R. Bradshaigh maryed. Lady Clifton's dream. Jack Clifton's ruin.

1673-4-5.

November 1673, Mr. William Martin dyed sodainly in drink at Leverpool. James Anderton, Esq. dyed December 16. My aunt, Elin Brad- shaigh, at Roan, December 28. Mr. Robert Mayl. Mr. Peter Stanley. Mr. Andrew Holland. Lame Gervise Clifton. Dutches of Newcastle. Mrs. Gorsuch. About October 1673, Timothy, an old huntsman of Sir Richard Fleetwood's (who was well known at + B) fell from his horse as he came from the ale-house in ye evening, and was found dead (unhurt, yet warm) in ye morning, with ye whip in his hand. Mr. William Parker, of Woofhouse. Sir Thomas Haggerston, March 5, 1673 (or rather, perhaps, ye 6th). Mrs. Osbalston, of Osbalston. Mr. Richard Moore, P. Mr. John Mollins, P. Mr. Staninought, parson of Aughton,

February 28, 1674.

John Tildesley. Sir William Stanley, of Hooton. Mr. Edward Massey, of Puddington. Dr. Murton, parson of Sepbton, February 28, 1674. Mr. John Clifton. Mrs. Westby, of Burn. Sir Gilbert Ireland dyed April 1675. Captain Peter Slater slain May 5. My Lady Ireland. Mrs. Charles Westby. Mrs. Clifton, of Lithane Mr. Massey, of Rixton. Mrs. Ogles, of Whiston. Mr. John Tatlock. Mr. Cuthbert Clifton, sen. Mr. George Clifton. Robert Hesketh, of Meales, Esq., in December 1675. Mr. Holt, of Castleton.

The following notes occur in the margin:—

Mr. Parker lost the woof-house by a verdict at Lancaster. Sir Thomas Preston entered into ye Novitiat of ye Jesuites, 1674.

1677-9.

Mr. Richard Ashton, of Littlewood, who had formerly slain two men in Lancashyre, was barbarously slain at London. Sir Francis Anderton dyed at Parris, and his son Henry, in France. Sir Richard Hoghton. Thomas Arnold and William Hunt Mrs. Frances Latham. Mr. H. Latham. Sir Edward More, October 4, 1678. Mr. John Townley. The only son of Sir Charles Anderton. Mr. Walmsley, in April 1679. Mr. Bretherton, of ye Hey. Mrs. Massey, of Rixton, May 10, 1679. Mr. Alcock, about March. Mr. Gellibrond, of Chorley, about June. Mrs. Elinor Anderton. Mrs. Elizabeth Anderton.

Mr. John Cooke drowned in a ditch or pudle in December. Mr. Lancaster, of Rennel (Rainhill) about ye same time hardly escaped drowning, haveing fallen into a brook, put of which he got with much adoe, and died a few days after. Mr. Nich. Fazakerley, January 6, 1679. Mr. Robert Williamso. Mr. John Leigh. Mrs. Singleton, of Steinig (Stayning). In or about Rainford, a maid having filled a pail of water at a pit, whilst she sat it on her head, fell back into ye pit and was drowned. Another girl or maid-servant in Rainford, on Thursday, January 29, 1679, fell into a pit and was drowned as shee was stooping to take water.

Autobiography of Joseph Lister

Joseph Lister

Contents

Preface

The only object of this publication is to preserve a brief, but curious memorial of an eventful period of our national history. The original manuscript of the following narrative, or a transcript made from it by himself, was in the possession of my grandfather, and from it a small edition was printed by my father at Wakefield at the close of the last century; but copies of this edition are now so rare, that it has appeared to me to merit a reprint. In addition to the account of Joseph Lister and his family given in his own autobiography, and to what is said in the notes, the following notices have been kindly communicated to me by Mr. Hunter, to whom I am indebted for other observations on the text, and to whom I have taken the liberty of dedicating this little volume. I know nobody who is so intimately acquainted with the particular part of the history of the time to which it more especially belongs, and who, therefore, is so capable of appreciating the simple and unvarnished tale of Joseph Lister. It was he who, assisted by some private memoirs in my possession, first pointed out to me the connection between the Listers and my own family.

Joseph Lister is mentioned several times by Oliver Heywood, one of the non-conforming ministers under the Act of 1662 for the Uniformity of Public Worship, &c. in England, who left a large mass of auto-biographical manuscript. He was living at Allerton on the 26th of May, 1682, and on the 4th of June, 1686, when he was visited there by Mr. Heywood. Joseph himself sometimes preached as a 'gifted brother' in the dissenting congregation of Kipping, to which he belonged, in the absence of the pastor, as was the practice in the section of the non-conformists called Independents. They had for a time a minister who preached the Fifth Monarchy, from whom Lister and others withdrew. Kipping is near Thornton, which was a chapel to the church of Bradford, in which were several puritan ministers who prepared the way for the subsequent non-conformity of this rural district. Joseph Lister was buried in Thornton Chapel.

David Lister, the eldest son of Joseph Lister, who was intended by his father for the dissenting ministry, was first at school with David Noble of Morley, a Scotchman, author of a treatise on the book of Daniel, from whom he went to the academy kept by Richard Frankland, an ejected minister, then at Natland near Kendal, where he entered, May 12, 1675. He died therein November, 1677. Under the date of Dec. 1, 1677, Oliver Heywood observes, "Got out early: visited, prayed with, and was much afflicted with Joseph Lister's case, who buried his son at Mr. Frankland's on Monday last, a hopeful scholar."

Accepted Lister, the younger son, was born at Allerton, and baptized in March 1671, and was educated under Matthew Smith at Mixenden in the parish of Halifax, who was a non-conformist minister there, and author of various theological treatises. He was ordained by Mr. Frankland, Mr. Heywood, and Mr. Thorpe, (all ministers who had been ejected in 1662), other ministers being present, on the 6th of June, 1694, at the meeting place at Horton near Bradford. His thesis was, *An vere fideles de sua salute certi esse possunt?* He took the affirmative. He was then examined in Hebrew, Greek, and other parts of learning, delivered his confession of faith, and answered to various interrogatories respecting his objects in entering the ministry, &c.

After this Mr. Thorpe prayed over him, and in the midst of his prayer the ordaining ministers laid their hands upon him. A bible was then presented and they gave him the right hand of fellowship. Then followed an exhortation to the ministers ordained (two others were ordained with him) and to the people. The service appears to have lasted about six or seven hours, after which they dined at Mr. Sharp's. Accepted Lister first settled as a minister at Kipping, but removed thence to Bingley in 1695, from whence he went to Thornton, and finally appears to have returned to Kipping. He published a sermon preached at the dissenting chapel in Call Lane in Leeds, entitled *Christ's Coming the Believer's Comfort*; it was a funeral sermon for Benjamin son of Joshua Dawson of Leeds. On Sunday, Feb. 21, 1708-9, he preached twice, and administered the Lord's Supper, and on the Thursday following, 25th Feb., he died of apoplexy.

Oliver Hey wood has the following entries relating to Accepted Lister.

18 March, 1694-5, "Called of Mr. Accepted Lister: did a weighty business with him about Bingley."

11 Dec. 1701, "Set myself to write a letter to Mr. Lister, in answer to his concerning that great dispute of his removing from Bingley."

On this subject see Joseph Lister's *Narrative*. According to the testimony of his friend and neighbour Mr. Thomas Dickenson, who succeeded Mr. Hey wood in his congregation at Northowram in the chapelry of Coley, Accepted Lister was "an excellent preacher; a little helpless body, but a great and sound soul."

John Dunton[1] says, "Mr. Accepted Lister, of Thornton in Bradford-Dale, is a little man, but one that has a great soul, rich in grace and gifts, of a strong memory, good elocution, accepted with God and all good men, and one that serves God faithfully in the Gospel of his Son; naturally caring for the good of souls, and longing after them in The bowels of the Lord Jesus."

On the 11th of April, 1705, Accepted Lister, being then minister of Kipping, married Mary Whitehead. His widow afterwards (21 July, 1713) married Robert Richmond, minister at Cleckheaton, and (18 Sept. 1728) she married a third husband, John Willis of Wakefield. Her sister, Martha Whitehead, was married to Thomas Cordingley of Halifax, whose daughter,

---

1. Panegyrick on eminent Persons; in the *Life and Errors of John Dunton*, Nichols's edition, London, 8vo. 1818, p. 421.

Elizabeth Cordingley, was married to John Wright of Bradford. Their son, Thomas Wright of Birkenshaw near Cleckheaton,[2] was my grandfather, and this distant family-connection with the Listers may have been the cause of the Memoirs being preserved by him, and has been in some measure an inducement to me to undertake the present edition.

In reprinting the text of Joseph Lister's *Narrative*, I have endeavoured to increase its interest by a few illustrative notes, chiefly gathered from the communications of two kind friends, the Rev. Joseph Hunter and Sir Cuthbert Sharp of Sunderland, gentlemen deeply conversant in the history and antiquities of the North of England. I have also reprinted at the end a rare tract preserved among the King's Pamphlets in the British Museum, relating to two important incidents in Lister's Autobiography. The only other copy of this tract known to me is among a very valuable collection of Yorkshire pamphlets in the possession of Mr. Thorpe of Piccadilly.

Thomas Wright

---

2. Of whom a short biographical sketch will be found in the second (posthumous) edition of his *Familiar Religious Conversation, in verse*, 12mo. Leeds, 1812, published originally in 1778 under the title of, *A modern Familiar Religious Conversation, among People of Differing Sentiments.*

An Historical Narrative

I propose to keep an account of some of the most remarkable passages of Providence towards myself, and some of the chief public occurrences that happened within my observation during the course of my life. I was born at Bradford, in Yorkshire, of godly and religious parents, June 7th, 1627. My father died when I was about six years old, and left five children, of whom I was the youngest but one. I was brought up at school, and my pious mother would gladly have had me a scholar, but I had no mind to learn; however a free-school being in the town,[1] I was continued there many years, but was averse to learning, and much inclined to play above my fellows.

My dear mother[2] took great care to instruct me; and though she was a woman that would pass by many trifling faults, yet could she not wink at sinful ones, but restrained me from them as much as she could, and corrected me when she found me

---

1. The Free-school at Bradford has sometimes been of considerable repute. John Sharp archbishop of York, and Dr. David Hartley were educated there.

2. It appears exceedingly probable, from several things in the narrative that his mother was sister of Edward Hill and Joshua Hill, two clergymen, one of whom, Edward, was M.A. and vicar of Huddersfield, and had the church of Crofton near Wakefield, from which he was ejected by the act of Uniformity, 1662. He died in 1668. Calamy, Account, p. 793, and Cont. 941. Joshua was minister of the chapel of Bramley, in the parish of Leeds, and died Dec. 13, 1632. Thoresby's *Ducatus Leodiensis*, p. 210. It was probably his widow who visited Lister's mother from Bramley, about 1636, as is mentioned in the narrative. Joseph Hill, B. D. a celebrated tutor in Magdalen College, Cambridge, a non-conformist, was son of Joshua. He removed to Holland in 1678, and died there in 1707. There is an edition of *Schrevelius* by him. In a subsequent part of the narrative, Joseph Lister speaks of an uncle Edward Hill, who was a minister.

guilty: I then thought she was too severe; but I have seen the contrary since. It was her custom before she corrected, to pray earnestly with me, that God would bless her correction of me for my good, yet I was often weary both of her praying and correction, though she did both for my good, and oh! what a mercy it was, how many parents are greatly defective in this, and can let their children sin without reproof or controul; or if they be offended with their faults, perhaps correct them in anger and passion, and so add their own folly to their children's wickedness.

When I was about nine or ten years old, I remember an aunt of mine came from Bramley to pay my mother a visit, and to spend the Lord's day with us; and at noon, after dinner was over, I did (unknown to any of the family) take my aunt's horse out of the stable, with a design to water him; the horse ran away with me, and I fell off, and was so stunned by the fall, that I lay insensible in the way, till word was brought to my poor mother; I was taken up for dead, but being brought home and means used, after a long time they perceived that I began to breathe; and I afterwards recovered, and came to myself, but I knew nothing of anything what passed after my falling off, but by information afterwards.

O how near was I to death at this time! and had I died then, surely I had gone down to the pit. My mother who was fond of me, endeavoured to impress this Providence upon my mind, and prayed over me many a time, and got many godly men to pray with me and for me: but alas! I soon forgot both my danger and deliverance, and not having broke any of my limbs, I was sent again to school.

As soon as I was thought fit, I was brought to public ordinances, and was carefully examined as to what I remembered; I was taught how to understand the minister's method,[3] and by degrees got the gift of memory; and pleased my good mother well with that, for I could have brought home most, if not all the heads and particulars of a sermon: I also got a catechism and

---

3. "The minister's method," *i. e.* his distribution of his subject in heads and particulars.

several chapters and psalms, by heart; and I learned to write both long and short hand, and characters very well, that I might be of use in the family. I went to many funeral sermons, lectures, and monthly exercises, and constantly repeated what I heard, by which means I gained a good deal of notional knowledge, yet no impression was made to purpose upon my heart all this time.

About this time, that is, about the years 1639, 1640, and 1641, that many good ministers and Christians amongst the puritans, (as they were called at that time,) reflected upon the times, with many sad and foreboding thoughts, concluding that Popery was like to be set up and the light of the gospel put out, many ministers were silenced, and great numbers for these three or four years past were posting away to New England, and many of these, both men and women, that I myself knew; [4] and sad apprehensions remained with those that stayed behind.

O what fasting and praying, publicly and privately, what wrestling with God was there day and night? Many of those weeping, praying, and wrestling seasons, both day and night, were kept in my dear mother's house, and the fasts were kept with great strictness and severity; not any of us, old or young, eating so much as a morsel of bread for twenty-four hours together; which was a great weariness to me, and went much against my carnal heart, (fool and wretch that I was) with shame and grief would I think of it.

About this time (in the year 1641) did the Rebellion in Ireland break out, and many thousand protestants of all ages, sexes, and degrees, were put to death, with great inhumanity and cruelty; and great fear came upon the protestants in England, these villains giving it out, that what they had done there was by the

---

4. It appears from the papers of Mr. Oliver Heywood, who was the minister of Coley Chapel, in the parish of Halifax, but only four or five miles from Bradford, that several families removed themselves at this time to New England, from that neighbourhood, but none of them seem to have been of note either in England, or in the country to which they removed. The apprehensions Lister speaks of were not of the war, so much as of further trouble from the ecclesiastical authorities of the time, who were determined to suppress non-conformity, if possible.

king's commission, and that in a little time the English protestants (or heretics as they called them) should drink of the same cup; and it was verily believed by many, it would be so, if God should suffer it; and what fears and tears, cries and prayers, night and day, was there then in many places, and in my dear mother's house, in particular! I was then about twelve or thirteen years of age, and tho' I was afraid to be killed, yet was I weary of so much fasting and praying, and longed to see those nights and days over.

I remember one public fast day (for godly ministers appointed many, and kept them in their respective places;) Mr. Wales kept many at Pudsey,[5] it was two miles from Bradford, and thither my pious mother and all the family went constantly upon these days; I have known that holy Mr. Wales spend six or seven hours in praying and preaching, and rarely go out of the pulpit; but sometimes he would intermit for one quarter of an hour, while a few verses of a psalm were sung, and then pray and preach again; and what confession of sin did he make! what prayers, tears, and wrestling with God was in that place on these days! what tears

---

5. Elkana Wales, minister for many years at Pudsey between Bradford and Leeds, born in 1588. There is a long and good account of him in *Calamy*, (Account p. 801-4) to which we refer, with the following remarks communicated by Mr. Hunter. (1) The clause at the foot of p. 803, "He was so zealous, &c. belongs not to him, but to Christopher Marshall, another of the ministers ejected. (2) A few additional particulars of his life may be gleaned from the account of him by Thoresby, among Birch's MSS. at the Museum, No. 4460. (3; He married Elizabeth Clavering, of Caliley in Northumberland, aunt to Sir James Clavering of Axwell, the widow of Thomas Butler, a merchant of Newcastle, who had many children, one of them a major in the Parliament army, another married to John Oxenbridge, M. A. of Magdalene College, Oxford, and another to Ambrose Barnes, a merchant at Newcastle, who had left a large volume of Biographical and Political matter, now in the library of one of the Societies of Newcastle. Sir Cuthbert Sharp has published (or printed) many extracts from this manuscript, chiefly of the biographical and historical parts. Of Elkana Wales, who was thus stepfather to his wife, Barnes says that he was of a mild disposition, and then when he wrote "of fragrant memory." He mentions particularly what we find in *Calamy*, that he was not to be drawn from Pudsey by the offers of Lord Fairfax. His wife is described as a person of a very severe and harsh temper, and there is a melancholy account given of the circumstances of religious depression in which she died. (4) One of the Presbyterian congregations in the west riding of Yorkshire was at Pudsey, established by persons who had lived under the ministry of Mr. Wales.

and groans were to be seen and heard in that chapel!

I am sure it was a place of weepers; but that day I say, which I am speaking of, I think about three o'clock in the afternoon, a certain man that I remember well, (his name was John Sugden) came and stood up in the chapel door, and cried out with a lamentable voice, "Friends" said he, "we are all as good as dead men, for the Irish Rebels are coming; they are come as far as Rochdale, and Littlebrough, and the Batings,[6] and will be at Halifax and Bradford shortly;" he came, he said, out of pity and good will, to give us this notice.

And having given this alarm, away he ran towards Bradford again, where the same report was spread about. Upon which the congregation was all in confusion, some ran out, others wept, others fell to talking to friends, and the Irish Massacre being but lately acted, and all circumstances put together, the people's hearts failed them with fear; so that the Rev. Mr. Wales desired the congregation to compose themselves as well as they could, while he put himself and them into the hands of Almighty God by prayer, and so he did, and so dismissed us. But O what a sad and sorrowful going home had we that evening, for we must needs go to Bradford, and knew not but Incarnate Devils and Death would be there before us, and meet us there. What sad and strange conjectures, or rather conclusions, will surprise and fear make! Methinks I shall never forget this time.

Well we got home, and found friends and neighbours in our case, and expecting the Cut-throats coming. But at last some few horsemen were prevailed with to go to Halifax, to know how the case stood. They went with a great deal of fear, but found matters better when they came there, it proving only to be some protestants that were escaping out of Ireland for their lives into England; and this news we received with great joy, and spent the residue of that night in praises and thanksgivings to God. And I well remember what sad discourses I heard about this time, the Papists being desperate, bloody men; and those

---

6. Rochdale, Littleborough, and the Batings are well-known places on the great highway from South-Lancashire to Halifax, which is continued to Bradford.

that were put into offices and places of trust were such as would serve the King and his design.

At that time all profaneness came swelling in upon us, swearing, and Sabbath-breaking, profane sports, and those even authorized by law;[7] and the people of God not knowing what the end of these things would be, they being almost at their wit's end, parliaments were broken up, and all things going to wreck both in church and state. Horse and foot were now brought into the town and quartered in it, who rode round about it swearing what they would do, like so many bloodhounds.

Mothers and children expecting daily when they should be dashed in pieces one against another; everyone now began to shift for themselves, but they had no way of escape left them in the world, that they knew of; some indeed, in time, got into New-England, but they were but few, and that too with a great deal of difficulty; some made their escape into Lancashire, hoping to pass thence, but always being shut up, few could make their escape. The army at length marching away for a time, the poor inhabitants, who seemed devoted to destruction, now being laid open to the enemy, what remained but that they would be given over to the sword of these bloody villains?

At this time I was about fourteen years of age, and my mother put me apprentice to a trade, to a godly man at Horton,[8]

---

7. Of course the *Book of Sports* is alluded to.

8. It appears afterwards that his master's name was Sharp, and that his master had a brother-in-law named David Clarkson. This shows us, on comparison with the pedigree of Sharp, (Thoresby's *Ducatus*, p. 36) that the master to whom he was apprenticed was John Sharp of Horton, who in 1632 married Mary Clarkson. These Sharps had a good property at Horton, and were the principal people there. They were non-conformists, and had a meeting at Horton. John Sharp had two sons: one of them was brought up a non-conforming minister, and was pastor of a large congregation at Leeds, in 1693. There is an affecting account of the circumstances attending his death in Thoresby's *Diary*, together with many other notices of him. The other son was Abraham Sharp, an eminent mathematician and astronomer, an assistant to Flamstead and correspondent of Newton. He died in 1742 at the age of 90. His Monument with Inscription is in Whittaker's *Loidis and Elmete*, p. 355. Both these Sharps were several years younger than Lister, but were no doubt among his friends, or acquaintance, living as they did in his neighbourhood, and having a community in religious feeling and practice.

near the town of Bradford, where I was to be seven years; but the Civil Wars broke out in 1642, and many good men in the town and parish took up arms for the defence of the parliament, which was then in being. My master was a man of a good spirit, had a plentiful estate, and was an active man about the town, and though the King's party came at sundry times to take the town of Bradford, yet they were very happily repulsed; but in the year 1643, came the Earl of Newcastle, with a strong army, to Wakefield, and stayed there. But methinks I should here give an hint by the way, how that Uncivil War that shed so much English blood was brought about.

King Charles the first, then upon the throne, to say nothing of his own wicked disposition, did by the constant solicitation of the bloody Queen, together with the swarms of Jesuits and evil affected Councellors, Bishops, and men of great estate, place, and trust, all put their heads together to destroy Christ's interest in the nation, and betray their trust every way to the utter ruin and overthrow of Religion, and to cut off the lives of all the Protestants, and so have enslaved this land to Rome, the mother of harlots; whose kingdom is established by blood.

These things being so plain to be seen, that he must be blind that did not see it; all the King's actions both at home and abroad, shew, and particularly his dissolving of Parliaments time after time, when they did but touch upon these things, as some of the bold seeing men did year after year; so now there seemed to be no hope or help left for England, but that it must shortly be destroyed as Ireland was by a bloody Rebellion.

About this time God put it into the hands of the good people of Scotland; foreseeing the ruin that was hasting upon England, and knowing it could not long go well with them if we were once destroyed, but they and what was dear to them must be sacrificed next; upon which they two several times came into England, to Newcastle, and Berwick-upon-Tweed, with a considerable army, upon design to prevent our ruin; upon which an army was raised in England, to go and fight with them, and upon what terms they returned home again the first time I cannot tell; but, however, they came again shortly, and a great army was raised and went to meet them.

The King also went in person, and a great number of the Noblemen, Bishops, and Gentlemen, in great fury, with design to fight with, and suppress them. What they propounded, and required, I know not, but I remember it was said the English army were not very fully resolved to engage; so a parley was proposed, and accepted, and the treaty was concluded, to see if peace could be gained, and the Scots sent home quietly again; and after a long debate it was concluded that upon several conditions the Scottish General should deliver up the towns that they were possessed of, and march his army in peaceable manner into Scotland and there disband them; and one of the conditions on the King's part was, that he should in a few days issue out his writs for a free Parliament, which should consider of, and in an honourable manner conclude all matters of difference and dissatisfaction, especially all in the manner of misdemeanours, or ill government by any evil Councellors and Ministers of State.

So both the armies did withdraw, and that being blown over, tho' variously resented as persons stood affected to Religion and the Cause of Christ, in the next place the King, according to the previous condition, did call a Parliament, who had not sat long before they presented an humble address, or petition, that seeing his Majesty had given his subjects some cause of discontent, by his so often dissolving of Parliaments, they begged his Majesty would be pleased to sign an act that they might sit as long as they pleased, without being dissolved, which was granted, and therein (as God ordered it) they got the staff out of his hand, which he could never get again.

Well, having got this power they presently began to fall upon Ministers of State; and calling evil Councellors in question, still laying all misgovernment at the door of his bad Councellors and Ministers of State, they clapped up some wicked Bishops, Deacons, and Prelates, and tried them for their lives, and executed them; and also some great Statesmen. I remember one above the rest called Lord Wentworth, he had several titles, as Earl of

Strafford, &c. he was said to be one of the greatest Politicians in England; it was thought he had but hard measure, being (as was said) condemned by a law then to make, for tho' he was guilty of many crimes, yet no one of them alone would cut him off; therefore they made an act that two such crimes put together should be high treason; but then the main difficulty was to get his execution signed, which the King long refused, but the House being resolved to have him down, they pressed the King till he was pleased to sign it, (which thing he repented to his dying day) so they cut him off, which being done, the House did order that the act by which Lord Wentworth was beheaded, should not be brought into example.

This seemed an odd thing to be done by a Parliament; there were many things in evil case, and the House acted so as did not please the King; and there were some few wise, bold, and resolute men that now feared no colours; and they had a great influence upon the rest in the House of Commons; and this his Majesty knew full well, and had an evil eye upon them, and by some means it got out that the King intended to go with a guard to the House and apprehend them. He did go; but when he came there, and had looked all over the House, he saw the birds had got wing and were gone, so he told the House he came in that manner to impeach and carry away by force the five Members that he named; and so went away, but, however the House justified them, and complained of the King's breach of the privileges of Parliament.

So the King required a guard for his person, pretending to be in fear; and the City offered the Parliament a guard also to defend them, there being such swarms of bloody Papists all over the City, and continually walking about the Parliament-House, so that the difference between the King and the House increased every day. The King being grieved and full of fury that things went so contrary to his desires and the desires of his bosom friends and favourites, he now withdrew himself, and went and resided at Hampton-Court, and would but seldom admit of addresses or petitions to return to his Parliament; and at last away he goes, and takes a great swarm of Gentry, Clergy, Jesuits, and wicked Papists, that were ill-affected, and the two Princes, and comes to York, but had not long been there, before the Yorkshire Gentlemen, and others, resolved to go and petition him to return to his Parliament, which they did; but not being well received, and there being such vast numbers of wicked and bloody Papists about him, with arms, riding up and down swearing and cursing like so many devils, the petitioners being naked men, and suspecting the issue, withdrew, and got away, being yet more increased in their fears for the end of these things.

Then the King went to Hull, and when became there, the gates were shut against him, the Parliament having sent one Sir John Hotham to be Governor for them; the King called, and commanded him to open the gates that he might come in; but Hotham, kneeling upon the wall, told his Majesty he could not do that, and be faithful to the Parliament who had commissioned him to the contrary; so his Majesty departed in a rage at the disappointment of his design; and away he marches to Nottingham, and there he set up his Standard, and proclaimed war against the Parliament, which occasioned them to take up arms in their own defence, for now no way was left but to decide the difference by the sword; by which very much blood was shed all over the Kingdom, and in this war, it so fell out, that fathers and sons, and many brothers, fought one against another, till many families were quite ruined.

In this war Bradford was deeply engaged; the generality of the town and parish, and the towns about, stood up for the Parliament, and it was made a little garrison, and though it was not easy to keep, yet they threw up bulwarks about it; and the inhabitants were firm to the cause, and to one another, to the very taking of the town.

When the enemies approached the town, horsemen were sent to Halifax, Bingley, and the small towns about, who presently took the alarm, and came with all speed, and such arms as they had, and stuck close to the inhabitants, and did very good service. The enemies lay at Leeds, Wakefield, and Pontefract-

Castle, and so were near Bradford. (*See note following*)

———

Note—At the beginning of the troubles, Yorkshire was the scene of an important part of the war. The king, after being shut out of Hull, marched towards the south, to set up his standard at Nottingham, and left the command of the four northern counties to William Cavendish, Earl of Newcastle, who garrisoned York. The parliament gave the direction of the war in those parts to Ferdinando, Lord Fairfax, who with his son Sir Thomas Fairfax, kept up a continual war of outposts. A party of Newcastle's forces under Sir William Saville, seized upon Leeds, and held some of the smaller places in the neighbourhood, particularly Wakefield.

Sir Thomas Fairfax occupied Bradford, as being an important position for communication with Lancashire. Between the two rival posts there were frequent skirmishes. The attack upon Bradford, mentioned above, was made on Sunday, the 18th Dec., 1642. A contemporary account of the fight is printed at the end of the present volume. From other authorities we learn that the royalists were commanded in person by Sir William Saville, Sir Marmaduke Langdale, Sir John Gotherick, and Colonel Evers. Their numbers are differently estimated fourteen or fifteen hundred, according to the periodicals of the time (*Special Passages*, No. 21), seven or eight hundred, according to Sir Thomas Fairfax's own estimate (*Memorials*).

They came suddenly before Bradford at about 10 o'clock on the Sunday morning, when the inhabitants were at church; and planted two drakes, which they had brought with them, in a barn, from which they fired at the church, where the Bradford men defended themselves till towards midday, when some men from Halifax came to their aid; then they sallied out, and drove the enemy away. (Lord Fairfax's letter. *Special Passages*, No. 21). One of the Bradford men, before the others issued from the church, had shot the "master gunner" with a fowling piece, which had already daunted the enemy.

The Bradford men were as yet in such an ill condition of defence, that in the pursuit they were armed with "swords, sithes, long poles with sickles fastened to the ends of them, flayles, spits, and such like weapons." (The *Kingdomes Weekly Intelligencer*, No. 2), Sir Thomas Fairfax (in his *Memorials*) gives the following brief account of what appears to be this affair.

The first action we had was at Bradford. We were about three hundred men, the enemy seven or eight hundred, and two pieces of ordinance. They assaulted us: we drew out close to the town to receive them; they had the advantage of the ground, the town being encompassed with hills, which exposed us more to their cannon, from which we received some hurt. But our men defended those passages by which they were to descend so well, they got no ground of us; and now the day being spent, they drew off, and retired to Leeds.

Sir Thomas Fairfax then went and occupied Leeds, deserted by the enemy at his approach; and thence preceded to his father's head quarters at Tadcaster, and was engaged in several severe skirmishes. Newcastle's forces were now considerably increased, he drove Fairfax from Tadcaster, and the latter fell back upon Selby, leaving the road to Leeds open to the enemy. That town was again occupied by Saville, with superior forces; and in the fear of being cut off from their friends in the West, Sir Thomas Fairfax was sent by his father:

"with about three hundred foot and three troops of horse and some arms to Bradford,"—"a town very untenable, but, for their good affection to us, deserving all we could hazard for them. Our first work there was to fortifie ourselves, for we could not but expect an assault. There lay at Leeds fifteen hundred of the enemy, and twelve hundred at Wakefield, neither place above six or seven miles distant from us. They visited us every day with their horse, ours not going far from the town, being very unequal in number: yet the enemy seldom returned without loss, till at last our few men grew so bold, and theirs so disheartened, that they durst not stir a mile from their garrisons."

Fairfax now called in the country, and raised about eight hundred foot, with which he went from Bradford to Leeds, garrisoned by Sir William Saville, and took that town by storm (Monday, Jan, 23). An account of the taking of Leeds is given in the rare tract reprinted at the end of this volume. Newcastle was so much alarmed by the defeat of Sir William Saville, that he drew in all his forces to York, and again left the intervening ground open to the Parliamentarians. The Earl, however, soon began to resume offensive operations; the Parliamentarians were defeated at Clifford Moor; and at the end of April (1643), and beginning of May, Newcastle advanced towards Leeds, which he threatened to attack, and Lord Fairfax wrote to the Parliament for men and money to defend it.

At the same time some parties of royalists had taken Rotherham and Sheffield. According to the *Mercurius Aulicus*, p. 212, (the Royalist Newspaper,) Newcastle drew off his forces on an understanding that negotiations were entered upon for the delivery of Leeds, and Lord Fairfax had taken advantage of this to strengthen his army there. Sir Thomas Fairfax had again been sent to occupy Bradford, with seven or eight hundred foot and three troops of horse. The enemy had seized upon Wakefield, and posted there three thousand men.

On the 21st May (Whitsunday), Sir Thomas, having marched with his forces from Bradford, gallantly attacked Wakefield and entirely defeated the royalists, the horse and part of the foot escaping to Pontefract. Goring was taken prisoner on this occasion (*Mercurius Aulicus* p. 283. Fairfax's *Memoirs*). After this success, the Fairfaxes were very active, and obtained reinforcements from Lancashire (*Continuation of Special, &c. Passages*, No. 52). This was followed by a defeat of part of Newcastle's army at "Barnham Moor." But Newcastle had now assembled all his forces, preparatory to proceeding towards Nottinghamshire, and in June marched towards Bradford, and brought on the catastrophe which Lister now goes on to relate.

I remember one day they came to a hill called Hunderscliffe, and brought two great guns with them, and planted them directly against the steeple, where we had men with several long guns, that did much execution when they came within our shot; but God so ordered it, that a great snow shower fell just then, and one of the great guns burst, which so disheartened them, that they went away of their own accord.

Another day they came down into Barker-end, a place within a very little way of the church, and they placed their guns directly against the steeple; and they were also in a line with a street called Kirkgate, and would probably therefore have done a great deal of mischief in the town. In the next place a stout, gallant officer, commanding a company of foot, came running down a field, shaded with a hedge, intending to come running into the church, and so cut off the men both in the church and steeple; but the men in the steeple having a full view of their design, ordered a few men to meet them, and give them a charge: and the commander coming first, two of the townsmen met him, and struck him down: he cried out for quarter, and they poor men not knowing the meaning of it, said "aye, they would quarter him," and so killed him. I think they said he was the Earl of Newport, or his son, as I remember; and they sent a trumpeter to request his corpse, which was the next day delivered to them. (*See following note*)

––––––

Note—Lister seems to have been deceived by the vulgar reports, in the name of the person who was thus slain. The Earl of Newport at this time was Montjoy Blount, a son of Charles Earl of Devonshire. He was in the military service of Charles I, being Master of the Ordnance, and of the council of war, and is said (*Peerage of England*, 8vo. 1711, vol. 2, p. 229) to have died at Oxford in 1665. He had three sons who succeeded him in his honours, one after the other. He might have another son slain at Bradford. The Newports of Shropshire who were made Earls of Bradford, in that county, seem not to be connected with Lister's conjecture concerning the person then slain. Whitaker is mistaken in saying that there was no Earl of Newport at the time. (*Loidis and Elmete*, p. 360.)

Lord Fairfax, in a letter giving an account of this attack upon Bradford, which was printed at the time, and of which a copy is preserved among the *King's Pamphlets* in the British Museum, mentions "Colonel Evers and Captain Bynnes and another commander reported to be killed," on the side of the royalists. In the *Kingdomes Weekly Intelligencer*, No. 2, we are told that "Colonell Evers, and one Colonell Moore were there slain," In the account printed at the end of the present volume, there are enumerated as "slaine of theirs Sir John Harper, as one Savile taken at Hallifax confesseth, . . . Captain Wray, and Captain Bins."Vicars, who has made up his account almost entirely from the *Pamphlet* last mentioned, gives Sir John Harp (instead of Harper), in his *Parliamentary Chronicle*. It is not improbable that this last mentioned person is the one whom Lister took for "the Earl of Newport or his son."

He being now fallen that was their champion, his men that had followed him thither were more easily driven back to the body of their army, which stayed within a little of where their guns were planted. So presently a panic fear fell upon Sir William Saville,[9] their commander, and they did not fire a gun more that I remember; but immediately ran away to Leeds, their den; and the townsmen fell in the rear of them, and some little skirmish was made, and some little work was done, but not much.

Having made this little disgression, shewing the breaking out of the war, I shall now say something of its carrying on about Bradford.

I said before that the Earl of Newcastle was come to Wake-

------

9. Sir William Saville, of Thornhill, near Wakefield, Baronet, which, his chief house, he fortified, and made a garrison for the king. He had a chief command in Yorkshire, under the Marquis of Newcastle, but died early in the war, 24th January, 1643-4. Some of his original correspondence relating to the war is printed in Mr. Hunter's History of Hallamshire, His lady, a daughter of Lord Keeper Coventry, was also a remarkable person of those times, as may be seen in the Life of Dr Barwick. Their son, Sir George Saville was made Marquis of Halifax.

field with a strong army, intending to overturn the country, which my Lord Fairfax, then commander for the Parliament, understanding, he gathered all the forces under his command, and sent into Lancashire for some assistance from thence, and some troops came, and I think some few foot. Sir Thomas Fairfax commanded the horse. So it was that the Earl of Newcastle had marched his army as far as Howley-Hall,[10] (another den of dragons) and Adwalton. So my Lord Fairfax got his men ready very early in the morning, and marched away to Adwalton; and charged them so warmly that they beat them off their great guns, and turned them against them, and the enemy began to run.

But there was one Major Jeffiries, keeper of the ammunition, who, proving treacherous, and withholding it from the parliament's men, who called for it, and could get none, were forced to slacken their firing; which the enemy perceiving, and probably had private notice from the traitor, they presently faced about, and fell upon Fairfax's men, with that fury, that they presently regained their guns, and put them to the route, and fell on hacking and hewing down the foot, many being slain, and as many as could escaped to Bradford, whither my Lord Fairfax got also.

But O, what a sad discouraging day was that! all the Lancashire men, horse and foot, ran away home, and could by no means be persuaded to stay in Bradford, though my Lord resolved to stay there, and as many as had any courage left stayed there also. (*See note following.*)

———

Note—The disastrous battle of Adwalton or Atherton Moor, is not much spoken of in the contemporary news pamphlets. But we have two accounts of it which come directly from the persons engaged in it on the two different sides, one by Sir Thomas Fairfax (in his *Memoirs*), the other by the Duchess of Newcastle, in her life of her husband, from whose mouth no doubt it

10. Howley-hall, the fine seat of Lord Saville of Howley. See a view of the ruins, and some particulars respecting it, in *Loidis and Elmete*, p. 238.

was taken. Fairfax tells us that as soon as they heard that the Earl was marching to attack Bradford, "which was a very untenable place," he and his father determined to go and meet him.

They were to have marched at four o'clock in the morning, but the unnecessary delays of Major General Gifford, whose office it was to get everything ready, kept them till seven or eight, "not without much suspicion of treachery;" so that the enemy was prepared, and his whole army "drawn up in battalia," on "Adderton Moor." Lord Fairfax had few horse, and they had to march up hill to the attack; but they first beat in the royalist foot, and then drove horse and foot together up to their cannons.

At this critical moment, the rashness of some of the parliamentarians gave the enemy a momentary advantage, which was increased by the ill conduct of Major General Gifford, "who did not his part as he ought to do," (no doubt, the 'Major Jeffiries' of Lister), and the royalists rallied and entirely defeated the Parliamentarian army. The horse, with Sir Thomas Fairfax, escaped to Halifax. Lord Fairfax, with part of the foot, reached Bradford, which was immediately besieged by the Earl of Newcastle. Lord Fairfax left Bradford, and went to Leeds, before the town was blocked up; and Sir Thomas Fairfax came with what men he could raise to Bradford, where at the time of the siege he had eight hundred foot and sixty horse. The remainder of the narrative will be best given in his own words,

> The Earl of Newcastle spent three or four days in laying his quarters about the town of Bradford, and brought down his cannon, but needed not to raise batteries, for the hills within half musket-shot commanded all the town. Being planted in two places, they shot furiously upon us, and made their approaches, which made us spend very much of our little store, being not above twenty-five or twenty-six barrels of powder, at the beginning of the siege. Yet the Earl of Newcastle sent a trumpet to offer us conditions, which I accepted, so they were honourable for us to take, and safe for the inhabitants.
>
> We sent two captains to treat with him, and agreed to

a cessation during that time; but he continued working still; whereupon I sent forth the commissioners again, suspecting a design of attempting something upon us. They returned not till eleven a clock at night, and then with a slight answer. Whilst they were delivering it to us, we heard great shooting of cannon and muskets; all run presently to the works, which the enemy was storming.

Here for three quarters of an hour was very hot service, but at length they retreated. They made a second attempt, but were also beaten off; after this, we had not above one barrel of powder left, and no match. I called the officers together, where it was advised and resolved to draw off presently, before it was day, and to retreat to Leeds, by forcing a way, which we must do, for they had surrounded the town.

Orders were dispatched, and speedily put in execution. The foot commanded by Colonel Rogers was sent out, through some narrow lanes, and they were to beat up the dragoons' quarters, and so go on to Leeds. I, myself, with some other officers, went with the horse, which were not above fifty, in a more open way. I must not here forget my wife, who ran the same hazard with us in the retreat, and with as little expression of fear; not from any zeal, or delight in the war, but through a willing and patient suffering of this undesirable condition.

I sent two or three horsemen before, to discover what they could of the enemy; who presently returned, and told us there was a guard of horse close by us. Before I had gone forty paces, the day beginning to break, I saw them up the hill above us, being about 300 horse. I, with some twelve more, charged them, Sir Hen. Fowles, Major General Gifford, myself, and three more, brake through; Captain Mudd was slain, and the rest of our horse being close by, the enemy fell upon them, and soon routed them, taking most of them prisoners, and among whom was my wife, the officer Will. Hill, behind whom she rid, being taken.

I saw this disaster, but could give no relief; for after I was got through, I was in the enemies rear alone, those who had charged through with me, went on to Leeds, thinking I had done so too; but I was unwilling to leave my company, and stayed till I saw there was no more in my power to do, but to be taken prisoner with them. I then retired to Leeds.

The like disaster fell among the foot, that went the other way, by a mistake, for after they had marched a little way, the van fell into the dragoons' quarters, clearing their way; but through a cowardly fear, he that commanded these men, being in the rear, made them face about, and march again into the town, when the next day they were all taken prisoners, only eighty, or thereabout of the front that got through, came all to Leeds, mounted on horses which they had taken from the enemy, where I found them when I came thither, which was some joy to them all, concluding I was either slain, or taken prisoner. (Lord Fairfax's *Memoirs*, pp. 46-50.)

Lady Fairfax was immediately sent by the Earl of Newcastle to her husband's quarters at Hull.

The Duchess's account of her husband's victory is evidently rather partial. She says that in June 1643, Newcastle, after having recruited his army marched towards Bradford, taking Howley-house on his way. They had brought "a vast number of musquetiers" out of Lancashire into Bradford. They went out to "a place full of hedges, called Atherton Moor, near to their garrison at Bradford;" Newcastle had, according to his wife's statement, a much smaller number of musquetiers, but was, she confesses, superior in horse. The Parliamentarians had good ground, and Newcastle's horse could not act for a long time:

> The foot of both sides on the right and left wings, encountered each other, who fought from hedge to hedge, and for a long time together overpowered and got ground of my Lord's foot, almost to the environing of his can-

non.

At last the horse attack them furiously, and some cannons being brought to bear on them with effect, they were routed; "those that escaped fled into their garrison at Bradford, amongst whom was also their general of the horse." (Sir Thomas Fairfax.) "After this, my Lord caused his army to be rallied, and marched in order that night before Bradford, with an intention to storm it the next morning. But the enemy that were in the town, it seems, were so discomfited, that the same night they escaped all various ways, and amongst them the said general of the horse."

It is quite clear, from Fairfax's account, compared with the *narrative* of Joseph Lister, that the Duchess of Newcastle was altogether wrong in stating that Bradford was taken the night after the battle of Atherton Moor. According to the Micro-Chronicon, the battle of 'Adwalton' was fought on the 30th of June, and Bradford was taken [in the night of] 2nd July.

———

At last a little army was formed, and got to the works and Gentries, but Sir Thomas Fairfax was forced another way, and so got to Halifax, with those few horse he had left, and he came to Bradford the next day; whose coming did greatly hearten the soldiers in the town; but alas! their joy was but short, the enemies were encamped at Bowling-Hall, so near the town on that side of it, that they planted some of their guns against the town, and some against the steeple, and gave it many a sad shake. The townsmen had hung wool-packs at the side of the steeple, and they cut the cords with their spiteful shot, and shouted full loudly when the pack fell down.

But on the Lord's-Day morning they beat a drum for a parley, and all that day (during the parley) they spent in removing their guns, just against the heart of the town, and into the mouth of it, into that end of the town called Good-Man-End, and also brought their army, both horse and foot, round about the town, no way being left of making their escape, and but few men in the town, and most of the arms and ammunition, being either lost, or left at Adwalton, and no match but what was made of untwisted cords dipped in oil.

And about the going down of the sun, the parley broke up, and off goes their guns, before the inhabitants were aware; and at the first shot they killed three men sitting on a bench, and all that night it was almost as light as day, with so many guns firing continually. So in the dead of the night the captains were called, and a council sat to resolve what was best to be done; it was presently resolved that the soldiers should be told they must all shift for themselves, only the officers were resolved to make a desperate adventure of breaking through the enemies' army, at the upper end of the town, and all that were willing might forthwith repair thither.

But because my Lord had no garrison nearer than Hull, and no use could be made of their arms for want of match, and powder, he would not command the soldiers to go along with him, but leave them to their own choice, what to do, for he saw they could no longer keep the town, and so they did, and broke through, and made their way by dint of sword, and so got away towards Hull. And among the rest my godly master, Mr. Sharp, was one that broke through, and yet, he having no mind to go so far as Hull, he then left the army, and took toward Lancashire, and got that day to a town called Coln, where he stayed some time.

But oh! what a night and morning was that in which Bradford was taken! what weeping, and wringing of hands! none expecting to live any longer than till the enemies came into the town, the Earl of Newcastle having charged his men to kill all, man, woman, and child, in the town, and to give them all Bradford quarter, for the brave Earl of Newport's sake. However, God so ordered it, that before the town was taken, the Earl gave a different order, (*viz.*) that quarter should be given to all the townsmen.

It was generally reported that something came on the Lord's Day night, and pulled the clothes off his bed several times, and cried out with a lamentable voice, "pity poor Bradford!" that then he sent out his orders that neither man, woman, nor child, should be killed in the town; and that then the apparition which had so disturbed him, left him, and went away; but this I assert not as a certain truth; but this is true, that they slew very few in the town. Some desperate fellows wounded several persons, that died of their wounds afterwards; but I think not more than half a score were slain; and that was a wonder, considering what hatred and rage they came with against us. But we were all beholden to God, who tied their hands, and saved our lives.

My master being gone, I sought for my mother, and having found her, she, and I, and my sister, walked in the street, not knowing what to do, or which way to take. And as we walked up the street, we met a young gentleman (called David Clarkson) leading a horse.[11] My mother asked him where he had been with that horse. Says he, "I made an essay to go with my brother Sharp, and the army, who broke through the enemies leaguer; but the charge was so hot I came back again, and now I know not what to do."

Then I answered, and said, "pray mother, give me leave to go with David, for I think I can lead him a safe way;" for being born in that town, I knew all the bye-ways about it.

David also desired her to let me go with him, so she begged a blessing on me, and sent me away, not knowing where we could be safe. So away we went, and I led him to a place called the Sill-bridge, where a foot company was standing; yet I think they did not see us, so we ran on the right hand of them, and then waded over the water, and hearing a party of horse come down the lane, towards the town, we laid us down in the side of the corn, and they perceived us not. It being about daybreak, we

---

11. "David Clarkson." This "young gentleman" was fellow and tutor of Clare Hall, Cambridge, and is remarkable as well for his own worth and learned writings, as for having been tutor to Tillotson. See Birch's *Life of Tillotson*, 8vo. 1753, p. 4. He was son of Robert Clarkson of Bradford, and brother of Mary Clarkson, who married John Sharp of Horton. See Thoresby's *Duc. Leod.* p. 36. He was turned out of the living of Mortlock by the non-conformity act. See Calamy, Account p. 667. Many of his practical and controversial writings are in print.

staid here as long as we durst for being discovered, it beginning to be light.

Well, we got up, and went in the shade of the hedge, and then looking about us, and hoping to be past the danger of the leaguer, we took to the high way, intending to go to a little town called Clayton; and having waded over the water, we met with two men that were troopers, and who had left their horses in the town, and hoped to get away on foot, and now they and we walked together, and hoped we had escaped all danger, and all on a sudden a man on horseback from towards the beacon had espied us and came riding towards us, and we, like poor af-frighted sheep, seeing him come fast towards us, with a drawn sword in his hand, we foolishly kept together, and thought to save ourselves by running. Had we scattered from one another, he had but got one of us.

We all got into a field; he crossed the field and came to us, and as it pleased God, being running by the hedge side, I espied a thick holly tree, and thought perhaps I might hide myself in this tree, and escape, so I crept into it, and pulled the boughs about me, and presently I heard them cry out for quarter. He wounded one of them, and took them all prisoners, and said, "there were four of you, where is the other?" but they knew not, for I being the last and least of them, was not missed; so he never looked after me more; but I have often thought since how easily we might have knocked him down, had we but had courage; but alas! we had none.

Having passed this day, skulking in the hedges, when it was dark I betook myself to travelling towards Coln, the place to which I thought my good master was gone, and there I found him, and glad we were to see each other. He enquired of me (because I stayed in Bradford longer than he did) what was done, and what I knew I told him; and in the conclusion he asked me if I knew the way, and durst go back again to Bradford and see if I could find my dame, and bring him word where she was, and how she did, and what was done in the town; "yes Master," said I, "if you please to send me, I am ready and willing to go."

So in the morning he sent me away, and to Bradford I came, and found some few people left, but most of them scattered and fled away. I lodged in a cellar that night, but oh! what a change was made in the town in three days time! nothing was left to eat or drink, or lodge upon, the streets being full of chaff', and feathers, and meal, the enemies having emptied all the town of what was worth carrying away, and were now sat down and encamped near Bowling-Hall, and there kept a fair and sold the things that would sell.

In the morning I crept out of the poor cellar where I lay, and walked in the street to enquire after my dame; at last I heard that she and my mother were both well, and gone the day before to Halifax.

The women were gathering meal in the streets; for when the soldiers found anything that was better than meal, they emptied the sacks, and put that which was better into them, so that there was good store of meal thrown out, both in the houses and streets. But here I stayed not, but went after my dame to Halifax, and there I found her, and delivered my message from my master, and gave her some gold that he sent her, and what information I could: so she sent me back to my master, and desiring him to direct her what to do, and desired me to come back again to her. So away I went, and gave my master an account of all I could. "Well," said he, "dare thou go back again to thy dame?"

"Yes, Sir," said I, "if you please to send me."

"Go, then," said he, "and tell thy dame to go back home; and go thou with her, and go to the camp, and buy a cow, to give you some milk, and get the grass mowed, and help to get the hay; and perhaps the enemy will be called away shortly, and you may be quiet."

He also gave me money to buy other necessaries. Upon this I returned to my dame, and away we went to Horton, to my master's own house, and I went and bought a cow in the forenoon, and brought her home; but before night other soldiers came, and took her away from us, and carried her back to the camp.

Another day she sent me to buy another cow, and so they

did likewise by that. Then she sent me to my master again, to let him know what we had done, and to ask his counsel further. He was then much troubled, and desired me to go back, and tell my dame that he was wholly at a loss to know what to advise her to do, but must leave her to find out her own way, and act accordingly: and for himself, he was now determined to remove to Manchester; and if he could find out Sir Thomas Fairfax, he would fall in with him, and go with the army, for he could not stay in that place as he was; and "as for thee, Joseph," says he, "I would have thee to go and stay with thy dame, till I come home, and then I promise to teach thee thy trade; but if thou hadst rather be set free, I leave thee to thy liberty, and to make thy own choice, and I will be satisfied, for I know not what will become of me."

"Well, then, Sir," said I, "I chuse to be at liberty, and shall seek for another master."

"It shall be so," said he, "only go home, and tell thy dame what I say, and what thou and I have concluded upon."

"Yes Sir," said I, "that I purpose to do."

So I took my leave of him, and turned to my dame, who did sadly resent the tidings that I brought her; and in a short time afterwards I took my leave of her, and enquired for another master, and got one at Sowerby, in Halifax vicarage, where I lived very comfortably all the time of my apprenticeship, in which time I had many convictions, yet I made a wicked shift to stifle them all. But I remember one exercise-day at Halifax, I was hearing one Mr. Briscoe preach from that scripture in the *1st Peter*, 2. 12. last clause: *that they may by your good works, which they shall behold, glorify God in the day of visitation.*

He laid down this doctrine that all persons that live under the gospel have a day of gracious visitation; and he said this is but a day, and may be lost, and if once lost, all the angels in heaven and saints upon earth could not help that soul, and to prove this truth, he brought that scripture in the *15th Jeremy*, 1st: *Then said the Lord unto me, though Moses and Samuel stood before me, yet my mind could not be towards this people.* This fell upon me like a thunder-bolt.

I went home with a troubled heart: And whose case can this be, but mine, thought I; and if God's mind cannot be towards me I am undone for ever; and in this state I remained many a long day. The time of my apprenticeship was now just out, and I went and tabled with one Isaac Platts, about two years, and traded for myself, and my soul-trouble began to wear off, as I was taken up with other things.

It so fell out, that my master's daughter, and I, had formed a connexion, with my master's approbation, and having entertained an affection for her, it took up too much of my time. This circumstance, together with my mother's disapprobation of the match, and especially my fears that she would prove too much like her mother, who was a woman of the most frozen ill-contrived temper that, I think, I ever knew; always fretting and quarrelling with my master, who was, surely, a man of the most sweet and obliging behaviour that could be imagined; so that I thought how shall I ever bear such heart-breaking work, as I saw frequently in our family, this lay with such pressing weight upon my spirit, especially when the time drew near that we should put it to an issue, that I durst not proceed, but broke off the match as quietly as I could, to the great dissatisfaction both of the girl, my master, and dame, though I never durst tell my dame that the cause of it lay so much at the door of her unworthy carriage to her husband.

In a little time I fell sick, and so came home to my mother, at Bradford, and then were my soul-trouble and fears revived, and were more sharp and piercing than before; and my apprehensions of the approach of death, made the same cut more deep. In this agony I lay some weeks oppressed under the burden of gilt, and a death-threatening distemper. Yet at last God was pleased to step in with light, and love, and clear satisfaction; and I could not hold, but cried out aloud, "He is come! He is come!" which made the affliction on my body the more light and easy, the remainder of the time that I was under it, and in this sweet sense of comfort I walked many days; yet had I many clouds, fears, and doubts afterwards.

Being recovered of this distemper, I returned to my old land-lords, and paid off some debts I had contracted, and disposed of what goods I had of my own; and not having much left, I came to Bradford, and told my dear mother what case I was in with respect to my worldly affairs, and that I had traded what I had away.

"And what thinkest thou to do now, then?" said she.

"Why," said I, "mother, with your good leave, I will go to London; perhaps I may there get a place to serve some gentle-man." But this she was not at first willing for me to do. However she called in some good men, and desired they would first seek the Lord for my direction and guidance in this affair; which they willingly did; and in the close of the day, having laid all circum-stances together, they gave their opinion, though it was a place where I might be exposed to temptation, and be in great danger of being led into sin, yet on the other hand, there were many godly persons there, and choice religious ordinances; and that God might have a design of mercy towards me.

So they moved for my going, which pleased me very well. We next considered which would be the best manner of travelling thither; and it was resolved I should go with a carrier: So I went to Sowerby, to a London carrier, a good-conditioned man, to know when he went, and how to meet with him. It happened that a young man, of my acquaintance, was designed to go with him that journey, and glad we were both of going together.

The day being come, my dear mother sent me away, though she was loath to part with me, and told me I might live well enough upon my land at Bradford, being about ten pounds a year.

However, I left her, and my two sisters, to meet the carrier, and my fellow-traveller, at the end of the first day's journey; and having so done, we travelled together to the city.

Jonathan Walsh (for so was this young man called) went, as I did, with an intent to serve some gentleman. Being come thither, and while we were in the inn with the carrier, God so ordered it, that the carrier was in a room drinking with some persons for whom he carried goods, and there happened to be two gentlemen enquiring about a servant to wait upon one of them.

Says the carrier, "there came two young men up with me that want places; and I durst be bound for one of them."

So they desired him to call for that which he commended. He came to the stairs-head, and called for me. I went, not knowing the meaning of it, and being come into the room, one of the gentlemen asked me if I wanted a place of service.

"Yes Sir," said I, "if I can light upon a good place."

Says he "what employment are you for?"

"Sir," said I, "I may chuse my master, but will submit to any employment that a good man will please to set me to."

"You say well," say he, "will you come and take a trial what sort of a master I am, and what kind of a house I keep, and what your business will be?"

"Sir," said I, "I am a stranger here, and desire to gratify my curiosity a few days, and then, if God permit, I will come."

Then the other man spoke, and said, "this gentleman that hath been speaking to you is my father-in-law, and we live near together, and I want a man as well as he, you therefore need not be discouraged; but come, as you say, to my father's, and it is likely one of us may give you content."

"Well, Sir," said I, "I am a little surprised at this unlooked-for providence, at my entrance into the city, and among strangers, and I purpose to come on Monday, for tomorrow is a public fast-day, which I intend to keep, and observe as well as I can, and the three next days I shall look about me in the city."

I thought the son took more notice of what I said than the father did, and I liked him the better of the two; yet I thought to make trial of the father first.

Having proceeded thus far, I took my leave of them for the present, and went to look for my fellow traveller, but he was gone into the city, so I did not see him anymore.

The next day being a fast-day, I went to Aldermanbury, where Mr. Calamy was pastor, and two preached, and three prayed; and

Mr. Simeon Ash concluded with prayer.[12] Well, thought I, God hath brought me into Goshen, a rich and fat pasture! The rest of the week I spent in going to White-Hall, the Exchange, and the Tower, as I wished to see everything that was worth seeing; and on the Lord's-Day, I went to hear at Mr. Calamy's place again, where he and Mr. Ash preached, for Mr. Ash was an assistant to Mr. Calamy; and in the afternoon he went to Hackney, and preached with Dr. Spurstow.

So on the Monday I went to Hackney to my old gentleman, and when I came there it proved to be a school for young gentlewomen to learn to play and dance and sing, which did not at all suit with me, however I shuffled over three or four days as well as I could, and then told the old gentleman that I thought I must leave him, which he took ill, and told me my business would be easy; all I had to do was only to go into the city, and to carry or bring any message from the parents of the young gentlewomen, that were scholars there; on the Lord's-Day to carry bibles to church, and bring them home at night; and for my wages he would give me five pounds a year, and the vails of the house would be as much more.

But that contented me not, though the wages were more than I expected, yet I could not sit down with the employment of the house, and there being no family duty morning nor evening. So when he could not persuade me to stay, he desired me to go to his son's; I had got a little acquainted with him during my few day's stay; so I took my leave of the old man, and went to the young man's house.

I found the master a very good man, but the mistress was as bad; she opposed praying what she could, and would always be in bed both morning and evening at prayer, which was a great affliction to my good master; there were also maids in the house who were such swearers and cursers, and enemies to everything

---

12. Edmund Calamy and Simon Ash were very eminent preachers during the Commonwealth and Protectorate. Calamy was incumbent of Aldermanbury; and Ash was one of the Cornhill lecturers. They were ejected from their benefices at the Restoration. For an account of them see Dr. Calamy's Account of the Ejected or Silenced Ministers.

that was good, that they frighted me; alas! thought I, surely I have got into the suburbs of hell; and it will be my wisdom to haste away from hence, and if I cannot find some family better than these, it will be best for me to think of returning to Bradford again. So I told my master one morning that I thought I must leave him.

"No!" says he, "by no means, you shall not leave me, what is the matter?"

"Sir," said I, "I cannot like, and I pray you, give me leave to go away."

He then pressed me to tell him the reason, and if anything in his family was not to my satisfaction, it should be amended.

"Sir," said I, "it is not meet for me to reproach your family, but I shall venture to say so far, that though I was born in Yorkshire, in the cold north quarter of England, yet the worship of God was set up there, and religion and holiness were held in esteem, and profaneness and wickedness discountenanced; and I looked for better things in this warm southern climate than yet I find, and if all families be like those I have already met with, I purpose to return to the place from whence I came, for I think there is more of the power of godliness to be met with there. But, sir, I hope you will pardon my plain dealing, I do not mean to reflect upon you; I must needs say, I love your person, and your conversation; but your family does not consist of such persons as I was bred up amongst, and therefore I beg leave of you to go away."

He persuaded me to stay a few days longer, and so I did, and then we parted. He wished me good speed, gave me seven shillings, and I returned to the inn, where we first alighted, but the man who came with me was gone to Yorkshire again, not finding any encouragement, and I knew not then but I must follow him the next time the carrier came up to town.

But one day I thought I would take another walk to see Westminster and White-Hall, so I walked over the park to St. James's, and there found a Major and a Captain exercising their men; the Captain drew off his men and they marched away. I then drew near to the Major, and watched them exercise; I perceived the Major took some notice of me, and by and by he comes walking up to me, and asked me if I had any mind to be a soldier.

"No sir," said I, "I have no military spirit."

"Well," said he, "what brings you to the city; for I see you are a countryman?"

"Sir," said I, "my desire is to serve some gentleman, if I could meet with a good man, and a good family."

"Well," said he, "come along with me to my quarters."

So he ordered another officer to dispose of the soldiers, and went with me. He then asked me several questions, and at last told me that there had been a gentleman with him lately that was enquiring if any of his soldiers had a mind to leave the army and betake themselves to a private place: "But," said he, "I knew of none then, but perhaps I may see him again shortly, and if he be not provided, tell me where you lodge, and I will inform you."

So I thanked him, and went away, scarcely believing that I should hear any more of him; but the providence of God had a hand in it which I was not aware of, for the next morning but one, by that time I had well come down from my bed chamber, comes a soldier and enquires for me, and being come to him, he told me his Major had sent him for me, to come to his quarters at White-Hall, but he told me nothing of the business. So I went with him, and came to the Major, and he asked me if I had got a place.

"No sir," said I, "I have not."

"Well," said he, "the gentleman of whom I spake to you the other day, was with me yesterday, and if you please to go and speak with him, my sergeant shall go along with you to the custom-house, and there you will find him."

"Sir," said I, "you shew great kindness to a stranger, I heartily thank you."

So the sergeant brought me to the gentleman, (his name was Mr. Rye,) and told him his major had sent him with me who was the man they had talked about last night. Mr Rye took us to

211

a tavern, called for sack, and having well drunk, he sent the sergeant away, and bade me come to the custom-house about four o'clock, and wait on him, and I should know more of his mind; so I did, and after I had stopped some time, he came from his business, and away he led me quite out of the city to Islington Fields; and then he began to talk with me and told me it was not himself, but his mother-in-law, that wanted a man.

"But be not dismayed," said he, "for she is a good woman, and you will have a good place, if you stop with her. At present her summer-house is in Highgate, whither we are going."

Then he asked me some questions, as, what I knew of a work of grace upon my heart? what I thought of many scriptures, and what my judgment was as to different things in religion? was I a Baptist, or a Presbyterian, or a Congregational, or what was I? to which I answered according to my knowledge and apprehension. At last we came to the house. He led me into the kitchen, and he went himself into the hall, where his mother and his wife were; and after salutation, I heard him say, "Mother, I have brought you a new man."

"That is well," said she, "if he be a good one."

"I hope well of him," says he, "however you may make a trial of him."

So by and by I was called into the hall, and the old gentlewoman asked me what countryman I was.

"A Yorkshire man," said I, "a widow woman's son there."

"What occasioned your coming to London, and leaving your mother, being a widow?"

"Truly," said I, "having served my apprenticeship I thought to become a tradesman, and hoped to live upon it, but I went back, and saw I could not buy and sell and get gain, as other men did, and I was afraid of running into debt, and so in good time gave over, and came to London with a design to put myself in the situation of a servant, if it would please the Lord to dispose of me into some good family."

"Well" said she, "you and I are strangers, are you willing to stay here a month, and we shall have a trial of each other, and if

I like you not, then I will pay you well for that month, and so we shall part?"

"Yes," said I, "your proposal pleaseth me well."

So I went into the kitchen again, till supper time, and made observation of the man that she had, and how he did, and I thought I could do as he did well enough.

On the morrow I told Mr Rye, that had I known my mistress had a man, I should not have been willing to come. Says he, "you need not be troubled at that, for my mother has given him warning to provide himself another place; he is so in love with strong drink and bad company, that his stay has been burdensome to my mother long, but that she could not meet with another man to her mind."

So I was satisfied, neither did the man appear to be angry with me at all; thus did God in his kind providence provide for me by strangers. In two days time the man went away, and in the mean time my mistress had told me what my employment should be, (*viz.*) to wait upon her at table, bring the tablecloth and spread it, lay on the trenchers, salt, and bread; then set her a chair, and bring the first dish to the table, then desire her to sit down, and so wait till she called for beer or any other thing; then to fetch another dish and clean the trenchers, and so wait upon her till she had done, then to take off and draw the table, and carry away her seat, and then the two maids and myself to feed on what she left; and to wait on her to hear sermons almost every day.

I always wrote the sermon, and repeated it, and as I did at noon so I did at night at supper, and then all my work was done, and this was my business day after day. Thus God provided for me time enough and rich and fat ordinances, for she would hear the best preachers; O! what cause have I to wonder at the merciful providence of God in a strange place!

Well, a month being run about, Mr. Rye being at home, for he stayed mostly with Oliver Cromwell and godly officers of the army, and did but come home on Saturday night, my mistress called me into the hall, and said, "Come, Joseph, now the time that we appointed for trial is over, how do you like?"

"Alas! mistress," said I, "it is a small matter how I like, the thing upon which depends, my going, or staying, is how you are satisfied with me."

"Well," says she, "in a few words I must tell you, I like you well, and shall not be willing to part with you, if reasonable wages will please you."

"I am glad of that," said I, "for I like so well of your person and my employment, that you shall see I will not be willing to leave your service: and as for wages, prove me a year if I so long live, and at the end thereof give me what you please."

"You say well and like a servant that intends to be faithful, and you shall fare no worse for leaving it to me, only" says she, "I expect that you should be finer in your apparel, for you see, you and I must go amongst many great persons."

"Well," said I, "my inclination is to be fine enough, if I had wherewith to maintain it."

"O!" says she, "I will maintain you not like your mother's son, but as my servant;" upon which she bid me call the maid, who being come, she ordered her to bring the apparel to her that she had fetched; so she gave me a hat, bands, doublet, coat, breeches, stockings, and shoes, a cloak, and half a dozen pairs of cuffs, saying, "whatever I give you at the year's end, you shall have these things freely given you."

So I gave her hearty thanks, and went about my business, and thus the providence of God ordered things for my good. Here I had an easy life, brave ordinances, a great deal of time, and ten pounds wages, and many great gifts both from my mistress and Mr. Rye. God was pleased many a time to meet with my heart in ordinances, both by way of conviction and consolation; but above all the rest, under Mr. Collings, from that scripture in the *2nd. Galatians*, 20th. *who loved me and gave himself for me*; he here spoke of the freeness of Christ's love to vile sinners, yea to the very worst of sinners, and three things:

First, that is free love that was never deserved, and again, secondly, that is free love that was never desired, and thirdly, finally, that is free love that can never be requited. O! how these particulars suited my case, as if it had been fitted for none but me, and how did it soften and melt my hard heart. I scarce knew how I got home.

In this comfortable state of mind I went many a day; also, met with something encouraging under Mr. Griffith,[13] and Mr. Vening.[14] I had a brave time of it during my stay in the city, and I heartily wished it might have lasted long; but having served a little short of three years, to my mistress and my own satisfaction, my dear mother grew impatient of my stay, and sent letter after letter, importuning me to come to Bradford again; so I did at last tell my mistress, and shewed her some of the letters, which grieved her much, being loath to part with me. She offered me very great and kind offers to persuade me to stay with her, but at last she submitted, and gave me leave to go, but would often tell me, that none other but my mother should have got me from her.

I left her, and met with a friend who solicited me to go to one Alderman Andrews, who offered to give me ten pounds a year, from the report he had of me, and if he liked me he would not stick to give me twenty pounds a year; and whenever I left him he would promote me to some place of trust and profit; but my duty to my mother carried me against the stream and tide of pleasure, ease, and profit, so that I came down to my native soil again, having been wonderfully favoured by divine providence, and had got as much money as bought me a house of Mr. Home.

And thither I removed my dear mother, where she, and I, and one sister, lived together some time; but afterwards Samuel Bayley, a worthy man and a good friend of my good mother's, by his solicitations with her had prevailed to get her consent that I should go into the north, to a place called Gretam Hospital to be

13. Probably Mr. George Griffith who was at the Charter House, and preached a week-day Lecture at St. Bartholomew's near the Exchange. See *Calamy, Account*, &c. p. 57.
14. Ralph Venning, M. A. of Emanuel College, Cambridge, Lecturer of St. Olave's, Southwark, a popular preacher of the time. See *Calamy, Account*, &c. p. 22.

a steward for his wife's father, one Captain Askwith,[15] who had a place given him there worth 400 or 500 pounds a year, which the parliament had given him for what he had laid out in raising a troop of soldiers, and maintaining them in the wars.

To this place and employment I went, and I bless God I did discharge my place and trust faithfully and to great satisfaction, so that my master himself said that he never saw a finer account in all his life. Here I stayed scarcely two years. It is true I had power and authority enough, having all the servants at my command, and all that was my master's to dispose of.

All the people in the town were my master's tenants, and I in a remote sense set over them to receive rents, bargain with them for renewing of leases, repairs of houses, and what fell out any way to dispose and order. But, O! what a world of business had I to go through, to go to markets and fair, to buy and sell cattle and corn, some thousands of bushels of all kinds of corn, to sell to the merchants to go to the sea, all the summer-time especially, my hands being full all the day, and all that I did on the day I wrote down before I went to bed, so that I got very little sleep.

I remember one night I was writing at a little chamber table, and had a wax candle burning, and dropt asleep. But, by a good providence, one of the maids being late up, and coming near my chamber door as she went to bed, thought there was a greater light in my chamber than usual: so she called upon me, and I presently awaked, and saw my candle all on a flame, and it had made some impression on the table; yet I quickly put it out, and prevented any further harm, or danger.

Bless the Lord, my soul, for this merciful providence! It became an effectual warning to me ever after; so that when, at any time, I found myself inclined to sleep, stepping up and taking two or three turns in the chamber, I could shake it off, and go

---

15. Greatham Hospital is in the parish of Greatham, county of Durham, endowed in 1272 by Peter de Montfort. The Hospital presents to the Church. Captain Simon Askew (as he is called in some documents) was appointed Master in 1653, by the Parliament. (*Commons' Journals*, vol. 7. p. 328.) At the Restoration he accepted the Breda pardon, and signed a declaration to that effect at Hartlepool, 8th June, 1660, in which document he spells his name Ask with, as in Lister's narrative.

to my business again.

As we had but poor preaching here, I thought of what I had at London, and frequently thought of going there again; and knowing a merchant at Hartlepool, who had a ship, and traded much to London with corn and butter, (it being a very fruitful country, and I sold him great quantities of corn.) I consulted with him, and told him my purpose was to go to London again. He said he would take me in his ship for nothing, and, if the wind was fair, we might reach London in two or three days. But I could not get my mind to it without my mother's leave.

All my thoughts of this nature were, in a short time, at an end, for I had one day occasion to go to Hartlepool to receive a good quantity of money of the merchant above-mentioned; but it proved to be a day wherein the head officers of that city[16] met about' some weighty matters, and this merchant was mayor that year, and staid there late, and then I had to receive my money after he came, which made me late in the evening.

Near the city was a little arm of the sea, that went up into the land; it was low when the tide was gone in, that one might wade it, and it would but take one to the knees; but when the tide was up, a good large vessel might ride there. Now had it been light, as it was dark, I could have known by stoops whether I could ride it safely or no; and by riding two miles about, I might have gone and not come in the water. I sat on horseback at the side, debating what to do. I knew that the way was exceeding deep and dirty, and I should be starved in going that way, and my head ached very much.

On the other hand I concluded the tide was so far out that it was very dangerous to venture over. Yet, thought I, could I but get through, though with difficulty, if I get but to the land I may gallop home in a little time. Yet had I many fears upon me, for I had one time before this ventured when the tide was high, but going back, and so weak, and in the day time; yet then I was taken off my horse, and laid on my back in my cloak, and

16. Hartlepool is an ancient corporate town in the county of Durham. It is singular that Lister should call it a city.

it bore me up, and the seamen seeing me, came quickly with a boat, and saved my life. what a hand of mercy did appear in this salvation! One would think I should never have forgotten it, and yet within half a year's time I made this foolish and desperate adventure again.

Well, in I went, but by the time I had got fifteen or twenty yards into the water, I would have given a kingdom, if I had had one, to have been back again, but durst not, by any means, turn my horse about; if I had, surely I had been lost, every tide did flow so high, that my boots and pockets were full. Great streams went over the horse's neck, and behind me, over the saddle.

Now, thought I, my life is gone, my horse can never be able to swim to the far side, and I expected that every wave that came rolling upon us, would drive us down, and I had no human help, no apparent means to save our lives, only as the waves came upon us, I endeavoured to bear up my horse's head and breast as well as I could against them, lest, coming full upon his broad-side, they should force him down, and overwhelm both him and me.

Then I cried unto the Lord, who can do everything; and I thought, though I be in the sea, I am not in the whale's belly; and if I was, yet God could command deliverance for me; so I depended upon his ability to save me; and though I expected every minute to be cast away by every succeeding wave, yet the Lord had me in his hand all the while, and though my fears began to sink my spirits, yet God enabled the horse to grapple with the flood, and swim safe to shore: yet even then I was so overwhelmed with affright that, though I was safely delivered and upon dry land, yet could I hardly believe it, or tell where I was, though God's almighty arm had brought me safe to the dry land.

O! what a wonderful deliverance was this! Bless the Lord, O my soul, and all that is within me praise his holy name. I hasted home in a sad bath, and sent a man to take good care of the horse. I called one of the maids to warm me a shirt, another to warm my bed, and a third to get me something hot to drink, hoping to secure me from harm; so to bed I went, and got some little sleep. But in the morning I was so sick and ill that I could not rise, and my food began to be disagreeable to me, and that day, and the next night, my appetite and sleep departed from me.

The day after that I sent my water to a physician, who sent me word he could make no judgment of my case, but I might send my water to him the next day, and he would give me his thoughts upon it; but then, also, he said he could not tell what my disorder should be, except the person had been under some sad overpowering fear. All this time he knew nothing of my being in the water. But I knew my danger and fear had been great, almost too great for me to bear.

Well, in a short time, I fell into a violent fever, in which, after I had laid some weeks in great extremity, and the doctor ordering me nothing but some easy cordial things, I desired him to give me a bill, for I purposed employing another man, for though I was not against cordials for relieving and strengthening nature, yet I thought it very proper to have some working physic that might be likely to weaken and remove the distemper, which he was not willing to give me.

So, having paid him off, I sent to a physician at Durham, twelve miles off. He was a good man, I believe, and they said a young convert. His name was Doctor Tunstall. He sent me something by my messenger, and said he would come tomorrow and see me, which he did: He first let me blood, and then gave me what he thought proper; and God so blessed his prescriptions, that I did soon recover; but one very warm day, I desired to be helped down the stairs; and being down, I longed to go into the garden, and did so a few minutes, but soon repented my folly, for next morning I was confined to my bed, and much worse than before. I sent to the doctor again, and when he came, and had seen, and consulted with me a little, he was much discouraged, concluding my case far more dangerous than it was before: yet I desired him to do his best for me, and the will of the Lord be done.

I now lay long in a languishing condition, expecting nothing but death; and being easy, and well satisfied about my future state, was borne up comfortably. But one day he told my master's daughter, that if I had any friends or relations that would desire to see me alive, it was needful to let them know immediately, for he despaired of my life.

"Oh! Sir," says she, "he hath an own mother, but she is three-score miles off, or near it."

"Alas!" says he, "I fear he will be gone before she can see him."

However, she sent a man with all speed to Bradford, to my dear and tender mother, and she, and a brother-in-law that I had, came that long and tedious journey to see me.

She found me alive, but I did not know her; yet in two days I was a little better, and knew my dear mother; and I believe it did me much good, and helped on my recovery, to have her with me, forever afterwards I was better, but was brought exceeding low. After all this I fell into an ague, and shaked every day for twelve weeks. Then the doctor told me that unless my own country air would be of use to recover me, I was a dead man: so, as soon as I could conveniently, I resolved to try if, by short and easy journies, I might possibly get home.

I took my leave of all friends at Gretam, and rode upon an easy going horse, and two men to attend me; and though I was like an anatomy, and much afraid of riding in the cold air, and shaking by the way, (the last fit of which I had at Knaresborough,) yet at last I got home, and God so graciously ordered it, that there I shook hands with that shaking distemper, and never had the least return of it to this day! what a mercy was it that God then shewed towards me! and how often have I stood wondering at it; for at this very time there was a man that used to trade to Hartlepool weekly, and who had many years known when the water was rideable, and yet he ventured in as I did, and he and his horse were both drowned at the very time when I lay sick; and they told me when the tide was gone in he was found, and the fishes had eaten his hands and face. Now this might have been my case as well as his; and yet he was lost, and I was saved. O that now I could live more to God than ever I did, and prepare for my last summons!

Well, being now got back to Bradford again, among my old Christian friends, they assisted me in returning a thanks-offering to the Lord for his past mercies, for I had been under a series of gracious and merciful providences for a long time past, and had experienced many gracious impressions upon my spirit, and my case was sweetly spoken to by one Mr. Pearson, from that text, in the *13th Luke*, 24. *Strive to enter in at the strait gate, for many, I say unto you, will seek to enter and shall not be able.*

Well, being now got home, and about thirty years of age, I began to think of changing my state by marriage. I therefore desired my dear mother's advice and counsel in this case. I also consulted with and begged the advice of my Christian friends, who commended to me one Sarah Denton, a young virgin, that I did not know. She was the daughter of one John Denton, a gracious holy man.

I contrived to see her, and liked her very well. After this, having my honoured mother's approbation and consent, after some time spent in prayer about it, I waited for an opportunity to speak to her father; So having been at an exercise at Bradford one day, I walked up the town with him, and told him I had heard a good report of his daughter Sarah; and my friends thought she might be a suitable wife for me: so I begged his good leave and consent to speak to her, in order thereunto. He told me he was very willing, and I should be welcome to his house on that errand, whenever I pleased: for which I thanked him; and begged his leave to say a word or two more.

"Well," said he, "say on."

"Well," said I, "though I have heard your daughter much praised, yet I have no personal knowledge of her. If I be not satisfied when I come to discourse with her, will you not be offended, if I let her alone, and proceed no further?"

"No, no," said he, "you shall be welcome to talk with her any time, and act according to your own discretion; and if you go no further in the affair, I shall be satisfied."

Upon this bottom and encouragement I went one afternoon, and the good man was just coming into the fold, so he went back again with me into the house, and I said, "you may easily imagine what makes me be here."

"Well," said he, "you are welcome."

We then walked into the chamber, and he told me his daughter was making hay, but he would go to her, and send her to me; he did so; but she had not the confidence to come to me by herself, but brought her elder sister with her, she herself being a very bashful girl. I conversed with her at this time, and many times afterwards, and found her to be a woman of clear experience, and of a sweet natural temper; and after some time spent in courtship, she and I were well satisfied with each other.

So we told her father and my good mother that we desired them to settle whatever they intended about our portions; upon which John Denton aforesaid, and Joshua Bailey, his brother-in-law, came to my mother's house to consult about it. So after a short preamble my mother told them, that my portion was well known, being those houses and land that lay all together in that end of the town; as for money she knew I had little or none.

"Now brother," said Joshua Bailey, "you must tell Sarah what you will give your daughter."

"Well," says he, "I have, as you know, three daughters, and I purpose to give them all alike, but what that may be I know not; but however above an hundred pounds."

"Well," said my mother, "I do heartily give my son to your daughter, with what he hath, or I can help him to; and I desire you will give your daughter for a wife to my son, heartily and chearfully, and with her person give her for a portion what you please, for I am satisfied; I hope my son will find all that in your daughter that I have desired and looked for."

Then I asked when they would have us put an end to the affair by marriage: this they left to our own choice, when we saw it convenient. So both sides having got something ready, we resolved upon a day. Now at this time there was a law that justices should marry people; so we purposed to be married first by a justice more privately, and went to Halifax to Justice Farrar, none but my bride, and her father, and a brother-in-law, and my uncle and aunt Spencer, that met us there, being with us.

So we brought the bride home to her father's house, and there left her for fourteen days, and then we intended to have the company of our friends; and I having an uncle who was a parson, one Mr. Edward Hill,[17] he offered to give us a wedding sermon, and if I had not known my wife since the justice married us, he would, after the sermon, marry us again; which he did, and after this we settled in our own house; and in a convenient time, my dear mother went to her house also.

With this wife I had two sons, David and Accepted; and though she was not a woman that made any great show in the world to attract people's notice, yet I think she was one of the meekest, wisest, and holiest women that lived in the days of her pilgrimage. Though I might have had a great deal more wealth with another woman, yet I was always abundantly well satisfied in the choice which God had made for me in her. What a mercy was it that the moving providence of God did direct me to this woman, though to me unknown; and ordered all the concurring circumstances to the great satisfaction both of ourselves and our parents on both sides; so great goodness has God manifested towards me!

Having been married something above a year, my wife was safely delivered of a son, whom we called David, and did dedicate him to the Lord's work and service in the Lord's ministry, if he would please to accept of him.

We kept him at school, but greatly to his disadvantage, for some years, by being under bad masters. At last we found him a better master; but I was obliged to table him from home for near five years. Then I got Mr. Noble to examine him, who found him to have been well instructed: but in a little time his master left the school, and became a popish priest. I was then

17. Edward Hill was turned out of the living of Crofton, near Wakefield, in 1662, and died in 1669. See *Calamy, Account*, &c. p. 793.

at a loss where to send him; however, I went to Morley, where Mr. Noble[18] taught a school at that time, and put my son under him. He was a diligent and faithful man, and my son profited much with him, till he was fit for university-learning, but it was not convenient for me to send him to the university at this time, I therefore let him remain another year with his old master, to learn logick; and in that time he became a good proficient in the art, before he went to Mr. Frankland;[19] and when he came from Morley he gave me a very satisfying account of a work of grace upon his heart, which made me hope that God designed him for his own service.

So having previously wrote to Mr. Frankland on the subject, I sent him thither in the seventeenth year of his age,[20] and there he remained about three years and a half, and then Mr. Frankland sent a messenger to inform me my son was fallen sick of a fever, and was dangerously ill. I went to see him, and found him very weak. I staid about a week with him, and all that time he seemed better, and there was a great probability of his recovery. It being the beginning of winter, I thought it best for him to come home, and having ordered for his journey as soon as he should be able to travel, I left him, expecting him to follow

18. Mr. Noble was a self-taught man, who had a school in good report at Morley. He was admitted to the ministry among the Independents, and had the charge of a congregation at Heckmonwicke. He published in 1700, *The Vision and Prophecies of Daniel explained*, &c.

19. Richard Frankland, M.A. who was ejected from the living of Bishop Auckland, by the Uniformity Act, in 1662. He was a man of considerable learning, and being in the prime of life at the time when he was removed from the public ministry, he undertook to conduct an academy for the education of men who were designed for the ministry among the Non-conformists. For this employment he was thought to be singularly well qualified. When Cromwell had formed the design of establishing a college at Durham for the education of ministers and others, Mr. Frankland was one of the persons intended to be the tutors. His own academy was conducted by him from 1669 to the time of his death in 1698, in which period near three hundred persons, most of whom were ministers among the Dissenters, were educated by him. He was not able, owing to the state of the times, to remain in one place, and we find him at Rathmel and Calton in Craven, at Atterclifte near Sheffield, and at Natland near Kendal in Westmoreland. The academy was at the last named place when the two Listers were studying under him.

20. In the seventeenth year of his age. He entered the academy May 12, 1675, according to a MS. list of the pupils.

me; but in fourteen days all our hopes were overturned, for Mr. Frankland sent another messenger to tell me he was worse after I went away, and desired me to go again; which I did, and got thither on Thursday, in the afternoon.

My son was glad to see me, yet feared I should get my death by those long journies, being very cold, frosty, and snowy weather. He was now grown very weak, yet very sensible of his case, and on Saturday, in the evening, he died very comfortably, having only preached three times to great satisfaction, in the one and twentieth year of his age. So I had the happiness to be with him at his death; and wrote a letter to my dear wife that night, sent it to her on the Monday, and on the Tuesday I laid him in his grave at Kendall, and on the Thursday I got home again. I feared this sad stroke would break my wife's heart, but, blessed be God! she bore it with uncommon fortitude.

A long time before this, my wife, and myself, were admitted into the church at Kipping,[21] with which we walked satisfyingly many years. The church called one Mr. Whitehurst to be pastor to them, and he gave content some years; yet he proved, at last, so wedded to the doctrine of the Kingdom of Christ, as he called it, together with other notions, from which he could not be got, that it made a breach in the church: some of his hearers left him, and others walked with him till new matters of dissatisfaction broke out, and then they also left him to provide for himself. He then went to Burlington, and died. After he was gone, the church at Kipping was again united, and walked sweetly together, but could not get a pastor.

I had but two children with my wife, and the name of the

---

21. Kipping is in the West Riding of Yorkshire, a few miles north-west of Bradford. Here was one of the congregations formed by the ejected ministers, which continues to exist at the present day. This tract contains perhaps the best information that can now be collected concerning the early history of the society, which appears to have been more than usually distracted by variety of opinion. Of Mr. Whitehurst, whose doctrine of *The Kingdom of Christ* was probably that better known by the appellation of *The Fifth Monarchy*, there is some account by Dr. Calamy. Of Matthew Smith, who was suspected of being less orthodox than the generality of his brethren in the non-conformist ministry in Yorkshire, there is an account in Watson's *History of the Parish of Halifax*.

younger was Accepted: the reason why I called him so was this; my dear wife had been, for some years, comfortably satisfied about her spiritual welfare, and her interest in Christ, yet at this time the Lord was pleased to carry it towards her so strangely, that she fell under doubts and fears about her interest in him, and relation to him, when she was great with this child.

This cloud and darkness, occasioned by Christ's withdrawing from her, had such an effect upon her, as caused her to walk with an unwonted sadness for most part of three days; but then the Lord was pleased to shine in upon her soul again, to her great satisfaction, and she was filled with peace and joy through believing; in consideration of which, we resolved to give him this name; and God hath made him acceptable to many souls, though it pleased the Lord to afflict him with a great weakness in his joints, so that he could not go without crutches, yet he was enabled to pray and preach two or three hours together upon them, to the awakening, warning, and comforting of many that came to hear him, and attend upon his ministry.

We lived at Bradford about two years, and then an uncle of my dear wife's, called Samuel Bailey, died at Allerton, who, upon his death-bed, desired that we might remove thither, and have one half of the land, and his wife the other half, it being all too much for her to deal with.

So in a short time, as we were desired by all that were concerned in it, we went, there being two houses, and land enough for us both. All the inhabitants shewed great respect to us, and thanked God for bringing us thither. Joshua Bailey, my wife's uncle, abated forty shillings in the year of the rent, for which it had been let before; and one time he saw we had too few cows for the pasture, he went and bought us a new calved cow, and sent his man with her, and gave us her freely.

Another time he brought us a purse with twenty pounds in it; nay, he and his wife too, were open-handed to us every day; which exceeded all expectation, but it lasted to his dying-day. By his will he gave my wife and her heirs forever, the land he lived on, worth twenty pounds a year, and we lived very comfortably many years; during which time my uncle, aunt, and wife's mother died; my father-in-law was left alone, of which he grew weary, and solicited us to come and live with him, and he offered us such profitable terms that we thought of going.

Before the time came in which we purposed to remove, he fell sick, and his master sent for him to heaven, where he longed to be. He would sometimes say to me in the times of God's withdrawments, "O! son, I am not able to bear under God's absence"; and in a few days he died. He was as gracious and holy a man as ever I knew.

My mother died after she had long followed and faithfully served the Lord; being an honour to her profession, a woman of a thousand, every way exemplary in her conversation, a pattern of holiness, an heiress of a kingdom that fades not away, and which she is now possessed of forever. She left me rich in a stock of prayers, the answers to which I am reaping every day.

After the Black Bartholomew act was passed, when so many godly ministers turned non-conformists, and when preaching and praying were such crimes in England, as to incur great fines and imprisonments, we had several houses where we met, as that at Kipping, and John Berry's, and our house, and sometimes at Horton. We had Mr. Ryther one year, and then he had a call to London; sometimes Mr. Root, sen.; Mr. Root, jun.; Mr. Ness; Mr. Marsden; Mr. Coats; Mr. Bailey, and others; and at last we got a man called Mr. Whitehurst, and he became our pastor.[22]

After some years, a difference fell out betwixt him and several of the church members, and they withdrew from him, and I was one of those that did so. And about two years afterwards, we heard of one Mr. Smith, a young man that lived with his father

---

22. All these persons except Mr. Bailey were ministers who had left the Church on the passing of the Act for Uniformity, and whoever is curious to know something of them may consult the writings of Dr. Calamy, who has done ample justice to the ministers excluded by that Act, and performed a most valuable service for the non-conforming body, or at least that small portion of it who are solicitous to know something of the founders of their interest. Mr. Bailey was one of the first persons who entered the non-conforming ministry as a non-conformist. Much was expected from him for he was pious, zealous, rich and hospitable: but he died at an early period of life.

at York, and a man of fine parts. To this man we sent, and desired him to come and preach with us, so he did, and stopped about a month, till we had a proof of him in part, and found he was not altogether of our judgment, yet we dealt plainly and faithfully with him, and gave him an account of the breach that happened amongst us.

We gave him a call to preach the gospel to us, which he accepted. Having been with us about seven or eight years, the good people about Mixenden and Warley invited him to preach with them on some week days, and they began to covet him, and made some offers to him to come and preach every other Lord's-Day with them, which he consented to. I went there winter and summer, many years, but my dear wife was deprived of the means, not being able to travel so far.

Our son Accepted being now fit for university learning, we spoke to Mr. Smith to instruct him, which he was willing to do; knowing him to be a good scholar; he remained with him about three years, and in the last year he broke his thigh, in consequence of which we feared he would not be able to stand to preach, so we purposed to provide a school for him, and built a very convenient room for that purpose; but a neighbouring schoolmaster who pretended much respect and kindness for him, betrayed him into the Spiritual Court at York, by which he was prosecuted, for teaching without a licence, and though he had good abilities, and I had some friends that used their utmost endeavours to obtain a licence for him, yet all would not do, unless he would subscribe and swear against his conscience.

He therefore desisted from his purpose for the present, and gave himself up to the study of the scriptures, the better to prepare himself for the work of the ministry; and about this time Mr. Smith, upon some slight occasion, resolved to leave Kipping, and go to Mixenden, which he did, and in a little time repented, and would have come again, but we had no desire of him, having gone away in such a blameable manner. We got the neighbouring ministers, and others, to supply the place; and after a certain time, the church that used to meet at Kipping, solicited my son to preach there, which he long refused to do upon a double account; first, the great weakness of his body, fearing he would not be able to stand; secondly, the deep sense he had of his own inability for it.

Yet they continued to importune him from time to time, but he put them off a long season, but he did preach a little in our own house, where many came to hear him. At last he was prevailed upon, chiefly by the moving arguments of the good Doctor Hall,[23] to accept of their invitation. The people gave him a call to preach the gospel to them, which he accepted; and promised to continue with them one quarter of a year, which he did, and they renewed their call every quarter.

Upon the 17th day of October, in the year 1693, my son fell from his horse, and broke both his thighs, having been at Leeds to preach, and he lay nine Lord's-Days, and then he was enabled to preach again. During this time he had a call to Clifford,[24] and went thither some few days, but he could not see his way clearly, so he resolved not to go, but continued at Kipping; yet not to his satisfaction, for though they often pressed him to become their settled pastor, yet they were so divided among themselves, by contrary opinions, and the members of the church being some of them old men, and most of them living at so great a distance, that they could with difficulty enjoy communion with their brethren, that he could not accept of their call to office.

But, however, he preached the gospel to them, and often told them, that he would advise them to look out for a man that was fitter to serve them. It happened that some of the good men of Bingley,[25] came and desired that my son might go every other Lord's-Day, and preach there; unto which, after some discourse about it, the people at Kipping consented and my son was willing to go for one quarter of a year to make trial. So it was concluded.

---

23. Dr. Hall, a physician, who appears to have been the principal person in the congregation at Kipping.
24. Clifford is an obscure village not far from Tadcaster, where was one of the chapels founded by the non-conformists of the first race.
25. At Bingley also was one of the original chapels of the non-conformists.

He went one quarter, and at the end thereof, they renewed their call. But during this time, having been preaching at Kipping, upon the 20th day of January, in the year 1695, his horse's foot stuck fast in a hole of the ice, and in endeavouring to get it loose, my son fell off, and broke both his thighs again, and lay silent other seven Lord's days, and then he was enabled to stand and preach again.

But now our fears of future dangers were so great, that we durst not think of his riding on horseback anymore; and the good people of Bingley now renewed their call to my son for good and all, and had one strong argument on their side, and that was, the house and chapel were both under one roof. This was a capital consideration under our circumstances; and as we knew they wanted a settled pastor at Kipping, and seeing my son could not accept of that office with them, we thought it best to remove, so that a way might be made for another to come that might answer their desire; and not being under any promise of staying at Kipping any longer than from quarter to quarter, he inclined to go to Bingley, and, after long consultation, promised to go in a quarter of a year. Accordingly at the time they sent horses and carts, and fetched us and almost all we had away in one day.

We came to this place in the month of May, 1695, and the Lord gave us favour in the eyes of all the inhabitants of the town, (except two men,) who behaved with great love and kindness towards us; and yet but few of the town's people came to hear my son preach; but the congregation chiefly consisted of persons that came from other places. Having been here about two years, my dear wife died, and she lieth asleep in this place till the blessed morning of the resurrection, when the great jubilee-trumpet shall sound, and all the prisoners of death and the grave shall arise, and then she shall appear a blessed and glorious creature indeed.

Here she left my son and me in an evil, tempting, and ensnaring world, to shift for ourselves as well as we could. About three years after my dear wife's death, I was attacked by a most violent fever, which was then very fatal in the neighbourhood. Under this distemper I was afflicted with very great sweatings, and extreme coughing for two or three hours together, with but very little intermission; and also with the most afflicting thirst I ever experienced; all which brought me very low, so that for a week or ten days I was, in the judgment of almost all spectators, a gone man; and I had received the sentence of death in my own apprehension; and yet, at last, even to a wonder, God was pleased to rebuke the distemper, and raise me up again. "Bless the Lord, my soul, and all that is within me praise his holy name!"

Now what shall I render to the Lord for all his benefits bestowed upon me? "I will take the cup of salvation, and praise his name." And I would pray that I may be helped to walk with God a little while as Enoch did, passing the time of my sojourning here with fear, looking for a city which hath foundations, whose builder and maker is God. During our stay at Bingley, my son had many calls from the church at Kipping, to return to them again, and all the good people at Bingley were often desiring him to accept of the office of a settled pastor amongst them.

With this circumstance my son was much embarrassed, and wrote to the neighbouring ministers, desiring them to meet and consult upon the case, and favour him with their opinion and advice upon the subject. They met accordingly, but arguments of considerable weight appearing on both sides, and they being unwilling to offend either party, returned doubtful answers, and came to no positive conclusion, but left it, at last, to my son, to act according to his own inclination. He was now more embarrassed than before: however, Mr. Whitaker,[26] and Mr. Noble, declared for his return to Kipping.

After a long time of debating, praying, and weighing matters over in his own mind, he thought he had a call from heaven to

---

26. Thomas Whitaker, A. M ., one of the first who entered on the ministry among the non-conformists, not having been in the ministry before the Act of Uniformity. His ministerial life was passed at Leeds, where he and his family lived a century in excellent reputation and esteem. He preached the funeral sermon on the death of Joseph Lister and his son Accepted, which sermon is printed in a posthumous volume of his sermons, 8vo. 1712.

that old broken and shattered church; and his heart inclined to see if the Lord would please to use him as repairer of the breaches there, and hoping there might be a prospect of some good to be done amongst the rising generation, as well of the children of the church-members, as of the other neighbours.

Having given the church at Kipping a promise to go thither, they sent thirty men and as many horses and carts as carried all we had away, on the 22nd of July, 1702.

My son continued their pastor for the space of seven years, and on Thursday, the 25th February, fell sick, and died, to our great loss and trouble, but to his great gain.

So far Joseph Lister

His father lived to see him buried; and he himself died exactly that day fortnight, and was buried on Sunday, March the 14th, 1709, being twelve weeks and four days short of completing his 82nd year. [27]

---

27. There was printed at the time *A Sermon on the death of Mr. Joseph Lister, at Kipping in Bradford-Dale, who died April 1709*. The text is *John 11. 16*. There is no biography. The only passage in which he and his son are particularly alluded to is this: "You have lost an able and faithful minister of the New Testament, whose route prospered under all the infirmities of a crazy tabernacle, and who knew how 'rightly to divide the Word of Truth.' You have lost also an able, serious and experienced Christian; whose advice, counsel, example, has been your glory for many years. Two such lives gone from this earth, and gathered to heaven, as it were both in one day! Oh what a wide gap has the removal of them made! and what a melancholy aspect hath it left on this assembly!" *Whitaker's Sermons*, 8vo. 1712, p. 154.
In the Preface to these Sermons, which was written by Thomas Bradbury, a popular divine among the early Dissenters, it is said of them:—"Mr. Joseph Lister was an old disciple of great eminency for knowledge and holiness: He and his son, Mr. Accepted Lister, died within a very little time of one another. The Sermon was preached to the Church, which the one served as Deacon, the other as Pastor."

The Rider of the White Horse and his Army, Their Late Good
Successe in Yorke-Shiere.
Or
A true and faithfull Relation of that famous and wonderfull victory
at Bradford, obtained by the Club-men there, with all the
circumstances thereof.
And of
The taking of Leeds and Wakefield by the same men under the
command of Sir Thomas Fairfax, with the manner and circumstances
thereof from good hands.
Seriously commended to the High Court of Parliament, and all
that are of Gods side for their incouragement.
London, Printed for Thomas Underhill, 1643.

Bradford's Deliverance

After the Lord Fairfax His Excellency had retired from Tadcaster, the Lord of Newcastle possessed himselfe of Pontefract, so making himselfe master of our western parts, block't up all passages betweene us and our strength, and there manifested his resolutions to sesse the whole county, but to exact extraordinary summes of those who had subscribed the Parliaments propositions.

We could expect nothing now, but that those townes should first suffer, who had bin most forward to assist the Parliament: Leeds, Bradford, and Halifax were princepally aimed at. In Leeds the malignant humour being predominant, easily converted the towne into their temper. Bradford was the next place in their way, the towne most unable to resist them; and indeed whoever considers their dangers, weaknesse, and discouragements, must judge their attempt as worthy admiration as their successe. The maine body of the Popish army was within a dayes march of Bradford, some amongst them grievously exasperated by a dishonourable repulse from this towne not long before. So fare were we from expecting help from the Lord Fairfax, as we thought it scarce possible to seeke it.

Our malignant spirits before charmed, now appeared breathing forth nothing but threatenings against those who had bin most active for the Parliament: and their apparition was so terrible, as it affrighted many of the best affected persons out of the towne; and thereupon, out goes our Royalists to bring in the Kings Catholick army. Some religious persons in the parish, considering what danger might result both to their consciences and country from such cowardize and treachery (instigated by feare of perjury, if they should contribute any assistance against the Parliament, and care of their lives and estates, evidently endangered by a bare refusall without resistance) resolved to stand upon their guard, invited all the well affected in the parish to assist them, and entred the towne.

When our malignants were returned with a letter from Sir William Saville, wherein he manifested an intention to burne and plunder, if we did not contribute to the maintenance of the Popish army. To which no other answer was return'd, then the apprehension of those who brought it, and had subscribed it; all couragious attempts, yea desperate in the account of many, who saw neither wisedome nor strength sufficient to manage them; there wanted both the head, body, and sinewes of warre, we had never a gentleman in the parish to command us, nor would any stranger be perswaded to undertake the charge.

All our trained souldiers with their armes, were with the Lord Fairfax, and the most of those who were fitted for service as voluntiers. Nor could it be expected, that the well affected of our poore parish, could pay a garrison any long time, and none would tarry one day without pay. Our neighbours perceived this, and therefore judging our attempt desperate (as in the eye of reason it was) and fearing the issue would be our ruine, refused to helpe us, least they should perish with us. Nor wanted we discouragements from our own men, to instance in no more; the very night before the enemy assaulted us, the greatest part of them left us.

This was on Saturday, Decemb: 17. The next morning about 9 of the clock, the enemy was discovered, approaching the east end of the towne; they were marshald in two bodies, the van was commanded by Colonel Evers (eldest sonne to the Lord Evers), wherein were three troopes of horse, two companies of dragooners, 100 foot, twenty pyoniers, two drakes, the traine of artillery commanded by Major Carew a Dutchman. The rere was commanded by Sir Francis Howard, wherein were his own and Captaine Hiliards troops, six companies of Collonel Eddringtons dragooners, and a 100 foote. Collonel Goring came along with them, and some say the Earle of Newport; but whether they had any charge or no in this expedition I heare not.

All these our Yorkshiere gentlemen had procured of the Lord of Newcastle, as though Sir William Savils regiment, Sir Marmaduke Langdale, Sir Thomas Gleman and Sir John Gothericks troopes, Sir Ingram Hopton, Captain Nevill, Captaine Batt, Captaine Bins companies had not bin sufficient to have swallowed our despicable towne. I should now shew how our men were marshald, but 'tis a hard matter to marshall those who had neither commanders, collours, nor distinct companies.

The night before, we had borrowed a commander of Hallifax, who had neere upon forty musquets and calievers, in towne about thirty fowling, birding, and smaller peeces, and well nigh twice as many club-men. These our Captaine disposed in severall parts of the towne, ten or twelve of our best marksmen upon the steeple, and some in the church; who being next the enemy, awaited not their warning peece, but at the first sight gave fire upon them bravely.

The enemy who expected a surrender, rather then resistance, being herewith something daunted: and perceiving how advantagious the steeple was to us, presently possest themselves of some houses not farre from the church, very convenient for the shelter of their men, and planting of their ordnance, and from thence sent out Sir John Gothericks troope, who partly to divert us from hindring them planting their canon, and partly to hinder the parish from comming to our aid, past through some parish villages on the one side of the towne, robbed a woman, most cowardly slew two naked men, and so came within sight of our sentinell at the west end of the towne.

Our musquetiers there discharged at them, shot two or three horses, whereof one of them lightly wounded was brought into towne; and in a short space (partly by our shot, partly by the approach of some club-men from Bingley) they were forced to retire back to their strength.

In the meane time their canons were planted in places most

convenient for battering the steeple, (which did most annoy them) and scowring of Kirkgate, downe which our men must upon necessity march to resist them. This done, Major Carew draws down some foot, and therewith takes two houses within thirty yards of the church, and this he did without any other impeachment then from the steeple; we having not any strength to sally out upon them, from these houses they plaid upon the church very hotly, and the church upon them.

Our steeple had a notable advantage of them, which our musquitiers there especially improved against them, for when any buffe or skarlet coat appeared, they laid two or three of their peeces in one hole, and discharged at once upon them with good successe, and thereby deterred the rest from relieving their men in the houses, and thus they continued till high-noone, about which time there came to our aid from Halifax some firemen and many clubbs, such of these as came to fight, were forthwith drawne downe to service, some of them were placed in the church, others in lanes neare the foresaid houses; the church and lanes kept the houses in play, and the steeple hindred the enemy from relieving the houses. But this was not the way to repell the enemy.

The largenesse of the church windowes, and smalnesse of the houses, made their assault secure, and our defence dangerous, which our men perceiving, resolved to win or lose all at once; watching an opportunity betwixt the discharge and charge of the enemy, they sallyed out of the church, and being seconded by those in the lanes, rushed in upon the houses, burst open the doores, slew those that resisted, tooke those who yeelded; the rest fled into the next field, whither some few of ours followed (the greatest part being employed in conveying the men and munition which the enemy had left behind them;) and in the field the skirmish was hotter then ever.

Our men were too eager to keepe ranke or file, though they had knowne howe to keepe it, and indeed their disorder was an advantage to us, for mixing themselves with the enemy, they fought securely in the mouth of the enemies canon, and in the eye of one body of their forces, both placed in the field above them; the enemy not daring to discharge, least with them they should slay their own men (otherwise, they having ten firemen for one, might have cut us off in an instant) nor could ours use their muskets otherwise then as clubbs. To speake ingeniously, their commanders exasperated by the cowardize of their common souldiers, manifested great courage, but they smarted for it; our sythes and clubbs now and then reaching them, and none else did they aime at.

One amongst the rest in a scarlet coate, our club-men had got hold of (and he in all probability, as some credible reports give us occasion to beleeve, was Collonel Goring) and were spoiling him. Their horse fearing the losse of such a man, became more couragious then they intended, leaped over the hedge and rode full upon our men, forcing them to give a little ground; too much (alas! that they had known him) to lose such a man, but they quickly recovered the ground 'tho they lost the man; doubled their courage, would neither give nor take quarter; (nor was this their cruelty, as the enemy complaines, but their ignorance) and in the end forced both men and horse to leave the field; and yet could not we keepe it, for we being separated from theirs, the musketiers had liberty to play upon us; and indeed they rained such a shower of lead amongst our men, as forced them to retreat for shelter to the next hedge, and so hindred them from pursuing, till they had removed their canons.

Their ordnance all this time played upon us, one of them ranged an 8 pound bullet; yet see the Lords mercy to us: that which was planted against the steeple never hit it; another intended for the skouring of Kirkgate, 'tho planted in as advantagious a place as they desired, 'tho the street was continually crowded with people; yea, though many of their bullets hit the houses, and some the street, yet was nobody at all hurt therewith; they bored indeed three or four houses, yet (which is observable) did most harme to a malignants; and thus the terror of the Lord, and of us, falling upon them, sending their foot and artillery formost, away they went, (using their feet better then they used their hands) and about fifty of our clubbs and muskets after them; which courage in ours, did most of all astonish the enemy; who say, no fifty men in the world, excepte they were madd or drunke, would have pursued a thousand.

Our men, indeed, shot as they were madd, and the enemy fell as they were drunke, and so we will divide it. Some discharged ten some twelve times in the pursuit; and having the whole body of the enemy for their butt, it may easily be imagined what good execution they did in a miles march (for so farre they pursued them) even to the Moore, where fearing to be environed by their horse, they retired, some of them so wearied with this eight houres hot service, as they could scarce returne to the towne.

One thing I cannot omit, a hearty round-head left by his comrades, environed with the enemies horse, discharged his musket upon one, strooke downe anothers horse with the thick end of it, broke a thirds sword, beating it backe to his throat, and put them all to flight; which (though as the rest wonderfull) I dare pawne my credit to be true. And thus ended our skirmish; wherein there was.

Slaine of theirs, Sir John Harper, (as one Savile taken at Halifax confesseth), Captaine Wray (in whose pocket was found good store of gold, and a commission directed to Major Williams, which made us think him to be the man), and Captaine Bins (whom they carried to Leeds scarce dead, and buried two daies after), and many common souldiers, more I am perswaded then we shall ever know of. Of ours, I cannot heare of two that perished by the enemy in the fight.

Sir John Gothericke got a bastinado, had his horse killed with a syth, and about a 100 common souldiers were wounded, as we are informed from Leeds were they are billeted: Of ours, about twelve, all curable except one or two.

Taken of theirs, Serjant Major Carew, (a man of great account, borne in the Low Countries of English parents,) twenty-six common souldiers, about ten horses, 180 weight of pouder, and about forty muskets; and thus God supplied our wants out of their store, giving us as many more muskets as we had, and well-nigh as much powder as we spent.

This was the issue of the fight, wherein nothing can be scene but God, and the wonderfull effects of his glorious attributes: Let us and our enemies both see it, that they may feare and shame, that we may trust and praise our God, who hath manifested himselfe to be the Lord of Hosts.

A True Relation, &c.

Sir Thomas Fairfax, son to the Lord Generall Fairfax, marched from Bradford (six miles distant from Leeds) on Munday morning with 6 troopes of horse, and three companies of dragoones under the command of Sir Henry Fowles Knight, his Lieutenant Generall of the horse, and neare a 1000 musketeers, with 2000 club-men, under the command of Sir William Fairfax Colonell, and Lieutenant Generall of the foot.

One company of these being dragoones under Capt. Mildmay, and about thirty musketiers and 1000 club-men marched on the south side of the river of Ayr to Hunslet-more above halfe a mile from Leeds, on the south-east side towards Wakefield: and the rest on north-side Ayr by Aperley-bridge (twenty yards of Christall-bridge being broke downe by the enemy) to Woodhouse-more, on the west-side Leeds about a mile thence; where they commending the cause to God by prayer, Sir Thomas dispeeded a trumpeter to Sir William Savile, who commanded in chiefe in Leeds, requiring in writing that towne to be delivered him for the King and Parliament; which Sir William disdainfully answered and said, he used not to give answer to such frivolous tickets, being confident (it seems) that with the strength he had he could keepe the towne, wherein were about 2000 men. *viz.* 1500 foot, and five troops of horse and dragoons and two demi-iculverins.

Sir Thomas approached nearer the south-west side of the towne with his forts that came on the north-side Ayre, and coming within view of the towne with banners displayed (about thirty-six colours) sent another trumpetter to Sir William, who shortly after by a trumpetter assured him he should get nothing but by fight, wherupon he drew out of his companies five colours of his expertest souldiers, and appointed them to march downe with Serjeant Major Forbes, Captaines Briggs, Lee, Francke, and Palmer, with his dragoones on foot, towards the water along the trenches, drawn two yards breadth and height from Mr. Harrisons new church along the south-side of the towne to the water, an inner trench being devided and drawne on the inside that long trench neare the waterside, compassed about the declivity of the hill a little above the water.

Neare to and above which about a hundred musketiers were drawne out of the towne, and about two of the clock in the afternoone, gave fire from the inside of the works upon Sir Thomas his musketiers, who approaching nearer shrowded themselves under a hill at the south head of the great fields before the great long trench, and let fly at the said centry with no losse at all to either side, they within the trenches shooting too high, and the other at the trenches.

Meane while Sir William Fairfax, Sir Tho. Norcliffe, and other Captains leading their companies to the west-side of the new church, and the troopes of horse attending the enemies outroads in the lanes and fields on the west and north parts; and the forts of the south-side Ayre, approaching the bridge, forced the guarders to quit the works at the first centry, placed on the outside the houses towards Beiston, brake through the works, and shot at the other strong century at the bridge end, where the forts discharged upon them without any losse to either side, but seeing the very neare approach of the dragoons, musketiers, and many club men, and fearing the speedy forcing that place they instantly fetcht to the bridge the demiculverin.

And after about an hours time spent in vain shooting between the forts within and without the works on the south-side of the town, as aforesaid, Serjeant Major Forbes most bravely leading on his companies in the plain fields before the great trenches, his Lieutenant Horsefall of Halifax, Captaines Lee, Brigg, and Francke contended which should next follow, and Captain Chadwicks Lancashiere souldiers accompanied; the enemy shot most vehemently from the trenches, yet killed none.

It was perceived by the forts on the south side Ayre, that if they could get some musketiers over the fields to the water side without danger by the cannon and muskets from the bridge, they could force the great centries from their works on the other side the river (in regard they had made no other defence against the south side water) and so open an easie passage to Ser. Major Forbs and his forces; whereupon by single persons they got to the water-side, and hid them in a little lane (James Nayler one of the dragooners being first), whither they had no sooner got, then the demiculverin from the bridge plaid neare them, and about four muskets from that little lane, and two from under a stump of a tree, a little above by the water side, discharged amongst the centry, and one man being there slain, the rest perceived their errour, and in conclusion fled apace out of the lower centry, which being espied by those on the south side Ayre (Serjeant Major Forbes and his company not discerning them, for the height of their works hindered) a great shout from those on the south side of the water discovered it to the serjeant-major, who with his forces comming downe towards the water side was holpen by Lieutenant Horsfall, who lending him his shoulder to climbe the top of the works, he most furiously and boldly entred the works single; him his said Lieutenant (wading through the river side below the worke) next followed most resolutely, then the rest followed, and M. Jonathan Scholefield (the minister at Croston chappell in Halifax Parish near Todmerden) in their company begun, and they sung the one verse of the *68 Psalm, Let God arise, and then his enemies shall be scattered and those that hate him flee before Him.*

And instantly after the great shout on the south-side river, still informing of the enemies flight from the upper and next centry (where about 100 were) Serjeant Major entred that also, and M. Scholefield begun, and they sung another like verse. So these works being gained, the enemy fled into the houses, and shot again furiously at those who had entred their works, who pursuing their victory, went up along the inside the works to the third centry at the lane neare M. Metcalfes house, where fierce shot being made from a new house and all about, two men of Serjeant Major Forbes company were shot dead.

Here Captain Lee entring that centry from the lane leading from Chrystall-bridge, was shot in the leg above the ankle; some bones being broken and took out, he is likely shortly to recover. The victory they pursued, though with great difficulty; Captain Briggs drawing towards the old-church, was from an house shot under the chin neare the throat, and in the arme, though not mortally, as is hoped.

The enemy flying along a street or lane, from the two centries neare the water into the heart of the towne, where the other demiculverin lay to guard that passage, Sir William met them, and enquiring the cause of their flight, was answered that their workes were entered; he called on them, go beat them out, promising to lead them, yet they denyed: which he seeing, and that twelve musketiers, drawne on bothe sides that lane by Mr. Scholefield had gained that cannon by killing the cannoneere (though with losse of a gray cotes, the one wherof being shot, did fight beyond the strength of a man) he and the rest, perceiving the towne lost, about an houre after the first centry was entred, fled away, thinking to get over the bridge towards Wakefield, and some of them (upon occasion of the club-mens beating backe from that centry by shot from an house neare the bridge end) got, to the number of 40, by the south side water, downe toward Hunslet, but were many of them taken, amongst whom Captain Thirlwell. Sir William seeing that way blokt, with many others fled amain back to the old church, by the south-side wherof by fine force they made way through clubs and fouling peeces along the north-side Ayre towards Pomfret, Sir William being neare drowning in the passages. Many antients, Drums, and foot taken, and some slaine here, *viz.* Captain Widrington, Maud of Wakefield, Hunsworth of Leeds, and others; Captain Errington was drowned, so were M. Robinson vicar of Leeds and others, *viz.* M. Calvery of Calvery and M. Jackson of Leeds; and 460 common soulders taken, with about fourteen barrels of gunpouder, great store of match, two cannons and many muskets.

So the towne being taken about four a clock, notice hereof came to Wakefield about six, the garrison there about twelve quitted that place, and the malignants thereof, M. Nevile, Paulden, Reyser and the rest, conveyed what goods they could to Pomfret, whence also the next night they fled away with thirty carriages, and all except about 200, who keepe the castle; and Captains Birkehead and Wilson with about 200 muskets and neare 1400 club-men from about Almurbury, and three troops from Leeds, entred vacant Wakefield the same Tuesday, and that night, and Captain Radcliffe, and neare as many musketiers and club men on the next day from Quick, &c.

As the musketiers and club-men retreated from the water side after the first two centries were won, the cannon from the bridge played amongst them, and as they went on in the lane, leading to Beiston, it beat down the barrs of a tenter which flew amongst them; and the next shot from it crusht the top of an house, yet did no more harme; these of Halifax parish, *viz.* one Michael Woodhead was shot upon his tin-buttons, and his doublet burst neare his heart, and the bruised bullet fell downe into his breeches, and no more hurt; John Milnes man, had his coat, dublet, and two shirts shot through to his coller bone on his back, whence the bullet rebounded and no hurt, but a little rotting of the flesh since, one Lilly, M. Thos. Listers man, had a bullet shot into the hilt of his sword, whereby the hilt was drawn out almost as small as wyre where the bullet light, and no hurt.

About twenty slain, ten of Sir Tho. Fairfax part, wherof Sir Tho. Norcliffe lost two men, as they entered Leeds neare new church. The works cost about 500 lb. The 460 prisoners are all discharged (save about twenty) upon oath taken never to serve against King and Parliament; and Leeds and Wakefield strongly guarded.

LEONAUR

ALSO FROM LEONAUR
AVAILABLE IN SOFTCOVER OR HARDCOVER WITH DUST JACKET

LIFE IN THE ARMY OF NORTHERN VIRGINIA *by Carlton McCarthy*—
The Observations of a Confederate Artilleryman of Cutshaw's Battalion During the
American Civil War 1861-1865.

HISTORY OF THE CAVALRY OF THE ARMY OF THE POTOMAC *by
Charles D. Rhodes*—Including Pope's Army of Virginia and the Cavalry Operations in West Virginia During the American Civil War.

CAMP-FIRE AND COTTON-FIELD *by Thomas W. Knox*—A New York Her-
ald Correspondent's View of the American Civil War.

SERGEANT STILLWELL *by Leander Stillwell* —The Experiences of a Union
Army Soldier of the 61st Illinois Infantry During the American Civil War.

STONEWALL'S CANNONEER *by Edward A. Moore*—Experiences with the
Rockbridge Artillery, Confederate Army of Northern Virginia, During the American
Civil War.

THE SIXTH CORPS *by George Stevens*—The Army of the Potomac, Union
Army, During the American Civil War.

THE RAILROAD RAIDERS *by William Pittenger*—An Ohio Volunteers Recollections of the Andrews Raid to Disrupt the Confederate Railroad in Georgia During the American Civil War.

CITIZEN SOLDIER *by John Beatty*—An Account of the American Civil War by a
Union Infantry Officer of Ohio Volunteers Who Became a Brigadier General.

COX: PERSONAL RECOLLECTIONS OF THE CIVIL WAR--VOLUME 1 *by
Jacob Dolson Cox*—West Virginia, Kanawha Valley, Gauley Bridge, Cotton Mountain, South Mountain, Antietam, the Morgan Raid & the East Tennessee Campaign.

COX: PERSONAL RECOLLECTIONS OF THE CIVIL WAR--VOLUME 2
by Jacob Dolson Cox—Siege of Knoxville, East Tennessee, Atlanta Campaign, the
Nashville Campaign & the North Carolina Campaign.

KERSHAW'S BRIGADE VOLUME 1 *by D. Augustus Dickert*—Manassas, Sev-
en Pines, Sharpsburg (Antietam), Fredericksburg, Chancellorsville, Gettysburg, Chick-
amauga, Chattanooga, Fort Sanders & Bean Station.

KERSHAW'S BRIGADE VOLUME 2 *by D. Augustus Dickert*—At the wilder-
ness, Cold Harbour, Petersburg, The Shenandoah Valley and Cedar Creek..